Adobe®
Illustrator® 10

Classroom in a Book®

Adobe

www.adobe.com/adobepress

Contents

Getting Started

Adobe® Illustrator® is the industry-standard illustration program for print, multimedia, and online graphics. Whether you are a designer or technical illustrator producing artwork for print publishing, an artist producing multimedia graphics, or a creator of Web pages or online content, the Adobe Illustrator program offers you the tools you need to get professional-quality results.

About Classroom in a Book

Adobe Illustrator 10 Classroom in a Book® is part of the official training series for Adobe graphics and publishing software developed by experts at Adobe Systems. The lessons are designed to let you learn at your own pace. If you're new to Adobe Illustrator, you'll learn the fundamental concepts and features you'll need to master the program. If you've been using Adobe Illustrator for a while, you'll find that Classroom in a Book teaches many advanced features, including tips and techniques for using the latest version of Adobe Illustrator.

Although each lesson provides step-by-step instructions for creating a specific project, there's room for exploration and experimentation. You can follow the book from start to finish or do only the lessons that correspond to your interests and needs. Each lesson concludes with a review section summarizing what you've covered.

Prerequisites

Before beginning to use *Adobe Illustrator 10 Classroom in a Book*, you should have a working knowledge of your computer and its operating system. Make sure that you know how to use the mouse and standard menus and commands, and also how to open, save, and close files. If you need to review these techniques, see the printed or online documentation included with your Windows® or Mac® OS documentation.

Note: When instructions differ by platform, Windows commands appear first, and then the Mac OS commands, with the platform noted in parentheses. For example, "press Alt (Windows) or Option (Mac OS)"; or "press Ctrl (Windows) or Command (Mac OS) and click away from the artwork." Common commands may be further abbreviated with the Windows command first, followed by a slash and the Mac OS commands, without any parenthetical reference. For example, "press Alt/Option"; or "Ctrl/Command-click."

Installing the program

Before you begin using *Adobe Illustrator 10 Classroom in a Book,* make sure that your system is set up correctly and that you've installed the required software and hardware. You must purchase the Adobe Illustrator software separately. For system requirements and complete instructions on installing the software, see the InstallReadMe file on the application CD.

Make sure that your serial number is accessible before installing the application; you can find the serial number on the registration card or CD sleeve.

Installing the Classroom in a Book fonts

To ensure that the lesson files appear on your system with the correct fonts, you may need to install the Classroom in a Book font files. The fonts for the lessons are located in the Fonts folder on the *Adobe Illustrator 10 Classroom in a Book* CD. If you already have these on your system, you do not need to install them. If you have ATM® (Adobe Type Manager®, Adobe's font management application), see its documentation on how to install fonts. If you do not have ATM, installing it from the CIB CD will automatically install the necessary fonts.

Note: *ATM is not compatible with Mac OS X. As an alternative for Mac OS X users, Adobe recommends that customers evaluate DiamondSoft Font Reserve and Extensis Suitcase products.*

To install the Adobe Illustrator Classroom in a Book fonts:

1 Insert the *Adobe Illustrator 10 Classroom in a Book* CD into your CD-ROM drive.

2 Install the font files from the CD to your hard drive, according to your operating system:

• In Windows (not XP), from the desktop navigate to the ATM installer file on the CD, located in the Fonts/ATM®/Setup directory. Double-click the installer file (Setup), and follow the on-screen instructions to install ATM and the fonts.

• In Mac OS (not Mac OS X), from the desktop navigate to the ATM installer file on the CD, located in the Fonts/Fonts/ATM® 4.6.1 + Fonts Installer folder. Double-click the ATM® 4.6.1 + Fonts Installer to install the fonts.

💡 *You can also install the Classroom in a Book fonts by copying all the files in the Fonts folder on the* Adobe Illustrator 10 Classroom in a Book *CD to the Program Files/Common Files/Adobe/Fonts (Windows) or System Folder/Application Support/Adobe/Fonts (Mac OS). If you install a Type 1, TrueType, OpenType, or CID font into these local Fonts folders, the font appears in Adobe Applications only.*

• In Windows XP, locate the Fonts folder in your directory (usually under c:/WinNT/Fonts). Open the Fonts folder, and then select each font from the CD and drag its PFB and PFM files to the Fonts folder. You can group and drag the fonts to install them, but you cannot drag the entire folder to install the fonts.

• In Mac OS X, navigate to the Fonts/Fonts/ATM® 4.6.1 + Fonts Installer folder on the CD. Open the Fonts folder, select all of the fonts, and drag them into the Library/Fonts folder on your hard drive. You can group and drag the fonts to install them, but you cannot drag the entire folder to install the fonts. Do not install ATM.

Copying the Classroom in a Book files

The *Adobe Illustrator Classroom in a Book* CD includes folders containing all the electronic files for the lessons. Each lesson has its own folder, and you must copy these folders to your hard drive to do the lessons. To save room on your drive, you can install only the necessary folder for each lesson as you need it, and remove it when you're done.

To install the Classroom in a Book files:

1 Insert the *Adobe Illustrator Classroom in a Book* CD into your CD-ROM drive.

2 Create a folder named AICIB on your hard drive.

3 Copy the lessons you want to the hard drive:

• To copy all of the lessons, drag the Lessons folder from the CD into the AICIB folder.

• To copy a single lesson, drag the individual lesson folder from the CD into the AICIB folder.

If you are installing the files in Windows, you must unlock them before using them. You don't need to unlock the files if you are installing them in Mac OS.

4 In Windows, unlock the files you copied:

• If you copied all of the lessons, double-click the unlock.bat file in the AICIB/Lessons folder.

• If you copied a single lesson, drag the unlock.bat file from the Lessons folder on the CD into the AICIB folder. Then double-click the unlock.bat file in the AICIB folder.

Note: As you work through each lesson, you will overwrite the Start files. To restore the original files, recopy the corresponding Lesson folder from the Classroom in a Book CD to the AICIB folder on your hard drive.

Restoring default preferences

The preferences file controls how palettes and command settings appear on your screen when you open the Adobe Illustrator program. Each time you quit Adobe Illustrator, the position of the palettes and certain command settings are recorded in the preferences file. If you want to restore the tools and palettes to their original default settings, you can delete the current Adobe Illustrator 10.0 preferences file. (Adobe Illustrator creates a preferences file if one doesn't already exist the next time you start the program and save a file.)

You must then restore the default preferences for Illustrator before you begin each lesson. This ensures that the tools and palettes function as described in this book. When you have finished the book, you can restore your saved settings.

To save your current Illustrator preferences:

1 Exit Adobe Illustrator.

2 Locate the AI Prefs (Windows) or Adobe Illustrator 10.0 Preferences (Mac OS) file.

Note: The default location of the Illustrator preferences file varies by operating system. Use your operating system's Find command to locate this file.

3 Drag the preferences file to your desktop.

To restore preferences to their default settings before each lesson:

1 Exit Adobe Illustrator.

2 Locate the Illustrator preferences file, named AI Prefs (Windows), or Adobe Illustrator 10.0 Prefs (Mac OS), as follows:

• In Windows 98 and ME, the AI Prefs file is located in the Windows®\Application Data\Adobe\Adobe Illustrator 10 folder. In Windows NT, this file is located in WinNT\Profiles\user name\ Application Data\Adobe\Adobe Illustrator 10 folder. In Windows 2000 and XP, it is in the Documents and Settings\username\Application Data\Adobe\Adobe Illustrator 10 folder.

• In Mac OS 9.x, the Adobe Illustrator 10.0 Prefs file is located in the System Folder\Preferences\Adobe Illustrator 10 folder. In Mac OS X, it is located in the Mac OS X\Users\Home\Library\Preferences\Adobe Illustrator 10 folder.

Note: *The default location of the Illustrator preferences file varies by operating system. Use your operating system's Find command to locate this file.*

If you can't find the file, either you haven't started Adobe Illustrator yet or you have moved the preferences file. The preferences file is created after you quit the program the first time, and is updated thereafter.

3 Delete or rename the AI Prefs file (Windows) or Adobe Illustrator 10.0 Prefs file (Mac OS).

4 Start Adobe Illustrator.

To locate and delete the Adobe Illustrator preferences file quickly each time you begin a new lesson, create a shortcut (Windows) or an alias (Mac OS) for the Illustrator 10.0 or Preferences folder.

To restore your saved settings after completing the lessons:

1 Exit Illustrator.

2 Drag the preferences file from the desktop back into the Adobe Illustrator 10 folder.

3 In the warning dialog box that appears, confirm you'll replace the existing file.

Note: You can rename the preferences file with your current settings, rather than moving it or throwing it away. To restore your current settings when you have finished the lessons, change the preferences filename back. Exit Illustrator, and return the renamed preferences file to the Illustrator 10.0 folder (Windows) or the Preferences/Adobe Illustrator 10 folder (Mac OS).

Additional resources

Adobe Illustrator 10 Classroom in a Book is not meant to replace documentation that comes with the program. Only the commands and options used in the lessons are explained in this book. For comprehensive information about program features, refer to these resources:

• The Adobe Illustrator User Guide. Included with the Adobe Illustrator software, the user guide contains a complete description of all features. For your convenience, you will find excerpts from these guides, including the Quick Tours for the software, in this Classroom in a Book.

• The Quick Reference Card, a useful companion as you work through the lessons.

• Online Help, an online version of the user guide and Quick Reference Card, which you can view by choosing Help > Contents. (For more information, see Lesson 1, "Getting to Know the Work Area.")

• The Adobe Web site (http://www.adobe.com), which you can view by choosing Help > Adobe Online if you have a connection to the World Wide Web.

Adobe certification

The Adobe Training and Certification Programs are designed to help Adobe customers improve and promote their product proficiency skills. The Adobe Certified Expert (ACE) program is designed to recognize the high-level skills of expert users. Adobe Certified Training Providers (ACTP) use only Adobe Certified Experts to teach Adobe software classes. Available in either ACTP classrooms or on-site, the ACE program is the best way to master Adobe products. For Adobe Training and Certification Programs information, visit the Partnering with Adobe Web site at http://partners.adobe.com.

A Quick Tour of Adobe Illustrator

This interactive demonstration of Adobe Illustrator is designed to give an overview of key features of the program in about one hour.

Getting started

You'll work in one art file during this tour. Before you begin, you need to restore the default preferences for Adobe Illustrator. Then you'll open the finished art file for this lesson to see what you'll create.

Note: *If you're new to Adobe Illustrator or to vector-drawing applications, you may want to begin with Lesson 1, "Getting to Know the Work Area."*

1 To ensure that the tools and palettes function exactly as described in this tour, delete or deactivate (by renaming) the Adobe Illustrator 10.0 preferences file. See "Restoring default preferences" on page 4.

2 Start Adobe Illustrator.

3 To open the finished art file, choose File > Open, and open the TourEnd.ai file in the Lesson00 folder, located inside the Lessons folder within the AICIB folder on your hard drive.

4 If you like, choose View > Zoom Out to make the finished artwork smaller, and leave it on your screen as you work. If you don't want to leave the image open, choose File > Close.

For an illustration of the finished artwork in this lesson, see the color section.

Now open the start file to begin the tour.

5 To open the start file, choose File > Open, and open the TourStrt.ai file in the Lesson00 folder, located inside the Lessons folder within the AICIB folder on your hard drive.

Cambria Museum of Art
Join us for an evening of live music, refreshment, and art in celebration of our new location at the heart of downtown Cambria. Featuring a true Cambria treasure: 100 years of local artwork.

6 Choose File > Save As, name the file **Cambria.ai**, and select the Lesson00 folder. Leave the Format option set to Adobe Illustrator® Document, and click Save. In the Illustrator Native Format Options dialog box, select Illustrator 10 Compatibility and click OK.

Creating basic shapes

Adobe Illustrator includes a variety of tools and commands for creating basic geometric shapes, as well as specialized tools for precision drawing and patterns.

You'll begin this tour by adding some basic shapes to the artwork.

Drawing a star

First, you'll draw a star and modify the shape to create the flower.

1 Double-click the zoom tool (🔍) in the toolbox to enlarge the view to 100%.

2 Hold down the mouse button on the rectangle tool (▭) in the toolbox to display a group of tools. Select the star tool (☆), and then click once at the top left of the flower stem.

Clicking once with the star tool rather than dragging it in the artwork lets you precisely specify the shape's dimensions.

3 In the Star dialog box, specify the shape of the star. (We specified 60 points for Radius 1, 15 points for Radius 2, and 10 for the number of points on the star.) Click OK.

Now you'll change the direction of the star points.

4 In the toolbox, select the twist tool (⑤) from the same group as the rotate tool (⟳). In the artwork, click on the top point of the star but don't release the mouse button. Drag the point to the right or left. Release the mouse button when you are satisfied with the effect.

Painting the fill and stroke

In Illustrator, color within an object is called a *fill* and color on a line is called a *stroke*. The current fill and stroke colors are shown in the large Fill and Stroke boxes near the bottom of the toolbox and in the Color palette.

Now you'll paint the flower's fill and remove the stroke.

1 With the flower still selected, click the Stroke box in the toolbox and click the None button to remove the stroke. Then click the Fill box to specify you want to edit the fill of the star.

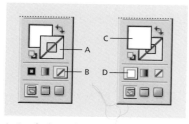

A. *Stroke box selected*
B. *None button selected*
C. *Fill box selected*
D. *Color button selected*

2 Click the Swatches tab to bring the Swatches palette to the front of its group, or choose Window > Swatches.

The Swatches palette contains a premade set of colors, gradients, and patterns that you can edit, save, and apply.

3 Click any swatch in the palette to change the flower's color. (We chose the Yellow & Orange Radial gradient.)

For information on how to create your own gradients, see Lesson 8, "Blending Shapes and Colors."

Now you'll change the stroke weight of the flower stem.

4 Choose the selection tool ( ) in the toolbox, and then click the left line of the stem to select it. If the Stroke palette is not visible, click the Stroke tab to bring the palette to the front of its group or choose Window > Stroke.

5 In the Stroke palette, type a larger value in the Weight text box (we increased it to 3 points) and press Enter or Return to apply the change.

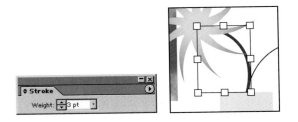

6 Choose File > Save.

Combining shapes

Adobe Illustrator includes numerous tools and commands that let you modify the shapes of objects. The Pathfinder commands change the shapes of objects by adding and subtracting the outlines, or *paths,* around them.

Uniting shapes into one

Now you'll add a circle shape to the rectangular flower vase and unite the shapes into one object.

1 Choose View > Smart Guides to turn them on. Smart Guides give you information about the objects as you point to them.

2 Choose Select > Deselect to deselect the artwork, and then click the Default Fill and Stroke button in the toolbox to deselect the current settings of the flower stem.

*Default Fill and
Stroke button*

3 Select the ellipse tool (◯) from the same group as the star tool (✪) in the toolbox. Hold down Shift+Alt (Windows) or Shift+Option (Mac OS) and drag to draw a circle that's almost as tall as the rectangular flower vase. (Holding down Shift constrains the ellipse to a circle. Holding down Alt/Option draws from the center rather than from the left side.)

4 Select the selection tool (▶) and select the circle's center point, but don't release the mouse button. Drag the circle to the center of the rectangle. When you release the mouse button, the Smart Guides snap the circle's center to the center of the rectangle.

5 Now select the circle's center point. Drag the circle straight down the vertical guide until its center reaches the intersect point of the table. Then release the mouse button.

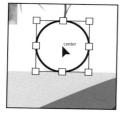
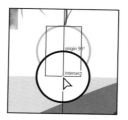

Select center point.　　　　*Drag down to intersect point.*

Now you'll unite the circle and rectangle into one object.

6 With the circle still selected and using the selection tool, Shift-click the rectangle to select both objects.

7 Choose Window > Pathfinder, and Alt/Option-click the Add to Shape Area button ( ) in the Pathfinder palette.

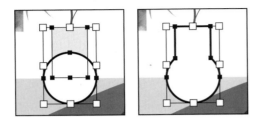

Note: If you click the Add to Shape Area button without holding down the Alt/Option key, the shapes become a compound shape. *They are still two separate paths but appear as though they are combined into one shape. You can release a compound shape and it reverts to the original shapes. By Alt/Option-clicking the Add to Shape Area button, you permanently combine the shapes (also called* expanding) *into one shape. You cannot retrieve the original shapes once a compound shape has been expanded.*

Sampling a color

Now you'll paint the vase with a color from the window curtain.

1 With the vase still selected, select the eyedropper tool ( ) in the toolbox and click the middle stripe of the curtain to pick up, or *sample,* its dark blue color. Sampling a color copies the color's fill and stroke into the Color palette and into any objects that are currently selected.

2 Choose Select > Deselect to deselect the artwork.

Subtracting one shape from another

Now you'll use a Pathfinder command to change the shape of the bottom of the flower vase.

1 Select the rectangle tool (▭) from the same group as the ellipse tool, and draw a rectangle over the bottom portion of the vase.

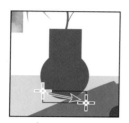

2 Click the selection tool (▸) to select the rectangle, and Shift-click the vase to select both objects.

3 In the Pathfinder palette, Alt/Option-click the Subtract from Shape Area button (▢).

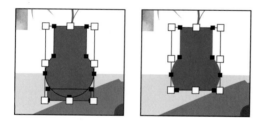

The rectangle shape (the front shape) is subtracted from the round shape of the vase, creating a straight line at the base.

Creating blends

Adobe Illustrator lets you blend shapes and colors of objects together into a new object that you can modify. Now you'll blend two different-sized and colored circles to create a bunch of grapes.

1 Click the largest circle on the napkin to select it, and then Shift-click the smallest circle to select it.

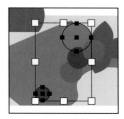

2 Choose Object > Blend > Blend Options. In the Blend Options dialog box, for Spacing choose Specified Steps, type **5** for the number of steps, and click OK.

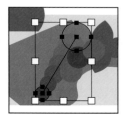

3 Choose Object > Blend > Make to create five intermediate objects that blend the colors and sizes of the two circles.

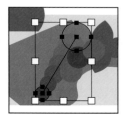

Editing your drawing

Adobe Illustrator has tools that let you edit, erase, and smooth what you draw, and a Navigator palette to help you move around in the artwork as you work.

Zooming in

Now you'll use the Navigator palette to zoom in closer on the blended grapes so you can change the direction of its path.

1 If it isn't visible, click the Navigator tab to bring the palette to the front of its group or choose Window > Navigator.

2 In the Navigator palette, move the slider or click the Zoom In button (⌂) to zoom in closer to the artwork (to about 300%) and use the hand pointer to move the red view box over the grapes.

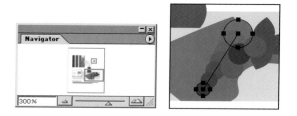

Diverting a path

You can change the straight path of the blended grapes to a curved path by moving the direction points of an anchor on the path.

1 Select the convert-anchor-point tool (⌐) from the same group as the pen tool (✎) in the toolbox. Experiment with moving the path of the grapes by selecting an end anchor point and dragging it to the left or right. You can also drag the direction handles on the anchor point.

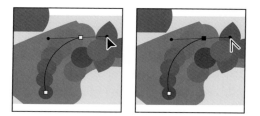

2 Press Shift+Ctrl+A (Windows) or Shift+Command+A (Mac OS) to deselect the artwork, and then choose File > Save.

Editing a shape

Now you'll use the pencil tool to change the shape of the table napkin under the grapes.

1 Select the selection tool ( ) in the toolbox, and click the napkin to select it.

2 Select the pencil tool ( ) in the toolbox, and position the pointer over the anchor point at the right corner of the napkin. (If necessary, scroll to the right to see it.)

3 Press the mouse button and drag the pencil tool down along the right side of the napkin to straighten out the shape, starting from the right corner and ending on the bottom corner of the napkin. When you release the mouse button, the napkin is reshaped.

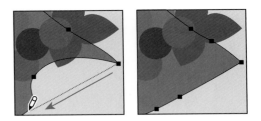

4 If you make a mistake, choose Edit > Undo Pencil and then redraw the shape.

5 When you've finished, choose Select > Deselect to deselect the napkin.

6 In the Navigator palette, click the Zoom Out button ( ) a few times to zoom back out to 100%, and then move the view box to the center of the artwork.

Drawing straight lines

Now you'll draw some straight lines to create a window frame on two sides of the window.

1 Click the Default Fill and Stroke button ( ) in the toolbox to deselect the settings of the napkin.

2 Choose View > Outline, and then select the pen tool ( ) from the same group as the convert-anchor-point tool ( ) in the toolbox.

3 Make sure that the Smart Guides are turned on in the View menu, and click the anchor point on the bottom left corner of the window to begin drawing the first straight line. Then hold down Shift and click directly beneath the window to end the line.

Each time you click, you create an anchor point, and Illustrator connects the anchor points with a straight line. Holding down Shift constrains the line to vertical, horizontal, or diagonal paths.

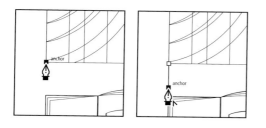

4 Shift-click five more times to draw the window frame in a counterclockwise direction, ending with the same anchor point you started with. As you move the pen tool over your starting point, the pen tool displays a small circle, indicating that your last click will close the object's path.

5 Click the selection tool ( ) to select the frame. Then Shift-click the top of the wall to the right to select it also.

6 Choose View > Preview. Notice that the window frame you just drew is on top of the flower. Objects are tiled in the order that they're created with the most current on top.

7 Choose Object > Arrange > Send to Back.

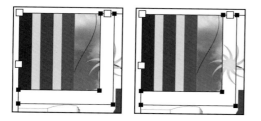

Many of the objects in this illustration were created using the pen tool. For information on drawing with the pen tool, see Lesson 4, "Drawing with the Pen Tool."

Painting

In Adobe Illustrator, you can paint an object in many ways. So far, you've painted the flower with a color or gradient from the Swatches palette and copied a color from the curtain to the flower vase using the eyedropper tool. You can paint objects in Illustrator artwork with black, white, shades of gray, process and spot colors, gradients, and patterns. You can also use the Brushes palette to apply patterns to the stroke or path of an object.

Painting with a spot color

Now you'll paint the wall and the window frame with the same spot color and change the tint.

1 With both the window frame and the wall still selected, make sure the Fill box is selected in the toolbox. (The Fill box appears in front of the Stroke box to indicate that it's selected.)

2 Click the Swatches tab to bring the palette to the front of its group or choose Window > Swatches.

3 Position the hand pointer over the swatches to see their names, and select the Aqua swatch in the fourth row. You can identify this swatch as a spot color by the triangle and dot in the bottom right corner of the swatch.

In Illustrator, a color swatch can be a predefined spot color (such as a PANTONE® color) or any color you save and name in your artwork.

4 Shift-click the wall to deselect it and keep the window frame selected.

5 In the Color palette, drag the Tint slider to the left to lighten the color. (We used 65%.)

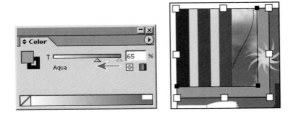

6 In the Color palette, drag the None button up and drop it over the Stroke box to remove the window frame's stroke.

Painting with brushes

You can paint with four types of brushes—Calligraphic, Scatter, Art, and Pattern. You can also create your own brushes to draw with or to apply to existing paths. Now you'll apply a custom-made Art brush to the flower's stem and a Pattern brush to the picture frame on the wall.

1 Click the right side of the flower stem to select it, and choose Window > Brushes, or click the Brushes tab behind the Swatches palette to bring the Brushes palette to the front.

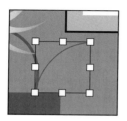

2 Position the mouse button over the triangle in the top right corner of the Brushes palette, press the mouse button to display the palette menu, and choose List View. The names of the brushes are grouped by type (Calligraphic, Scatter, Art, or Pattern) and then listed alphabetically with each group. Scroll down to the list of Art brushes and select the Leaf Art brush.

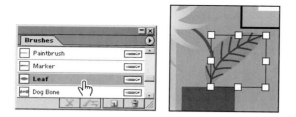

3 Now click the outer edge of the picture frame on the wall to select it, and select the Picframe Pattern brush in the Brushes palette.

See Lesson 5, "Working with Brushes," for information on creating your own custom brushes and using the Brushes palette.

Painting with a pattern swatch

Now you will use the Swatches palette to add a pattern fill to the tablecloth.

1 Click inside the tablecloth to select it. If necessary, click the Fill box in the toolbox to select the tablecloth's fill.

2 Click the Swatches tab to bring the palette to the front of its group, click the Show Pattern Swatches button at the bottom of the Swatches palette, and click the pattern you want. Try out other pattern fills for the tablecloth. (We used Tablecloth Pattern #1.)

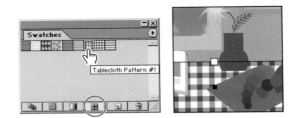

Scaling and rotating objects

You can easily scale and rotate objects—either by dragging or by specifying precise values. Now you'll scale and rotate the book to enlarge it and turn it at an angle.

1 To scale the book, first click the book to select its bounding box. Then hold down Shift and slowly drag the bottom right corner of the bounding box about halfway to the napkin.

Holding down Shift as you drag increases the size of the book proportionally while keeping the left side of the book in its original position.

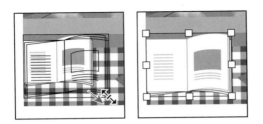

2 To rotate the book, move the cursor down to the bottom right corner of the book, just outside the bounding box. (The pointer changes from a scale symbol to a rotate symbol.) Press the mouse button and drag the pointer down and to the left to rotate the book in a clockwise direction.

3 Choose Select > Deselect to deselect the artwork, and then choose File > Save.

Using layers

The Layers palette in Adobe Illustrator lets you organize artwork into layers, groups, and objects that can be selected, displayed, edited, and printed individually or together.

1 If the Layers palette is not visible, click the Layers tab to bring the palette to the front of its group or choose Window > Layers.

The artwork has been organized into four layers. New objects are created on the layer that is selected in the Layers palette. You can view, select, and edit each layer, group, or object within a layer using the Layers palette.

2 In the Layers palette, click the triangle (▶) to the left of the Draw&Paint layer name. The list expands to display the thumbnails of the paths that are on the Draw&Paint layer.

3 Click the triangle again to collapse the Draw&Paint layer's path list.

Collapsed layers   *Expanded layers*

4 In the Layers palette, click Photo to select that layer. Then drag the Photo layer up, just above the Curtain layer but below the Draw&Paint layer, to move the photo to the front of the window.

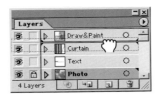

5 Notice how the curtain is hidden behind the clouds in the window. Now drag the Curtain layer in the Layers palette back up to just above the Photo layer to bring the curtain to the front of the artwork.

Photo layer in front hides curtain. *Curtain layer in front reveals photo.*

Moving layers in the Layers palette changes the order in which objects appear in the artwork, with the layer at the top of the palette containing the frontmost objects.

You can also change the transparency or apply effects to layers or nested layers.

6 In the Layers palette, click the hollow circle to the right of the Curtain layer name.

Curtain layer targeted

Selecting the circle changes it to a hollow double-circle, indicating that all objects on the Curtain layer are now targeted and will be affected by changes to their appearance or transparency. (If you want to select the objects on a layer without changing their appearance, click in the area to the right of the circle.)

7 Click the Transparency tab to bring the Transparency palette to the front of its group, or choose Window > Transparency.

8 Change the Opacity setting to **70%**. All objects on the Curtain layer are now slightly transparent. Notice that the double-circle now appears solid, indicating that the layer has appearance attributes applied to it.

70% opacity   *Appearance attributes applied*   *Result*

See Lesson 10, "Working with Layers," for information on creating layers and nested layers, and using the Layers palette.

Creating an envelope from a preset warp shape

Envelopes are objects that distort or reshape selected objects. You can make envelopes out of objects in your artwork, or you can use preset warp shapes. In this section, you'll select the curtain and distort it using a warp shape as its envelope. The curtain will look like a breeze is blowing it into the room.

1 Using the selection tool, click the curtain to select it. (The curtain is actually several rectangles that are grouped.)

2 Choose Object > Envelope Distort > Make with Warp.

3 In the Warp Options dialog box, choose Rise from the Style menu. Select Vertical Bend, and enter **40**%. Set the Distortion to **0**% Horizontal and **40**% Vertical. Select Preview to view the results, and click OK.

4 Notice that the curtain now flows off the edge of the page. With the selection tool, Shift-drag the curtain to the right. Position the right edge of the curtain near the curved black line. The curtain will still flow off the edge a bit.

5 Choose Select > Deselect. Choose File > Save and save the file.

Applying bitmap image filters

Adobe Illustrator includes special-effects filters that you can apply to embedded bitmap images (also known as *raster images*) for a range of effects.

Filtering a bitmap image

Now you'll apply a filter to the embedded bitmap image of the sky to make it look less like a photo.

1 In the Layers palette, click the lock icon next to the Photo layer to unlock the layer, letting you modify artwork on that layer.

2 Click Photo to select the Photo layer. Hold down Alt (Windows) or Option (Mac OS) and click the eye icon in the column to the left of the Photo layer.

3 Holding down Alt/Option as you click the eye icon hides all of the other layers. Hiding layers is a useful way to isolate detailed artwork as you work.

4 In the Layers palette, click the area to the right of the circle to select all artwork on the Photo layer.

The image is an imported TIFF file from Adobe Photoshop®. You can import artwork in a wide variety of formats from other applications.

For information on embedding or linking image files to your artwork, see "Opening and Placing Artwork" in online Help or Chapter 2 in the Adobe Illustrator User Guide.

5 Choose Filter > Sketch > Water Paper. Experiment with changing the filter values. When the preview in the Water Paper dialog box appears the way you like, click OK to apply the filter to the bitmap image.

Original   *Water Paper filter applied*

6 In the Layers palette, Alt-click (Windows) or Option-click (Mac OS) the eye icon again to show all the layers.

Applying a live effect

Now you'll give the wall next to the window a textured surface by applying an effect to it. The effect is called a live effect because, unlike the filter you just applied to the image, you can edit or change the effect at any time by using the Appearance palette.

1 Click the Appearance tab to bring the Appearance palette to the front of its group, or choose Window > Appearance.

2 Click the wall to select it. The appearance attributes of the wall are displayed in the Appearance palette.

3 Choose Effect > Artistic > Rough Pastels. Experiment with different values, and then click OK.

4 Notice that the appearance attributes have changed in the Appearance palette.

  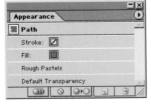

Original   *Effect applied*   *Appearance palette*

5 With the wall shape still selected, choose Effect > Artistic > Film Grain. Experiment with different values, and then click OK. (We used the default values.)

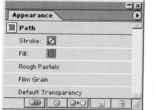

Appearance palette after   *Result*
Film Grain filter applied

You can alter the appearance of an object by changing the order of the effects in the Appearance palette.

6 In the Appearance palette, drag the Rough Pastels effect beneath the Film Grain effect. (To view all of the effects in the palette, you can drag the palette's lower right corner to resize the palette.) Notice how the effect changes when you apply the Film Grain effect before the Rough Pastels.

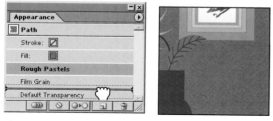

Changing order of effects   *Result*

7 Choose File > Save to save the changes.

Creating and using symbols

A symbol is an art object that you store in the Symbols palette and reuse one or more times in a document. You can create symbols from any Illustrator art object, including paths, compound paths, text, raster images, gradient meshes, and groups of objects. Symbols can also include active objects, such as brush strokes, blends, effects, or other symbol instances.

In this section, you will store one of the grapes as a symbol and then create a cluster of grapes. You will also change the color, size, and placement of the grapes with the symbolism tools.

1 Using the selection tool, select the grape that is on top of the leaves.

2 Choose Window > Symbols to display the Symbols palette.

3 Click the selected grape and drag it onto the Symbols palette. A thick black border appears in the palette to indicate that you are adding a new symbol. Release the mouse button to add the grape to the Symbols palette.

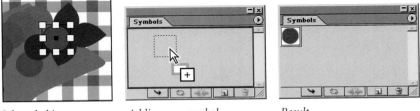

Selected object   *Adding new symbol*   *Result*

Using the symbolism tools

The symbol sprayer tool is one of the symbolism tools. The symbolism tools are used to create and modify instances or sets of symbol instances. Now you'll use the symbol sprayer tool to add more grapes to the illustration. Then you'll use the symbolism tools to modify the size, color, and position of the grapes.

1 Double-click the symbol sprayer tool ( ) in the toolbox to open the Symbolism Tools Options dialog box.

2 Enter a diameter of **100 pt** and leave the other settings at their default values. Click OK.

3 Position the symbol sprayer tool over the grape cluster and click and drag around until there are several grapes in the cluster.

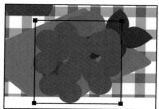

Set symbolism tools options.

Spray symbol instances.

Next you'll use the symbol stainer tool to change the colors of the grapes. The symbol stainer tool bases its color changes on the fill color in the Color palette. First you'll sample a color from another grape in the artwork, and then you'll use the symbol stainer tool to change the colors of the grapes in the symbol set you created.

4 Select the eyedropper tool (✐) in the toolbox and click the large purple grape at the top of the blend. By clicking the grape with the eyedropper tool, you sample its color and that color now appears in the Color palette.

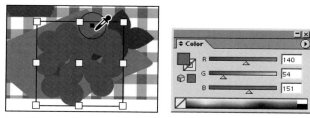

Sample color.

Sampled color is displayed in Color palette.

5 Select the symbol stainer tool (✎) in the same group of tools as the symbol sprayer (✎) in the toolbox.

6 With the symbol instance set still selected, click the symbol stainer tool over it a few times until you are satisfied with the color changes.

7 Select the symbol sizer tool (⟳) in the same group of tools as the symbol stainer (✐) in the toolbox.

The symbol sizer tool increases or decreases the size of symbol instances in an existing symbol set.

8 With the symbol instance set still selected, click the symbol sizer tool over it once to enlarge a few of the grape symbols.

9 Hold down the Alt/Option key and click again to reduce a few of the grape symbols.

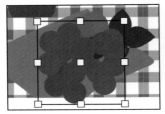 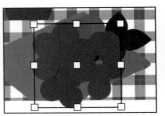 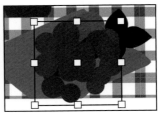

Symbols stained   *Symbols enlarged*   *Symbols reduced*

Now you'll reposition the grapes.

10 Select the symbol shifter tool (✺) in the same group of tools as the symbol sizer tool (⟳) in the toolbox.

The symbol shifter tool moves symbol instances around, and can also change the relative paint order of symbol instances in a set.

11 With the symbol instance set still selected, drag the symbol shifter tool over it to move the grape symbols to new positions.

12 Choose Select > Deselect to deselect the artwork, and then choose File > Save.

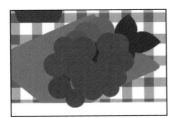

Symbols shifted

You're now ready to work with type.

Adding type

Adobe Illustrator lets you easily create type on a path or at any point in your artwork, as well as create and import text in columns or in other containers.

Now you'll add a headline to a path along the edge of the curtain.

1 In the Layers palette, drag the Text layer to the top of the palette.

Drag Text layer up to top of palette.

A curved line has been drawn along the edge of the window curtain.

2 Select the path type tool ( ) from the same group as the type tool (**T**) in the toolbox, and click once on the bottom end of the curved line to position the insertion point.

When you click a line with the path type tool, the line is converted to an invisible path (without any fill or stroke color) and a blinking insertion point appears.

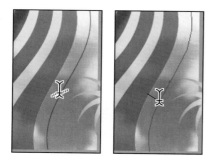

3 Type **Announcing our grand opening**.

The default characteristics of the type are Myriad® Roman 12 points.

Sampling type

Now you'll sample the type characteristics of the title at the bottom of the artwork and apply them to the new type.

1 Click the selection tool ( ). Clicking the selection tool after typing automatically selects the entire block of type.

2 Select the eyedropper tool ( ) in the toolbox, and click anywhere within the title "Cambria Museum of Art."

Sampling type with the eyedropper tool applies the characteristics to any selected type objects. It also copies the type characteristics to the Paragraph and Character palettes and the fill colors to the Color palette.

Changing type characteristics

Now you'll open the Character palette and change the character size of the poster's title to make it bigger.

1 Select the selection tool (▲), and click the title "Cambria Museum of Art" to select the block of type. (We specified this type as Adobe Garamond® Bold; you can use a similar serif typeface.)

2 Choose Window > Type > Character to display the Character palette. In the Size text box, double-click to select 15 pt and type **44**. Press Enter or Return to apply the change.

Wrapping text around objects

Now you'll wrap the type at the bottom of the artwork around the linked image of a leaf.

1 Click the leaf image to select it, and then Shift-click the text to the right of the image.

2 Choose Type > Wrap > Make to wrap the type around the leaf image.

3 Choose File > Save to save the artwork. Choose File > Close to close the file.

⍰ You can save Illustrator files in different formats depending on how you want to use the artwork. See "Saving and Exporting Artwork" in online Help or Chapter 14 in the Adobe Illustrator User Guide.

Congratulations! You've completed the Illustrator tour. Now you're ready to create your own Illustrator artwork.

Lesson 1

1 Getting to Know the Work Area

To make the best use of the extensive drawing, painting, and editing capabilities in Adobe Illustrator, it's important to learn how to navigate the work area. The work area consists of the artboard, the scratch area, the toolbox, and the default set of floating palettes.

In this introduction to the work area, you'll learn how to do the following:

- Open an Adobe Illustrator file.
- Select tools from the toolbox.
- Use viewing options to enlarge and reduce the display of a document.
- Work with palettes.
- Use online Help.

Getting started

You'll be working in one art file during this lesson, but before you begin you'll restore the default preferences for Adobe Illustrator. Then you'll open the finished art file for this lesson to see what you'll create.

1 To ensure that the tools and palettes function exactly as described in this lesson, delete or deactivate (by renaming) the Adobe Illustrator 10.0 preferences file. See "Restoring default preferences" on page 4.

2 Double-click the Adobe Illustrator icon to start the Adobe Illustrator program.

When you start Adobe Illustrator, the menu bar, the toolbox, and five palette groups appear on the screen. (The Transparency/Stroke/Gradient palette group is docked with the Color/Attributes palette group.)

Now open the start file to begin the lesson.

3 Choose File > Open, and open the L1start.ai file in the Lesson01 folder, located inside the Lessons folder within the AICIB folder on your hard drive.

For an illustration of the finished artwork in this lesson, see the color section.

4 Choose File > Save As, name the file **Parrots.ai**, and select the Lesson01 folder. Leave the Format option set to Adobe Illustrator® Document, and click Save. In the Illustrator Native Format Options dialog box, select Illustrator 10 Compatibility and click OK.

About the work area

In Adobe Illustrator, the work area occupies the entire space within the Illustrator window and includes more than just the printable page containing your artwork. The printable and nonprintable areas are represented by a series of solid and dotted lines between the outermost edge of the window and the printable area of the page.

__Imageable area__ is bounded by the innermost dotted lines and represents the portion of the page on which the selected printer can print. Many printers cannot print to the edge of the paper.

__Nonimageable area__ is between the two sets of dotted lines representing any nonprintable margin of the page. This example shows the nonimageable area of an 8.5" x 11" page for a standard laser printer.

__Edge of the page__ is indicated by the outermost set of dotted lines.

__Artboard__ is bounded by solid lines and represents the entire region that can contain printable artwork. By default, the artboard is the same size as the page, but it can be enlarged or reduced. The U.S. default artboard is 8.5" x 11", but it can be set as large as 227" x 227".

__Scratch area__ is the area outside the artboard that extends to the edge of the 227-inch square window. The scratch area represents a space on which you can create, edit, and store elements of artwork before moving them onto the artboard. Objects placed onto the scratch area are visible on-screen, but they do not print.

A. Imageable area B. Nonimageable area
C. Edge of page D. Artboard E. Scratch area

–From online Help and the Adobe Illustrator User Guide, Chapter 2

Viewing artwork

When you open a file, it is displayed in Preview view, which displays artwork the way it will print. When you're working with large or complex illustrations, you may want to view only the outlines, or *wireframes*, of objects in your artwork, so that the screen doesn't have to redraw the artwork each time you make a change.

1 Choose View > Outline. Only the outlines of the objects are displayed.

2 Choose View > Preview to see all the attributes of the artwork.

3 Choose View > Overprint•Pixel Closeup (at the bottom of the menu) to zoom in to a preset area of the image. This custom view was added to the document.

Note: To save time when working with large or complex documents, you can create your own custom views within a document to quickly jump to specific areas and zoom levels. You set up the view that you want to save and then choose View > New View. Name the view; it is saved with the document.

4 Choose View > Overprint Preview to view any lines or shapes that are set to overprint.

5 Choose View > Pixel Preview to view how the artwork will look when it is rasterized and viewed on-screen in a Web browser.

Outline view   *Preview view*   *Overprint preview*   *Pixel preview*

Working with tiled artwork

The artboard's dimensions do not necessarily match the paper sizes used by printers. As a result, when you print a file, the program divides the artboard into one or more rectangles that correspond to the page size available on your printer. Dividing the artboard to fit a printer's available page size is called tiling.

As you work with tiled artwork, be sure to consider how the artwork relates to the boundaries of the page grid and to the total dimensions of the artboard. For example, if the artwork is tiled onto six pages, part of the artwork will print on a separate sheet of paper that corresponds to page 6. If you specify printing only from pages 1 to 5, the part of the artwork that is on page 6 won't print.

If you have set up the file to view and print multiple pages, the file is tiled onto pages numbered from left to right and from top to bottom, starting with page 1. (The first page is always page 1; you cannot change the page 1 designation in Adobe Illustrator.) These page numbers appear on-screen for your reference only; they do not print. The numbers enable you to print all of the pages in the file or specify particular pages to print.

The page or set of pages is aligned with the upper left corner of the artboard by default. However, you can reposition pages on the artboard by using the page tool.

–From online Help and the Adobe Illustrator User Guide, Chapter 2

For more information on tiling, see "Tiling artwork and adjusting page boundaries" in online Help.

Using the Illustrator tools

The Illustrator toolbox contains selection tools, drawing and painting tools, editing tools, viewing tools, and the Fill and Stroke color selection boxes. As you work through the lessons, you'll learn about each tool's specific function.

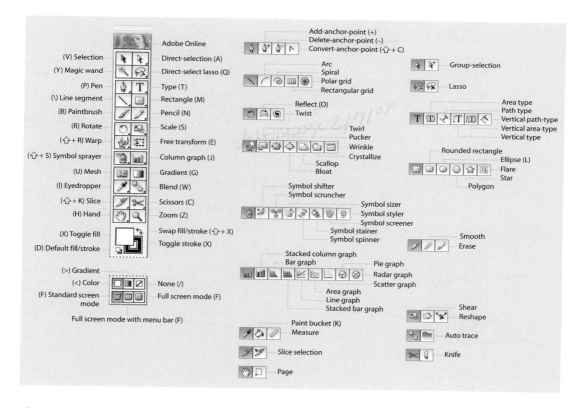

For an overview of the toolbox, see figure 1-1 in the color section.

1 To select a tool, either click the tool in the toolbox or press the tool's keyboard shortcut. For example, you can press M to select the rectangle tool from the keyboard. Selected tools remain active until you click a different tool.

2 If you don't know the keyboard shortcut for a tool, position the pointer over the tool to display the tool's name and shortcut. (All keyboard shortcuts are also listed in the Quick Reference section in online Help. You'll learn to use online Help later in the lesson.)

Some of the tools in the toolbox display a small triangle at the bottom right corner, indicating the presence of additional hidden tools.

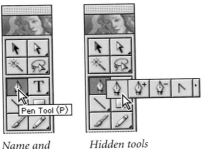

Name and   Hidden tools
shortcut

3 Select hidden tools in either of the following ways:

• Click and hold down the mouse button on a tool that has additional hidden tools. Then drag to the desired tool, and release the mouse button.

• Hold down Alt (Windows) or Option (Mac OS), and click the tool in the toolbox. Each click selects the next hidden tool in the hidden tool sequence.

Note: When you click a viewing tool to change the screen display of a document, you must return to the Standard screen mode to see the default work area displayed.

Standard
screen mode

Changing the view of artwork

You can reduce or enlarge the view of artwork at any magnification level from 3.13% to 6400%. Adobe Illustrator displays the percentage of the artwork's actual size in the title bar, next to the filename, and at the lower left corner of the Adobe Illustrator window. Using any of the viewing tools and commands affects only the display of the artwork, not the actual size of the artwork.

Using the View commands

To enlarge or reduce the view of artwork using the View menu, do one of the following:

• Choose View > Zoom In to enlarge the display of the Parrots.ai artwork.

• Choose View > Zoom Out to reduce the view of the Parrots.ai artwork.

Each time you choose a Zoom command, the view of the artwork is resized. Additional viewing options appear at the lower left corner of the window in a hidden menu, indicated by a triangle next to the percentage.

You can also use the View menu to fit the artwork to your screen.

1 Choose View > Fit in Window. A reduced view of the entire document is displayed in the window.

2 To display artwork at actual size, choose View > Actual Size. The artwork is displayed at 100%. (The actual size of your artwork determines how much of it can be viewed on-screen at 100%.)

3 Choose View > Fit in Window before continuing to the next section.

Using the zoom tool

In addition to the View commands, you can use the zoom tool to magnify and reduce the view of artwork.

1 Click the zoom tool ( ) in the toolbox to select the tool, and move the cursor into the document window. Notice that a plus sign appears at the center of the zoom tool.

2 Position the zoom tool over the parrot in the upper left corner of the illustration and click once. The artwork is displayed at a higher magnification.

3 Click two more times over the upper left parrot. The view is increased again, and you'll notice that the area you clicked is magnified. Next you'll reduce the view of the artwork.

4 With the zoom tool still selected, position the pointer over the upper left parrot and hold down Alt (Windows) or Option (Macintosh). A minus sign appears at the center of the zoom tool ( ).

5 With the Alt/Option key still depressed, click in the artwork twice. The view of the artwork is reduced.

In addition to clicking the zoom tools, you can drag a marquee to magnify a specific area of your artwork.

6 With the zoom tool still selected, hold down the mouse button and drag over the area of the illustration you want to magnify; then release the mouse button.

7 Drag a marquee around the lower parrot.

The percentage at which the area is magnified is determined by the size of the marquee you draw with the zoom tool (the smaller the marquee, the larger the level of magnification).

Area selected   Resulting view

Note: *Although you can draw a marquee with the zoom tool to enlarge the view of artwork, you cannot draw a marquee to reduce the view of artwork.*

You can also use the zoom tool to return to a 100% view of your artwork, regardless of the current magnification level.

8 Double-click the zoom tool in the toolbox to return to a 100% view.

Because the zoom tool is used frequently during the editing process to enlarge and reduce the view of artwork, you can select it from the keyboard at any time without deselecting any other tool you may be using.

9 Before selecting the zoom tool from the keyboard, click any other tool in the toolbox and move it into the document window.

10 Now hold down spacebar+Ctrl (Windows) or spacebar+Command (Mac OS) to select the zoom tool from the keyboard. Click or drag to zoom in on any area of the artwork, and then release the keys. The tool you selected in the previous step is displayed.

11 To zoom out using the keyboard, hold down spacebar+Ctrl+Alt (Windows) or spacebar+Command+Option (Mac OS). Click the desired area to reduce the view of the artwork, and then release the keys.

12 Double-click the zoom tool in the toolbox to return to a 100% view of your artwork.

Scrolling through a document

You use the hand tool to scroll to different areas of a document.

1 Click the hand tool (✋) in the toolbox.

2 Drag downward in the document window. As you drag, the artwork moves with the hand.

As with the zoom tool, you can select the hand tool from the keyboard without deselecting the active tool.

3 Before selecting the hand tool from the keyboard, click any other tool in the toolbox and move the pointer into the document window.

4 Hold down the spacebar to select the hand tool from the keyboard, and then drag to bring the artwork back into view.

You can also use the hand tool as a shortcut to fit all the artwork in the window.

5 Double-click the hand tool to fit the document in the window.

Using the Navigator palette

The Navigator palette lets you scroll a document at different magnification levels without scrolling or resizing artwork in the document window.

1 Make sure that the Navigator palette is at the front of its palette group. (If necessary, click the Navigator palette tab, or choose Window > Navigator.)

2 In the Navigator palette, drag the slider to the right to about 200% to magnify the view of the parrots. As you drag the slider to increase the level of magnification, the red outline in the Navigator window decreases in size.

3 In the Navigator palette, position the pointer inside the red outline. The pointer becomes a hand.

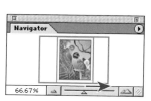

Dragging slider to 200%　　*200% view of image*　　*View in Navigator palette*

4 Drag the hand in the Proxy Preview area of the Navigator palette to scroll to different parts of the artwork.

You can also drag a marquee in the Navigator palette to identify the area of the artwork you want to view.

5 With the pointer still positioned in the Navigator palette, hold down Ctrl (Windows) or Command (Mac OS), and drag a marquee over an area of the artwork. The smaller the marquee you draw, the greater the magnification level in the document window.

Using the status bar

At the bottom left edge of the Illustrator window is the status bar. The status bar can display information about any of the following topics:

- The current tool in use.

- The date and time.

- The amount of virtual memory (Windows) or free RAM memory (Mac OS) available for your open file.

- The number of undos and redos available.

- The document's color profile.

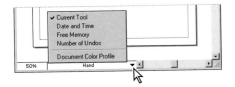

To specify the type of information you want to display in the status line, do the following:

1 Position the pointer over the triangle in the status bar, and hold down the mouse button.

2 Drag to choose the type of information you want from the pop-up menu.

Working with palettes

Palettes help you monitor and modify artwork. By default, they appear in stacked groups. To show or hide a palette as you work, choose the appropriate Window command. Selecting a Window command, as indicated by a check mark, displays the selected palette at the front of its group; deselecting a Window command conceals the entire palette group.

You can reorganize your work space in various ways. Try these techniques:

• To hide or display all open palettes and the toolbox, press Tab. To hide or display the palettes only, press Shift+Tab.

• To make a palette appear at the front of its group, click the palette's tab.

Click the Attributes tab to move the palette to the front.

• To move an entire palette group, drag its title bar.

• To rearrange or separate a palette group, drag a palette's tab. Dragging a palette outside of an existing group creates a new group.

Palettes are grouped.   *Drag a palette by its tab to separate the palette from its group.*

• To move a palette to another group, drag the palette's tab to that group.

• To display a palette menu, position the pointer on the triangle in the upper right corner of the palette, and hold down the mouse button.

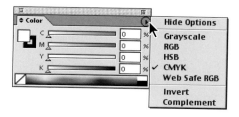

• To change the height of a palette, drag its lower right corner. (You cannot change the height of the Align, Attributes, Color, Info, Magic Wand, Options, Pathfinder, Stroke, Transform Type or palette.)

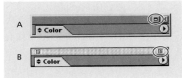

Click to collapse or expand palette.
A. Windows B. Mac OS

• To collapse a group to palette titles only, click the minimize/maximize box (Windows) or the resize box (Mac OS); click the box again to expand the palette group.

• To cycle through the available sizes for a palette, double-click a palette's tab or single-click on the double triangles to the left of the palette name. You can still access the menu of a collapsed palette.

Using context menus

In addition to the menus at the top of your screen, context-sensitive menus display commands relevant to the active tool, selection, or palette.

To display context-sensitive menus, position the pointer over the artwork or over an item in a palette list. Then click with the right mouse button (Windows) or press Ctrl and hold down the mouse button (Mac OS). (In Windows, you can also use context-sensitive Help or press F1 to get online Help. See "Using online Help" on page 52.)

Here you see the options for the pen tool, displayed in its context-sensitive menu. (You access these same options by selecting the Edit or Object menu.)

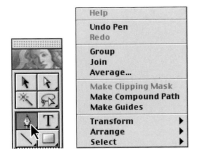

Calibrating your monitor

Whether preparing artwork for print or online use, you should begin by calibrating your monitor. This will ensure the closest possible match between your colors on-screen and those produced by a printer, a video display, or another computer monitor, and also between your colors in Illustrator and in other software applications. If your monitor isn't calibrated, the resulting colors may not even be close to what you originally saw on it.

Creating an ICC monitor profile

Your monitor will display color more reliably if you use color management and accurate ICC profiles. The Adobe Gamma™ utility, which is automatically installed into your Control Panels folder, lets you calibrate and characterize your monitor to a standard and then save the settings as an ICC-compliant profile available to any program that uses your color management system. This calibration helps eliminate any color cast in your monitor, make the monitor grays as neutral as possible, and standardize image display across monitors.

Although Adobe Gamma is an effective calibration and profiling utility, hardware-based utilities are more precise. If you have a hardware-based utility that can generate an ICC-compliant profile, you should use that instead of Adobe Gamma.

Depending on your workflow scenario, an ICC monitor profile can be either a source profile or a destination profile, or both.

Note: *Adobe Gamma can characterize, but not calibrate, monitors used with Windows NT. In addition, the ICC profile you create with Adobe Gamma can be used as the system-level profile in Windows NT. Its ability to calibrate settings in Windows 98 depends on the video card and video driver software. In such cases, some calibration options documented here may not be available.*

–From online Help and the Adobe Illustrator User Guide, Chapter 7

To calibrate your monitor with Adobe Gamma, do the following:

1 Make sure that your monitor has been turned on for at least a half hour to stabilize the monitor display.

2 Set the room lighting at the level you plan to maintain.

3 Turn off any desktop patterns and change the background color on your monitor to a neutral gray. This prevents the background color from interfering with your color perception and helps you adjust the display to a neutral gray. (For more on how to do this, refer to the manual for your operating system.)

4 Set your monitor to display thousands of colors or more.

5 Launch the Adobe Gamma utility:

• In Windows, double-click Adobe Gamma in Program Files > Common Files > Adobe > Calibration.

• In Mac OS, from the Apple® Menu, choose Control Panels > Adobe Gamma.

6 Click to reflect one of the following options:

• Step by Step (Assistant) and click Next for a version of the utility that will guide you through each step of the process. This version is recommended if you're inexperienced creating color profiles. If you choose this option, follow the instructions described in the utility.

• Control Panel and click Next for a version of the utility that is contained in a single dialog box. This version is recommended if you have experience creating color profiles.

Using online Help

For complete information about using palettes and tools, you can use online Help. Online Help includes all of the information from the *Adobe Illustrator 10.0 User Guide*, plus keyboard shortcuts and additional information, including full-color galleries of examples not included in the printed user guide. All of the illustrations in online Help are in color.

Online Help is easy to use, because you can look for topics in these ways:

• Scanning a table of contents.

• Searching for keywords or phrases.

• Using an index.

• Jumping from topic to topic using related topic links.

Displaying the online Help contents

First you'll look for a topic using the Contents screen.

To properly view online Help topics, you need Netscape® Communicator 4.0 (or later) or Microsoft® Internet Explorer 4.0 (or later). You must also have JavaScript active.

1 To display the Help Contents menu, choose Help > Illustrator Help, or press F1 (Windows).

2 Drag the scroll bar or click the arrows to navigate through the contents. The contents are organized in a hierarchy of topics, much like the chapters of a book.

Illustrator Help Contents screen

3 Position the pointer on the Looking at the Work Area chapter, and click it to display its contents.

4 Locate the Toolbox Overview (1 of 5) topic, and click to display it. An illustration of the selection tools and shortcut information appears.

The online Help system is interactive. You can click any blue text, called a *link*, to jump to another topic. The pointer icon indicates links and appears when you move the mouse pointer over a link or a hotspot.

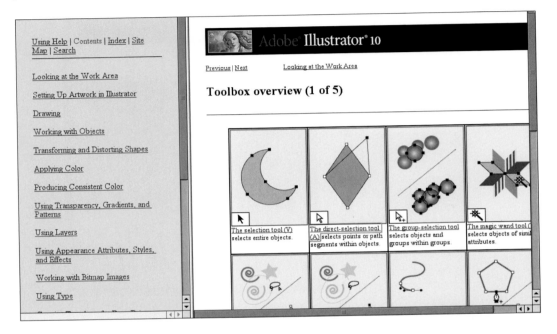

Using keywords, links, and the index

If you can't find the topic you are interested in by scanning the Contents page, then you can try searching using Search. You can search using keywords or phrases.

1 Click Search, and type **Brushes** in the text box. Click the Search button to go to that topic. A list appears of the items containing information about brushes.

2 Click Creating Brushes to learn about creating brushes. Notice that there are several subtopics available for further research.

3 Click Creating a Calligraphic Brush to read step-by-step instructions on how to create a calligraphic brush.

You can also search for a topic using the Index.

4 Click Index to go to an alphabetical listing of topics. You will see an alphabet.

5 Click the letter *H* to get a listing of all the topics starting with H.

6 Click the 1 or 2 next to the hand tool entry to get information about the hand tool and its functions.

Click Index for alphabet.

Click letter for topics; then click number.

Using Adobe online services

Another way to get information on Adobe Illustrator or on related Adobe products is to use the Adobe online services. Selecting the Adobe Online menu item takes you directly to the product page on Adobe.com that lists the latest information on Illustrator.

Visiting the Adobe Web site

If you have an Internet connection and a Web browser installed on your system, you can access the U.S. Adobe Systems Web site (at http://www.adobe.com) for information on services, products, tutorials, tips, and community events on Illustrator.

1 If you have an Internet connection, from Adobe Illustrator, choose Help > Adobe Online, or click the icon at the top of the toolbox.

2 Click Go Online to connect to the Adobe Illustrator 10 Web page.

You can also choose to update the Adobe Online contents or set preferences to automatically refresh its contents before you use it. For instructions, see the next section, "Updating Adobe Online contents" on page 57.

3 Click any button in the Adobe Online window to open the linked Web page. The splash screen for Adobe Illustrator 10 online services appears, with buttons above the Adobe Illustrator title linking to topics on the Adobe Web site.

Adobe Illustrator 10 online splash screen

You can easily find information specifically on Illustrator—including the latest tutorials, quicktips and other Web content for Illustrator. Using Adobe Online, you can also download and view the current version of the Illustrator Top Issues document containing the latest Illustrator technical support solutions. Or you can learn about other Adobe products and news. You can also click links and view Adobe-suggested Web sites related to Illustrator and Adobe.

4 When you have finished browsing the Adobe page, close and exit the browser.

Updating Adobe Online contents

Because Adobe Online is constantly changing, updating its contents lets you quickly access the most current content available and be notified immediately of new product updates or upgrades. Adobe's servers perform this check automatically and without disturbing your workflow. If new product fixes, updates, or downloads are available, you will be notified the next time you launch your software or access the Adobe Online menu item. You can choose to accept or reject any items to download.

1 To set preferences to update content automatically, choose Edit > Preferences > Online Settings (Windows and Mac OS 9) or Illustrator > Preferences > Online Settings (Mac OS X).

Note: If you have an Internet connection, you can also set Adobe Online preferences from Illustrator by choosing Help > Adobe Online or clicking the icon at the top of the toolbox, and then clicking Preferences.

2 Set the update frequency to daily, weekly, or monthly. Click OK to close the dialog box; or continue to the next step to update Adobe Online contents.

3 In the Adobe Online Preferences dialog box, click Updates to display the Adobe Product Updates dialog box.

You can also update content using the Adobe Product Updates dialog box by choosing Help > Downloadables; or by choosing Help > Adobe Online or clicking the icon at the top of the toolbox, and in the Adobe Online dialog box, clicking Updates. You can also get the most recent information and downloads at http://www.adobe.com/adobeonline.

4 In the Adobe Product Updates dialog box, choose a View option:

• New Updates to display only updates that are new since the last time you viewed downloadable files or were notified of them.

• All Updates to view all files on the Adobe Web site that are currently available for download.

5 To view a list of files, open the Downloadables folder (Mac OS) or the Download folder (Windows) and any other folder listed.

6 To see a description of a file, click a filename and view its description in the Item Description section.

7 To see the location where a file will be installed if downloaded, select a file and view its location in the Download Location section. To change the location, click Choose.

8 To download a file, click its checkbox and then click Download.

9 To close the Adobe Product Updates dialog box, click Close.

Now you're ready to begin creating and editing artwork.

Review questions

1 Describe two ways to change your view of a document.

2 How do you select tools in Illustrator?

3 Describe three ways to change the palette display.

4 Describe two ways to get more information about the Illustrator program.

Review answers

1 You can select commands from the View menu to zoom in or out of a document, or fit it to your screen; you can also use the zoom tool in the toolbox, and click or drag over a document to enlarge or reduce the view. In addition, you can use keyboard shortcuts to magnify or reduce the display of artwork. You can also use the Navigator palette to scroll artwork or change its magnification without using the document window.

2 To select a tool, you can either click the tool in the toolbox or press the tool's keyboard shortcut. For example, you can press V to select the selection tool from the keyboard. Selected tools remain active until you click a different tool.

3 You can click a palette's tab or choose Window > Palette Name to make the palette appear. You can drag a palette's tab to separate the palette from its group and create a new group, or drag the palette into another group. You can drag a palette group's title bar to move the entire group. Double-click a palette's tab to cycle through a palette's various sizes. You can also press Shift+Tab to hide or display all palettes.

4 Adobe Illustrator contains online Help, with all the information in the *Adobe Illustrator 10.0 User Guide*, plus keyboard shortcuts and some additional information and full-color illustrations. Illustrator also has context-sensitive help about tools and commands, and online services, including a link to the Adobe Systems Web site, for additional information on services, products, and Illustrator tips.

Lesson 2

2 | Creating Basic Shapes

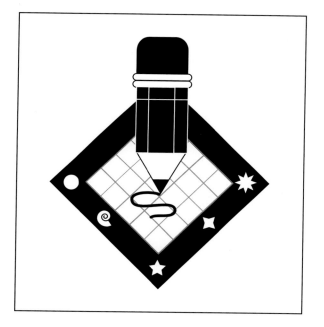

Many objects in the Adobe Illustrator program can be created by starting with basic shapes and then editing them to create new shapes. In this lesson, you will use some basic shapes to create a logo.

In this lesson, you'll learn how to do the following:

- Use tools and commands to create basic shapes.

- Copy and combine objects to create new shapes.

- Use rulers, guides, and grids as drawing aids.

- Use selection tools to select and change parts of objects.

- Paint objects.

- Scale objects using the bounding box.

Getting started

Before you begin, you'll need to restore the default preferences for Adobe Illustrator. Then you'll open the finished art file for this lesson to see what you'll create.

1 To ensure that the tools and palettes function exactly as described in this lesson, delete or deactivate (by renaming) the Adobe Illustrator 10.0 preferences file. See "Restoring default preferences" on page 4 in the Introduction.

2 Start Adobe Illustrator.

3 Choose File > Open, and open the L2end.ai file in the Lesson02 folder, located inside the Lessons folder within the AICIB folder on your hard drive.

4 If you like, choose View > Zoom Out to make the finished artwork smaller, adjust the window size, and leave it on your screen as you work. (Use the hand tool ( ) to move the artwork where you want it in the window.) If you don't want to leave the image open, choose File > Close.

Now create the start file to begin the lesson.

5 Choose File > New to open a new untitled document. Leave the Color Mode and Artboard Size at the default settings, and click OK.

6 Choose File > Save As, name the file **Logo.ai**, and select the Lesson02 folder. Leave the Format option set to Adobe Illustrator® Document, and click Save. In the Illustrator Native Format Options dialog box, select Illustrator 10 Compatibility and click OK.

Setting up the document

You'll begin the lesson by setting the ruler units to inches, displaying a grid to use as a guideline for drawing, and closing the palettes that you won't use.

1 Close all of the palettes by clicking their close boxes or by holding down Shift and pressing Tab once. For now, you won't need to use them.

You can also hide or show the palettes by choosing their Window commands. If a palette is grouped with others, choosing the Window command hides or shows the group. (Pressing Shift+Tab switches between hiding and showing the palettes. Pressing Tab alone hides or shows the toolbox and palettes.)

2 Choose View > Show Grid to display a grid that's useful for measuring, drawing, and aligning shapes. This grid won't print with the artwork.

3 Choose View > Show Rulers to display rulers along the top and left side of the window. The ruler units by default are set to points.

You can change ruler units for all documents or for only the current document. The ruler unit of measure applies to measuring objects, moving and transforming objects, setting grid and guide spacing, and creating ellipses and rectangles. (It does not affect the units in the Character, Paragraph, and Stroke palettes. These are controlled by the options in the Units & Undo Preferences dialog box.)

4 Choose File > Document Setup to change the ruler units for only this document. In the Document Setup dialog box, for Units choose Inches, leave the other settings unchanged, and click OK.

You can also set the default ruler units for all documents by choosing Edit > Preferences > Units & Undo (Windows and Mac OS 9) or Illustrator > Preferences > Units & Undo (Mac OS X).

Using basic shape tools

In this lesson, you'll create a simple logo using the basic shape tools. The shape tools are organized in two groups in the toolbox, under the ellipse and rectangle tools. You can tear these groups off the toolbox to display in their own palettes.

1 Hold down the mouse button on the rectangle tool (▢) until a group of tools appears, and then drag to the tear-off triangle at the end and release the mouse button.

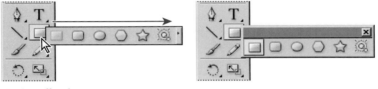

Tearing off tool group

2 Move the rectangle tool group away from the toolbox.

Drawing the pencil shape

In Adobe Illustrator, you control the thickness and color of lines that you draw by setting *stroke attributes*. A *stroke* is the paint characteristics of a line or the outline of an object. A *fill* is the paint characteristics of the inside of an object. The default settings will let you see the objects you draw with a white fill and a black outline.

First you'll draw a series of rectangles and triangles that make up the pencil. You'll display Smart Guides to align your drawing.

1 Select the zoom tool (🔍) in the toolbox, and click in the middle of the window once or twice until you are zoomed in to 150%. (Notice that 150% is displayed in the bottom left corner of the window.)

2 Choose View > Smart Guides to turn them on. Smart Guides automatically snap the edges of objects to nearby objects or their intersect points as you move them. Smart Guides also show Text Label Hints that display information on the position the pointer is currently snapped to (such as "center") as you manipulate the pointer.

You'll display the Info palette to check the dimensions of the rectangle you draw.

3 Choose Window > Info to display the Info palette.

4 Select the rectangle tool (▭), and drag it to draw a rectangle that's **0.75 inch** wide and **1 inch** tall. (Use the rulers and the grid as guides.) This will be the body of the pencil.

When you release the mouse button, the rectangle is automatically selected and its center point appears. All objects created with the shape tools have a center point that you can drag to align the object with other elements in your artwork. You can make the center point visible or invisible (using the Attributes palette), but you cannot delete it.

5 In the Info palette, note the rectangle's width and height. If necessary, choose Edit > Undo, and redraw the rectangle.

Info palette displays rectangle's width and height.

You'll draw another rectangle centered inside the first one to represent the two vertical lines on the pencil.

6 With the rectangle tool still selected, position the pointer over the center point of the rectangle, hold down Alt (Windows) or Option (Mac OS), and drag out from the center point to draw a rectangle that's centered inside it—release the mouse button when the rectangle is the same height as the first rectangle (1 inch).

Holding down Alt or Option as you drag the rectangle tool draws the rectangle from its center point rather than from its top left corner. Smart Guides indicate when you've snapped to the first rectangle's edge, by displaying the text label hint "path."

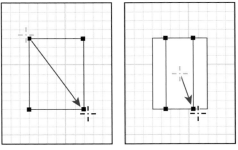

Drag to draw first rectangle.   *Alt/Option-drag to draw second rectangle.*

Besides dragging a tool to draw a shape, you can click with the tool to open a dialog box of options. Now you'll create a rounded rectangle for the eraser by setting options in a dialog box.

7 Select the rounded rectangle tool (⬭), and click once in the artwork to open the Rounded Rectangle dialog box. Type **0.75** in the Width text box, press Tab, and type **0.75** in the Height text box. Then press Tab again, and type **0.20** in the Corner Radius text box (the radius is the amount of the curve on the corners). Click OK.

💡 *To automatically enter identical Width and Height values in the Ellipse or either Rectangle dialog box, enter a Width or Height value, and then click the name of the other value to enter the same amount.*

You'll use Smart Guides to help you align the eraser to the top of the pencil body.

8 Choose View > Hide Bounding Box to hide the bounding boxes of selected objects. This will prevent you from accidentally distorting the eraser shape when you move and align it.

The bounding box appears as a temporary boundary around selected objects. With the bounding box, you can move, rotate, duplicate, and scale objects easily by dragging the selection or a handle (one of the hollow squares surrounding the selected objects). When you release the mouse button, the object snaps to the current border created by the bounding box, and you see the object's outline move.

9 With the rounded rectangle tool still selected, hold down Ctrl (Windows) or Command (Mac OS) to select the selection tool ( ) temporarily. Select the right edge of the eraser without releasing the mouse button, and then drag the eraser to the right side of the pencil body (Smart Guides indicate the path of the right side). Release the mouse button to drop the eraser on top of the pencil body.

10 Then hold down Ctrl (Windows) or Command (Mac OS), select the bottom edge of the eraser, and drag it up to the intersect point at the top of the pencil body. Release the mouse button.

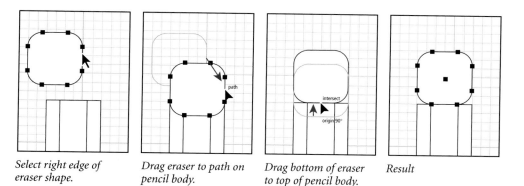

Select right edge of eraser shape.   *Drag eraser to path on pencil body.*   *Drag bottom of eraser to top of pencil body.*   *Result*

Next you'll create two shapes to represent the metal bands connecting the eraser to the pencil.

11 To create the first band, click once anywhere in the artwork to open the Rounded Rectangle dialog box again. Type **0.85** in the Width text box, **0.10** in the Height text box, and **0.05** in the Corner Radius text box. Click OK.

12 Click the selection tool ( ) to select the band, select the bottom left anchor point, and move the band to the top of the pencil body. Release the mouse button. (Smart Guides snap the anchor point to the top corner of the pencil body.)

13 With the band still selected, hold down Alt (Windows) or Option (Mac OS), select the anchor point again, drag straight up to make a copy, and move it above the original band. Release the mouse button. (Smart Guides snap the anchor point of the new copy to the top of the original band.)

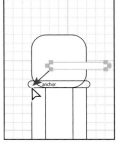 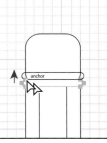 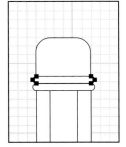

Move first metal band between eraser and pencil body. *Alt/Option-drag a copy above first metal band.* *Smart Guides snap objects into position.*

You've been working in Preview view. This default view of a document lets you see how objects are painted (in this case, with a white fill and black stroke). If paint attributes seem distracting, you can work with just the wireframe view of an object.

Now you'll draw two triangles to represent the pencil tip and its lead using Outline view.

14 Choose View > Outline to switch from Preview view to Outline view.

Illustrator lets you control the shape of polygons, stars, and ellipses by pressing certain keys as you draw. You'll draw a polygon and change it to a triangle.

15 Select the polygon tool (○), and position the pointer over the center point of the two rectangles.

16 Drag to begin drawing a polygon, but don't release the mouse button. Press the Down Arrow key three times to reduce the number of sides on the polygon to a triangle, and move the mouse in an arc to rotate one side of the triangle to the top. Before you release the mouse button, hold down the spacebar and drag the triangle down to position it below the pencil body. Release the mouse button when the triangle is positioned.

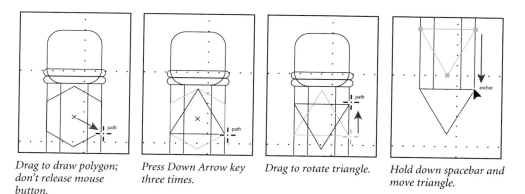

Drag to draw polygon; don't release mouse button. *Press Down Arrow key three times.* *Drag to rotate triangle.* *Hold down spacebar and move triangle.*

Now you'll create the second triangle for the pencil's lead tip using the scale tool.

17 With the triangle still selected, select the scale tool (⬚) in the toolbox and then Alt-click (Windows) or Option-click (Mac OS) the bottom corner point of the triangle.

Clicking the corner point of the triangle sets the reference point from which the new triangle will scale. Holding down Alt/Option as you click displays the Scale dialog box.

18 In the Scale dialog box, type **30%** in the Scale text box and click Copy. (Don't click OK.)

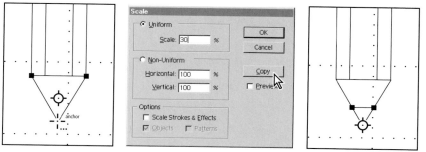

Alt/Option-click to set scaling reference point. *Set scale value.* *Result*

Next you will use the line segment tool to quickly draw a horizontal line segment near the top of the pencil.

19 Select the line segment tool (╲), and position the pointer over the left side of the pencil near the top. Click where you want the line to begin, and drag where you want the line to end. As you drag, hold down Shift to constrain the line horizontally.

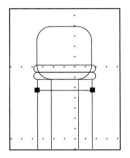

Note: The Line and Arc Segment Tool Options dialog boxes display the values of the last segment created. You can reset to the default values in the dialog box by pressing Alt (Windows) or Option (Mac OS) and clicking Reset.

20 Choose File > Save to save your work.

Drawing the piece of stationery

You can draw the diamond-shaped piece of stationery for the logo in a couple of ways. One way is to draw four-sided polygons (using the same methods you used to draw the triangles for the pencil tip). Another way is to draw using the rectangle tool, the rotate tool, and the Transform palette.

1 Select the rectangle tool (▭) in the toolbox, and position the pointer over the center point of the pencil body. Hold down Shift+Alt (Windows) or Shift+Option (Mac OS) and drag the tool to draw a square of any size from the center of the pencil.

Holding down Shift as you drag the rectangle tool constrains the rectangle to a square. Holding down Alt/Option draws the rectangle from its center point rather than from the top left corner.

Now you'll use the Transform palette to enter precise dimensions for the square.

2 Choose Window > Transform to open the Transform palette.

3 Type **2.25** in the W (width) text box and **2.25** in the H (height) text box. Press Enter or Return to apply the changes.

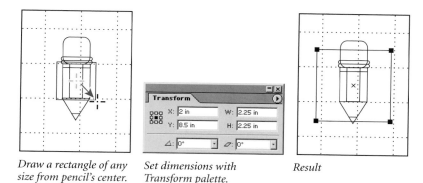

Draw a rectangle of any size from pencil's center. Set dimensions with Transform palette. Result

Next you'll create a smaller square that's centered inside the first one.

4 With the square still selected, choose Edit > Copy to copy the square to the Clipboard. Then choose Edit > Paste in Front to paste the copy of the square directly on top of the first one.

5 In the Transform palette, type **1.5** in the W (width) text box and **1.5** in the H (height) text box. Press Enter or Return to apply the changes.

6 Choose File > Save to save your work.

For information on using the transform tools and Transform palette in Illustrator, see Lesson 6, "Transforming Objects."

Drawing with the rectangular grid tool

With the grid tool you can create complex grids in one click-and-drag motion. You can use either the rectangular grid tool or polar grid tool to create rectangular grids or concentric circles, respectively, of a specified size with a specified number of dividers.

Now you'll add a grid to the stationary. Unlike the view grid, this grid can print.

1 To make this next part of the lesson easier to visualize, choose View > Hide Grid.

2 Select the hand tool in the toolbox ( ), and move to a clear area of the artboard so that you have a clear area in which to work for the next step.

3 Hold down the mouse button on the line segment tool (◥) until a group of tools appear, and then drag to the tear-off triangle at the end and release the mouse button.

First you'll practice how to draw a grid manually with the grid tool.

4 Select the rectangular grid tool (▦), and position the pointer in a blank area of the artboard.

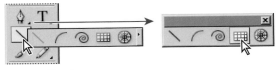

Tearing off tool group

5 Begin dragging without releasing the mouse, and experiment changing the number of horizontal and vertical lines in the grid by pressing the arrow keys. Without releasing the mouse button, press the Up and Down arrow keys as you drag to change the number of horizontal lines in the grid; press the Right and Left arrow keys to change the vertical lines in the grid until you have a grid that is five by five. Do not release the mouse button as you try the next few steps.

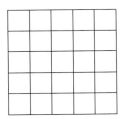

5 columns by 5 rows

6 While still drawing the grid, press the C, X, F, and V keys to change the space between the cells. C adds spacing to the cells on the left, and X adds spacing to the right. F adds spacing to the top cells, and V adds spacing to the bottom.

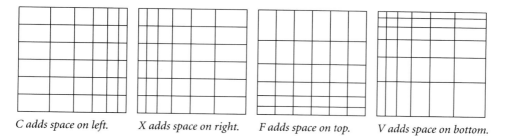

C adds space on left.   *X adds space on right.*   *F adds space on top.*   *V adds space on bottom.*

7 Because there is no shortcut to revert the space between the cells to the original setting, press the C or X keys as needed to equalize the horizontal spacing; and press the F or V keys as needed to equalize the vertical spacing until the grid is evenly spaced. The grid should have 25 (5 by 5) evenly spaced cells.

Next you'll adjust the grid to fit into the stationery using the Transform palette.

8 With the grid still selected, in the Transform palette enter **1.5** in the W (width) text box and **1.5** in the H (height) text box. Press Enter or Return to apply the changes.

You can also draw a grid precisely by selecting the grid tool, clicking in the artwork to display the Rectangular Grid Tool Options dialog box, and then setting values.

9 Select the selection tool ( ) in the toolbox. Position the pointer over the top right anchor point and move the grid to reposition it within the smaller stationery square at the same corner point. Notice that the pointer turns white when the points intersect.

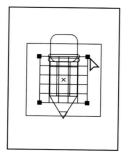

Reposition grid over smaller stationery square.

Now you'll rotate the grid and squares to create the diamond shape.

10 Using the selection tool, drag to marquee-select the large and small square and the grid. Be careful not to select any of the pencil.

11 Select the rotate tool (⟳) in the toolbox and position the pointer over the bottom right corner of the larger square. Shift-drag the corner to the left or right until a corner is at the top. (Smart Guides help to constrain the rotation to 45°.)

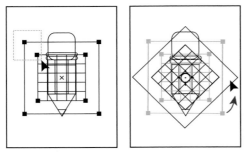

Use the selection tool to marquee-select the grid and squares.   *Use rotate tool to turn selected objects 45°.*

12 With the grid and two squares still selected, hold down Ctrl (Windows) or Command (Mac OS) to get the selection tool, and drag the top corner point of the larger square to move the squares down to just below the metal eraser bands on the pencil.

13 Choose View > Preview, and then choose Object > Arrange > Send to Back to move the squares and grid behind the pencil.

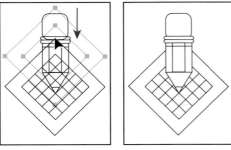

Drag squares down.   *Arrange squares in back of pencil.*

14 Choose Select > Deselect to deselect the artwork, and then choose File > Save to save your work.

Decorating the stationery border

You'll decorate the border of the piece of stationery with a circle, a spiral, and some star shapes, using different methods to create the shapes.

1 Double-click 150% in the status bar in the bottom left corner of the window, type **200**, and press Enter or Return to zoom in to a 200% view of the artwork.

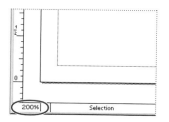

2 Select the ellipse tool (⬭), and position the pointer in the left corner of the stationery border. Hold down Shift+Alt (Windows) or Shift+Option (Mac OS) and drag the tool to draw a small circle.

Holding down Shift as you drag the ellipse tool constrains the shape to a circle; holding down Alt/Option draws it from its center point.

3 Now select the spiral tool (◉) next to the rectangular grid tool (▦), and position it in the bottom left side of the stationery about midway between the two corners. Drag the tool to draw a small spiral, release the mouse, and then use the arrow keys to adjust its position.

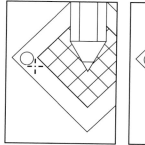

Press Shift+Alt/Option   *Draw spiral.*
and drag to draw circle.

You can drag the spiral tool to draw spirals or click once to open the Spiral dialog box and specify the characteristics before drawing the spiral. Illustrator lets you specify the radius, number of segments, and percent of decay (amount that the spiral uncoils).

Drawing spirals

The spiral tool creates a spiral-shaped object of a given radius and number of winds; that is, the number of turns that the spiral completes from start to finish.

To draw a spiral by specifying dimensions:

1. Select the spiral tool, and click where you want to place the center of the spiral.

By default, the Spiral dialog box displays the dimensions of the last spiral you drew. The unit of measure is determined by the unit of measure set in the Document Setup or Units & Undo Preferences dialog box.

2. In the Radius text box, enter the distance from the center to the outermost point in the spiral.

3. In the Decay text box, enter the amount by which each wind of the spiral should decrease relative to the previous wind.

4. Click the arrows or enter the number of segments in the Segments text box. Each full wind of the spiral consists of four segments.

5. For Style, select the counterclockwise or clockwise option to specify the direction of the spiral, and click OK.

–From the Adobe Illustrator User Guide, Chapter 3

Now you'll draw some stars using different methods.

4 Select the star tool ( ), and position the pointer in the bottom corner of the stationery. Drag the tool to draw the first star shape. By default, the star tool draws a five-pointed star.

5 With the star tool still selected, click in the bottom right side of the stationery (midway between the two corners) to create a second star. By default, the Star dialog box displays the dimensions of the last star you drew. In the Star dialog box, type **4** in the Points text box, and click OK.

6 To draw the last star, start dragging the star tool in the right corner of the stationery, but don't release the mouse button. As you drag, press the Up Arrow key to increase the number of points on the star (we created an eight-sided star), and then before releasing the mouse button, hold down the spacebar and move the star into position in the corner of the border.

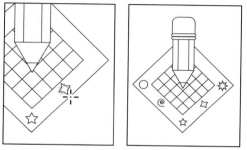

Draw star.   *Press Up Arrow key to add star points.*

7 Ctrl-click (Windows) or Command-click (Mac OS) away from the artwork to deselect the star, and choose File > Save.

Tips for drawing polygons, spirals, and stars

You can control the shapes of polygons, spirals, and stars by pressing certain keys as you draw the shapes. As you drag the polygon, spiral, or star tool, choose any of the following options to control the shape:

• To add or subtract sides on a polygon, points on a star, or number of segments on a spiral, press the Up Arrow key or the Down Arrow key before releasing the mouse button. The tool remains set to the last value you specified until you reset the number.

• To rotate the shape, move the mouse in an arc.

• To keep a side or point at the top, hold down Shift.

• To keep the inner radius constant, hold down Ctrl (Windows) or Command (Mac OS).

• To move a shape as you draw it, hold down the spacebar. (This also works for rectangles and ellipses.)

• To create multiple copies of a shape, hold down the ~ (tilde) key as you draw.

Now you're ready to add a fresh coat of paint.

Painting the logo

In Adobe Illustrator, you can paint both the fill and the stroke of shapes with colors, patterns, or gradients. You can even apply various brushes to the path of the shapes. For this logo, you'll use a simple method to reverse the default fill and stroke of your shapes, painting the fill with black and the stroke with white.

1 Select the selection tool (⬏) in the toolbox, and then click the eraser shape to select it.

2 Click the Swap Fill and Stroke button in the toolbox.

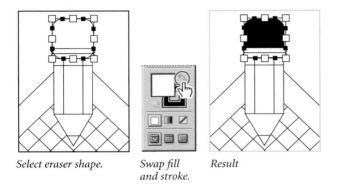

Select eraser shape.　　Swap fill　　Result
　　　　　　　　　　and stroke.

The black stroke of the rounded rectangle is transposed with the rectangle's white fill.

Next you'll paint the grid with a white fill and the stroke with a 50% screen of black.

3 Click anywhere on the grid, and choose Window > Color to open the Color palette.

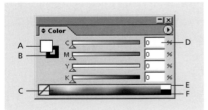

A. Fill box **B.** Stroke box **C.** Color bar
D. Color value **E.** White color box
F. Black color box

4 In the Color palette, make sure that the Fill box is selected (in front of the Stroke box); then click the white color box to the right of the color bar to paint the fill color of the grid white.

5 In the Color palette, click the Stroke box to bring it in front of the Fill box. The color value of the stroke is 100% black.

6 Change the black value from 100% black to 39% black by either typing **39** in the color value field or dragging the slider under the color bar to the left until the value is 39%.

7 Click the line beneath the bands on the pencil to select the line. In the Color palette, click the White swatch at the right of the color bar to stroke the band white.

8 Click one of the two rectangles that make up the pencil body to select it, and then Shift-click to select the other rectangle. Click the Swap Fill and Stroke button in the toolbox to swap the white fills of the pencil body with the black strokes and paint the pencil black with a white stroke.

9 Select the designs around the border by Shift-clicking them. Then select the Default Fill and Stroke button.

10 Click the outer rectangle (not the inner rectangle) of the stationery border to select it, and click the Swap Fill and Stroke button.

Now you'll paint the pencil's lead tip with both a black fill and a black stroke.

11 Click the small triangle that represents the lead tip to select it.

12 In the toolbox, click the Default Fill and Stroke button, and then drag the black Stroke box onto the Fill box to paint the triangle black.

To complete the design, you'll draw a curvy line using the pencil tool.

13 Click away from the artwork to deselect it.

14 With the Fill box selected, click the None button in the toolbox to indicate no fill setting. The Stroke is set to the default of black.

15 Select the pencil tool ( ) in the toolbox and draw a curvy line below the pencil's tip in the logo.

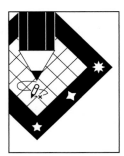

The curvy line remains selected after you draw it.

16 To adjust the path of the curvy line, drag the pencil tool along part of the selected line and then continue dragging.

17 If the Stroke palette isn't visible, choose Window > Stroke to display it, and then increase the stroke weight of the selected line to **3** points in the Weight text box. Press Enter or Return.

For information on drawing and editing shapes with the pencil tool, see "Drawing and editing freeform paths" in online Help or Chapter 3 in the Adobe Illustrator User Guide.

Copying and scaling shapes

A final step for creating logos is to scale the artwork to a 1-inch square and make sure that the resized logo still presents a clear image. You'll use the bounding box feature in Illustrator to make a scaled copy of the logo.

1 Double-click the zoom tool ( ) in the toolbox to zoom out to 100%.

2 Choose View > Show Grid to redisplay the grid.

3 Choose View > Show Bounding Box to display the bounding boxes of selected objects.

4 Choose Edit > Preferences > General (Windows and Mac OS 9) or Illustrator > Preferences > General (Mac OS X), and select the Scale Strokes & Effects option. Leave the other settings as they are, and click OK.

The Scale Strokes & Effects preference scales stroke weights and effects automatically, whether you scale objects by dragging or by using the Scale dialog box. You can also choose this command from the Transform palette menu.

5 Choose Select > All to select all the objects in the logo, and then click the selection tool ( ) in the toolbox to select their bounding box.

6 Hold down Alt (Windows) or Option (Mac OS) and drag the pointer from the center of the objects to the outside of the bounding box to make a copy of the logo.

7 Position the copy of the logo below the original, and line up the left corner point on the logo with a grid line to make it easier to measure as you scale the copy.

8 Using the selection tool, select the bottom right corner point of the bounding box, hold down Shift, and drag the corner up and to the left to scale down the logo—release the mouse button when the logo is about an inch wide.

Holding down Shift as you drag the corner of the bounding box scales the objects proportionally.

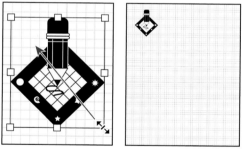

Shift-drag to scale   *Result*
proportionally.

You can use various zoom options to zoom in on the smaller logo and check its clarity. Illustrator's Navigator palette is useful for moving around in the artwork at a higher magnification.

9 Choose Window > Navigator to open the Navigator palette, and then click the Zoom In button ( ) at the bottom of the palette several times to zoom to 600%. As you click, the artwork in the window disappears and the red box in the Navigator palette becomes smaller.

The red square shows you where objects are located in relation to the artwork in the window. You can drag the red square to move the focus, or you can click where you want the red square to go.

10 In the Navigator palette, position the pointer so the hand is pointing to the smaller logo and click to move the red square over it.

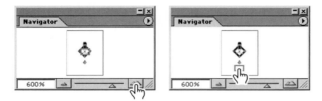

Click to zoom in.   *Click to move red view box.*

For more information on using the Navigator palette, see Lesson 1, "Getting to Know the Work Area."

11 Choose View > Hide Grid to hide the grid and clear the background.

12 Double-click the hand tool (🖐) in the toolbox to fit the artwork in the window.

13 Choose File > Save to save your artwork. Choose File > Close to close the file.

You've completed the basic shapes lesson and created the logo artwork.

For information on different ways you can add color to the logo, see Lesson 3, "Painting."

Review questions

1 What are the basic shape tools? Describe how to tear or separate a group of shape tools away from the toolbox.

2 How do you draw a square?

3 How do you draw a triangle?

4 Describe three ways to specify the size of a shape.

5 What is a quick way to transpose the color of an object's stroke with its fill color?

6 What is the difference between a view grid and a grid drawn with the rectangle grid tool?

7 How do you draw a rectangular grid? How can you control the size of the grid and its cells?

Review answers

1 There are six basic shape tools: ellipse, polygon, star, spiral, rectangle, and rounded rectangle. To separate a group of tools from the toolbox, hold the pointer over the tool that appears in the toolbox and press the mouse button until the group of tools appears. Without releasing the mouse button, drag to the triangle at the end of the group, and then release the mouse button to tear off the group.

2 To draw a square, select the rectangle tool (▭) in the toolbox. Hold down Shift and drag to draw the square, or click to enter equal dimensions for the width and height in the Rectangle dialog box.

3 To draw a triangle, select the polygon tool (⬡) in the toolbox, start dragging to draw the shape, and press the Down Arrow key to reduce the number of sides to three. Or click to enter the radius and number of sides in the Polygon dialog box.

4 To specify the size of a shape, you can do any of the following:

• Select the shape and specify new dimensions in the W (width) and H (height) text boxes in the Transform palette.

• Select the shape and then select the scale tool (⬚) in the toolbox. Alt/Option-click to set the point of origin and specify the dimensions in the Scale dialog box (click Copy to make a scaled copy of the selected object).

- Select the shape, and drag a side or corner handle of the shape's bounding box to resize its width, height, or both. (Shift-drag a corner handle to resize the selection proportionally.)

5 A quick way to transpose the color of an object's stroke with its fill color is to select the object and then click the Swap Fill and Stroke button in the toolbox.

6 The view grid is used as a guide for drawing and will not print with the artwork. A grid drawn with the grid tool can print.

7 To create a rectangular grid, you select the rectangular grid tool, and in the artboard either drag to draw a grid of the desired dimensions, or click to set the grid's origin and options. If you create a grid by dragging, you can use the Up and Down arrow keys to add or remove horizontal or vertical lines, or the Right and Left arrow keys to add or remove vertical lines; in addition, the V and F keys add space to the top and bottom cells, respectively; and the C and X keys add space to the left and right cells, respectively.

Lesson 3

3 | Painting

The Color and Swatches palettes let you apply, modify, and save colors in your artwork. You can paint with HSB, RGB, Web-safe RGB, or CMYK colors, grayscale, global process and spot colors, patterns, and gradients of blended colors. With the new Brushes palette, you can apply art or patterns to the path of an object.

In this lesson, you'll learn how to do the following:

- Paint with, create, and edit colors.

- Name and save colors, and build a color palette.

- Copy paint and appearance attributes from one object to another.

- Adjust the saturation of a color.

- Paint with gradients, patterns, and brushes.

Getting started

In this lesson, you'll learn about the variety of paint options in the Adobe Illustrator program as you paint an illustration of four hats. Before you begin, you'll restore the default preferences for Adobe Illustrator. Then you will open the finished art file for this lesson to see what you'll create.

1 To ensure that the tools and palettes function exactly as described in this lesson, delete or deactivate (by renaming) the Adobe Illustrator 10.0 preferences file. See "Restoring default preferences" on page 4.

2 Start Adobe Illustrator.

3 Choose File > Open, and open the L3end.ai file in the Lesson03 folder, located inside the Lessons folder within the AICIB folder on your hard drive.

4 If you like, choose View > Zoom Out to make the finished artwork smaller and leave it on your screen as you work. (Use the hand tool (🖐) to move the artwork where you want it in the window.) If you don't want to leave the image open, choose File > Close.

For an illustration of the finished artwork in this lesson, see the color section.

Now open the start file to begin the lesson.

5 Choose File > Open, and open the L3start.ai file in the Lesson03 folder, located inside the Lessons folder within the AICIB folder on your hard drive.

6 Choose File > Save As, name the file **Hats.ai**, and select the Lesson03 folder. Leave the Format option set to Adobe Illustrator® Document, and click Save. In the Illustrator Native Format Options dialog box, select Illustrator 10 Compatibility and click OK.

Filling with color

Painting objects with colors, gradients, or patterns is done using a combination of palettes and tools—including the Color palette, the Swatches palette, the Gradient palette, the Stroke palette, and the paint buttons in the toolbox, which let you select and change an object's paint and line attributes.

You'll begin by filling an object with color. Filling an object paints the area enclosed by the path.

When you reset the defaults, the Color palette and Swatches palette appear automatically on-screen when starting Adobe Illustrator.

1 Click the Swatches tab to bring the palette to the front of its group. (If the Color and Swatches palettes aren't visible, display them by choosing Window > Color and Window > Swatches; a check mark indicates that the palettes are open on-screen.)

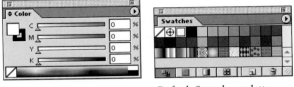

Default Color palette   *Default Swatches palette*

2 Click the close box or choose Window > Layers to close the Layers palette. (A check mark indicates that the palette is displayed.) You won't need this palette for this lesson.

3 Choose View > Hide Bounding Box. The bounding box is useful for moving and resizing objects. You won't need this option for this lesson.

4 Select the selection tool ( ) in the toolbox, and then click the rectangular border around the top left block in the artwork to select the object.

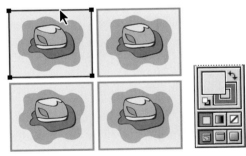

*The selected object's paint attributes
appear in the toolbox.*

In the toolbox, notice that the Fill box appears in the foreground, indicating that it is selected. (This is the default.) The box has a fill of a warm gray color. The Color button appears depressed, indicating that it is selected. In the background behind the Fill box, the Stroke box has a turquoise outline, indicating that the rectangle is outlined in turquoise. When the Stroke box or Fill box is in the background, its color is not the current selection.

The fill and stroke attributes of the selected object also appear in the Appearance palette. Appearance attributes can be edited, deleted, saved as styles, and applied to other objects, layers, and groups. You'll use this palette later in this lesson.

The Transparency palette displays the selected object's opacity and blending mode—both of which can affect the color of your artwork. You'll change transparency and blending modes later in this lesson. For more information on the Transparency palette, see "Using the Transparency palette" in online Help or Chapter 8 in the Adobe Illustrator User Guide.

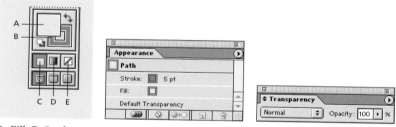

A. Fill B. Stroke
C. Color D. Gradient
E. None

Appearance palette
reflects selected object's
paint attributes.

Transparency palette displays
opacity and blending mode.

The Color palette displays the current color for the fill and stroke as well, and its CMYK sliders show the color's percentage of cyan, magenta, yellow, and black. At the bottom of the Color palette is the color bar. Now you'll use it to select a fill color of yellow.

5 In the Color palette, position the eyedropper pointer over the color bar. Hold down the mouse button and drag the eyedropper across the colors. As you drag, the color updates in the Fill boxes in the toolbox, in the Color palette and Appearance palette, and in the artwork.

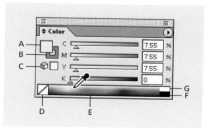

A. Fill box B. Stroke box C. Out of Web Color Warning
D. None button E. Color bar
F. Black color box G. White color box

The color bar lets you quickly pick a fill or stroke color from a spectrum of colors and select colors visually. You can also choose white or black by clicking the white color box or black color box on the right end of the color bar.

6 Now click a yellow color in the color bar to select the color. You can adjust the color by dragging the CMYK sliders in the Color palette. (We selected a yellow color with these values: C = 3.53%, M = 4.31%, Y = 48.63%, and K = 0%.) The color is updated in the Fill boxes in the toolbox and the Color palette, and in the artwork.

The paint attributes you choose are applied to all new objects you create until you change the attributes again. Depending on the last paint attribute applied, either the Fill box or the Stroke box appears selected and frontmost in the toolbox.

Stroking with color

Next, you'll outline the squiggly area around the bottom left hat. Painting just the outline of an object is called *stroking*.

1 Using the selection tool ( ), click the squiggly shape around the hat in the bottom left rectangle to select it.

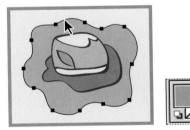

Select squiggly shape in bottom left rectangle.

The Fill box in the toolbox displays a pale green color. The Stroke box in the background has a red slash, indicating the squiggly shape's stroke is unpainted (a stroke of "None").

You'll start by swapping the fill color with the stroke color.

2 Click the Swap Fill and Stroke button to reverse the colors of the selected object's fill and stroke.

The Fill box now has no fill (a fill of "None"), and the Stroke box has a pale green color. (The color will become apparent in the next step.) With a fill of None, you can see through to the fill underneath—in this case, the gray color of the rectangle's fill.

Now you'll change the weight of the line that you just stroked using the Stroke palette. *Stroke weight* is the thickness of a line. In the Stroke palette (beneath the Transparency palette), the line has a weight of 1 point.

3 Click the Stroke tab to bring the palette to the front of its group. Then type **7** in the Weight text box and press Enter or Return to change the stroke weight to 7 points. The squiggly line now stands out.

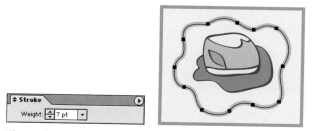

Change the Stroke weight to make the squiggly line stand out.

Next you'll use the Stroke palette's options to change the line from solid to dashed.

4 First, drag the Swatches palette by its tab to move the palette down and away from the Stroke palette.

5 In the Stroke palette, hold down the mouse button on the triangle in the upper right corner of the palette and choose Show Options from the palette menu. (You use this same technique for choosing options from other palette menus.)

You use the Stroke palette options to specify how to cap the ends, join the corners, and make lines dashed or dotted.

6 In the Stroke palette, select the Dashed Line option. The Dash and Gap text boxes become active.

To create a dashed or dotted line, you specify the length of the dash (or dot) and then the gap, or spacing, between the dashes. You can create a dashed or dotted line with as few as two values or as many as six values. The more values you enter, the more complex the pattern.

7 Type the following values in the Dash and Gap text boxes, pressing Tab to advance to the next text box: **12, 0, 12, 0, 12**. Leave the last Gap box empty. Press Enter or Return to apply the change.

Now you'll select a cap for the lines to create a dotted-line effect.

8 In the Cap options area of the Stroke palette, click the Round Cap button (the middle button). Click away from the artwork to deselect it and see the result.

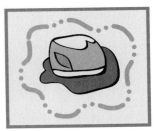

*Select Round Caps for   Result
dashed line.*

For examples of other effects you can create, and information on stroking lines, see "Using the Stroke palette" in online Help or Chapter 6 in the Adobe Illustrator User Guide.

You can select objects by a common paint attribute (such as their stroke color or weight) and change them all at once.

9 Select the border of one of the rectangles, and click the Stroke box in the toolbox to select the rectangle's stroke.

10 Choose Select > Same > Stroke Weight to select the strokes of all the objects that have the same stroke weight in the artwork (in this case, all of the rectangles).

11 In the Stroke palette, type **2** in the Weight text box and press Enter or Return to globally change the stroke weight to 2 points.

12 Click away from the artwork to deselect it, and choose File > Save.

Building a custom palette

Now you'll learn how to create your own custom palettes by mixing colors, naming them, and saving them in the Swatches palette.

Mixing your own color

You'll start to create a custom palette by mixing a color using the CMYK sliders in the Color palette. First you'll mix a fill color.

1 In the toolbox, click the Fill box to make it active.

2 Using the selection tool (▶), click the middle of the hat in the bottom left rectangle to select it.

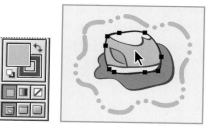

Select Fill box.   *Select middle of hat in bottom left rectangle.*

In the Color palette, notice that the hat color is grayscale—that is, a percentage of black—and only a K (black) slider shows a value. The color bar changes to display a scale ramp from white to black.

Now you'll change the color model to CMYK so that you can mix colors.

3 In the Color palette, choose CMYK from the palette menu.

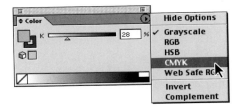

The Color palette lets you edit and mix colors—either colors that you create or colors that you have selected from the Swatches palette, from an object, or from a color library. In this case, you're choosing colors using the CMYK color model.

Now you'll select an orange color for the middle of the hat.

4 In the Color palette, drag the CMYK sliders to select a light orange color or type values in the text boxes and press Enter or Return to apply the changes. (We specified 0% cyan, 25% magenta, 54% yellow, and 0% black.)

You can use the different color models in conjunction with the Color palette sliders to select a color precisely by its different color values. However, if you mix color models (such as CMYK and RGB) in the same file, Illustrator will convert the colors to the mode in which the file is saved.

For information on the color models that Illustrator uses, see "Color Modes and Models" in online Help or Chapter 6 in the Adobe Illustrator User Guide.

5 Click away from the artwork to deselect it, and choose File > Save.

Saving colors

The Swatches palette stores the colors, gradients, and patterns that have been preloaded into Adobe Illustrator, as well as those you have created and saved for reuse. New colors added to the Swatches palette are saved with the current file. Opening a new artwork file displays the default set of swatches that comes with the Adobe Illustrator program.

You'll add the light orange color you just mixed to the Swatches palette so it will be stored with this artwork file. You can select a color to add from either the Fill or Stroke boxes in the toolbox, or from the Color palette. Even though you deselected the artwork, the light orange color is still the current color in the Fill box in the toolbox and in the Color palette.

1 Drag the orange color from the Fill box and drop it in the Swatches palette. It appears in the first empty spot in the palette.

As you drag a color into the Swatches palette, an outline appears around the palette, indicating that it is active and that you are about to drop the color.

Now you'll add another color to the Swatches palette.

2 Using the selection tool ( ), select the top left rectangle that you painted with a yellow fill.

3 Make sure that the Fill box is selected in the toolbox, and then click the New Swatch button at the bottom of the Swatches palette to store the color.

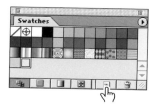

Clicking New Swatch button to store a color

You can make your own custom set of swatches for the file by deleting swatches from the Swatches palette that you don't use.

4 Click away from the artwork to deselect it, and then click the black swatch (C=0, M=0, Y=0, K=100) in the Swatches palette to select it. Click the Delete Swatch button at the bottom of the Swatches palette, and then click Yes in the warning dialog box to delete the swatch.

If you want to add a color back into the Swatches palette, you can drag the color directly from the Color palette or from the Fill or Stroke boxes in the toolbox. You can also restore the default set of colors to your artwork.

5 Choose Window > Swatch Libraries > Default_CMYK to retrieve the default set of swatches for CMYK files. (These swatches may look different from the swatches in your Swatches palette.)

6 In the Default_CMYK palette, select the black color swatch you deleted in step 4, and then choose Add to Swatches from the palette menu to copy the selected swatch back to your customized Swatches palette. The color appears as the last color in the bottom row of the Swatches palette.

You can add swatches from any color library palette to the Swatches palette.

7 Click the close box of the Default_CMYK palette to close it, and choose File > Save.

Naming a color

You can name colors and refer to that name as you paint. All colors—whether process colors or spot colors—can be named while still retaining all of the characteristics of the color mode (for example, RGB, Web Safe RGB, HSB, or Grayscale modes).

1 Double-click the yellow swatch you saved in the Swatches palette, or select it and choose Swatch Options from the Swatches palette menu.

2 In the Swatch Options dialog box, name the color (for example, "background-yellow") and click OK.

The Swatches palette lets you name, store, and select three types of colors: individual and global process colors (these include grayscale and CMYK, RGB, Web Safe RGB, and HSB color models), and global spot colors. Spot colors are special premixed colors used instead of, or in addition to, process color inks; they require their own separations and their own plates on press.

Working with process colors, spot colors, and registration colors

It is important to understand the different types of color used in Adobe Illustrator—global process color, non-global process color, spot color, and registration color—because the color type determines how colors are updated throughout the document, and how they are separated and printed.

Process colors *are the four inks used in traditional color separations: cyan, magenta, yellow, and black. In Illustrator, all five color models that are used in a CMYK file—that is, CMYK, RGB, Web Safe RGB, HSB, and Grayscale—will result in process colors. Avoid using process colors in documents intended for online viewing only, because CMYK has a smaller color gamut than a typical monitor.*

Global process colors *are process colors that automatically update throughout the document when the swatch is edited; that is, every object containing such a color changes when the corresponding swatch is modified.*

Nonglobal process colors *also can be assigned any of the five color models (CMYK, RGB, Web Safe RGB, HSB, and Grayscale), but do not automatically update throughout the document when the color is edited. Process colors are nonglobal by default; a nonglobal process color can be changed to a global process color using the Swatch Options dialog box.*

Spot colors *are special premixed colors that are used instead of, or in addition to, CMYK inks, and that require their own separations and their own plates on a printing press. When a spot color swatch is edited, the color is updated globally throughout the document.*

You can assign any of the five color models to a spot color. Spot colors may or may not fall within the CMYK gamut; for example, a spot color may be a neon or metallic ink that is not within the CMYK gamut, or it may be a shade of green that falls within the gamut.

Registration colors *are applied to objects that you want to print on all plates in the printing process, including any spot color plates. Registration colors are typically used for crop marks and trim marks.*

For an illustration of global and nonglobal process colors, see figure 3-1 in the color section.

Now you'll change the display of the Swatches palette so that you can locate the color by its name.

3 Choose List View from the Swatches palette menu to display the swatches by name and see the swatch you just named.

You can change how swatches are displayed in the palette—as large or small swatches, or by name. When you display swatches by name, the Swatches palette also displays icons indicating the color model and color type (individual process color, global process color, or global spot color).

Copying paint attributes

Adobe Illustrator lets you copy paint attributes of objects (such as their fill and stroke color) in various ways and apply the attributes to other objects.

You'll use the eyedropper tool to copy colors from your artwork into the Color palette. Also called *sampling*, copying colors lets you replicate paint attributes even when you don't know their exact values.

1 Select the eyedropper tool (✐) in the toolbox.

2 In the bottom left rectangle, click the orange brim of the hat to sample its color. This action picks up the fill and stroke attributes of the hat brim and displays them in the Color palette.

By default, the eyedropper tool affects all paint attributes of an object. However, you can restrict which attributes are affected (by double-clicking the eyedropper tool and selecting options in the dialog box).

3 To quickly apply the current paint attributes to the top of the hat, hold down Alt (Windows) or Option (Mac OS) to temporarily select the paint bucket tool (🪣), and then click inside the top of the hat to apply the paint.

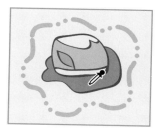

Select attributes with eyedropper.

Apply with paint bucket.

Copying appearance attributes

Adobe Illustrator lets you copy appearance attributes that include both the fill and the stroke of an object as well as its transparency and effects.

You'll create a drop shadow shape and change its transparency. Then you'll apply the shadow's appearance to another shape using the Appearance palette. You can save and name appearance attributes using the Styles palette.

1 Select the selection tool (▸) in the toolbox, and click the hat brim in the upper right rectangle.

2 Hold down Alt (Windows) or Option (Mac OS) and drag the brim slightly down and to the right. Release the mouse button to leave a copy of the hat brim. This copy will become a drop shadow.

3 Choose Object > Arrange > Send Backward to move the shadow shape underneath the hat brim. You should still be able to see both the shadow shape and the hat brim.

4 With the object still selected, use the Color palette to change its stroke to None.

5 Change the fill to a medium brown. (We specified 49% cyan, 65% magenta, 100% yellow, and 0% black.)

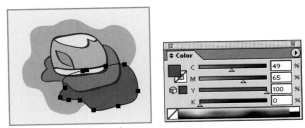

Move a copy of the brim and paint it brown.

6 Click the Transparency tab to bring the palette to the front of its group. Then choose Show Options from the palette menu to expand the palette.

7 With the shadow shape still selected, in the Transparency palette type **50** in the Opacity percentage box or use the slider, and press Return or Enter to change the opacity of the shape to 50%.

Change shadow's transparency to 50%.

8 In the Appearance palette, click the Path thumbnail to select it. Drag the Path thumbnail from the Appearance palette until the pointer is over the bottom right hat side. Release the mouse button to apply the appearance to the hat side and make it a transparent brown.

  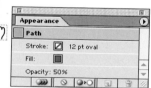

Drag Path thumbnail onto the hat side of bottom right hat.   *Release mouse button to apply appearance.*

9 Click away from the artwork to deselect it, and choose File > Save.

For more information on using the Appearance and Style palettes, see Lesson 9, "Using Appearance Attributes, Styles, and Effects," or see that topic in online Help or Chapter 10 of the Adobe Illustrator User Guide.

Saturating colors

Next, you'll adjust the saturation of the new color you added to the hat's top by changing the percentage of black in the color.

1 Using the selection tool ( ), click the top of the hat in the bottom left rectangle to select it. Make sure that the Fill box in the toolbox is selected.

2 In the Color palette, hold down Shift and drag the M slider to the left to desaturate the color. As you Shift-drag, the sliders move in tandem, and the color intensity changes.

 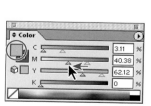

Select top of hat.   *Shift-drag left to desaturate magenta mix.*

Adjusting the saturation lets you change the strength of a color without affecting the hue. (However, if you drag a slider that is set to 0%, you will change the hue or color rather than the saturation.)

3 Click away from the artwork, and choose File > Save.

Painting with patterns and gradients

In addition to process and spot colors, the Swatches palette can contain pattern and gradient swatches. Adobe Illustrator provides sample swatches of each type in the default palette and lets you create your own patterns and gradients.

To learn how to create your own gradients, see Lesson 8, "Blending Shapes and Colors."

[?] For information on how to create patterns, see "Creating and working with patterns" in online Help or Chapter 8 in the Adobe Illustrator User Guide.

Now you'll fill some objects with a pattern, working with the hat in the top right rectangle.

1 Using the selection tool (▶), click in the center of the inner shape of the hat ribbon in the top right rectangle. The Fill box in the toolbox shows that the shape's current fill is gray.

Select inner shape of hat ribbon in top right rectangle.

The buttons at the bottom of the Swatches palette let you display swatches grouped as solid colors, gradients, or patterns.

2 In the Swatches palette, click the Show Pattern Swatches button (the fourth button from the left). All of the pattern swatches appear.

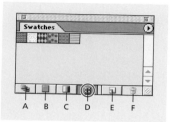

A. *Show All Swatches* **B.** *Show Color Swatches* **C.** *Show Gradient Swatches* **D.** *Show Pattern Swatches* **E.** *New Swatch* **F.** *Delete Swatch*

3 Click a pattern in the palette to select it, and fill the hat ribbon. (We selected the Confetti pattern.)

4 Now select the background of the top right rectangle. Make sure that the Fill box is selected, and paint the rectangle's fill with the same pattern.

Fill hat ribbon with a pattern.   *Select background of top right rectangle.*   *Fill background with same pattern.*

Now you'll apply a gradient to the first block in the illustration.

5 In the top left rectangle, select the squiggly line around the hat, and make sure that the Fill box is selected in the toolbox.

6 In the Swatches palette, click the Show Gradient Swatches button (third button from the left) to show only gradient swatches in the palette.

7 Click a gradient to apply it to the fill of the squiggly shape. (We selected the Yellow & Orange Radial gradient.)

Painting with a Pattern brush

Brushes can be applied to existing paths or objects. There are four types of brushes in the Brushes palette: Calligraphic, Scatter, Art, and Pattern. For information on how to create your own custom brushes, see Lesson 5, "Working with Brushes."

Now you'll paint the stroke of a shape with a Pattern brush.

1 Use the selection tool ( ) to select the squiggly shape around the hat in the bottom right rectangle.

2 Choose Window > Brushes or click the Brushes tab behind the Swatches palette to display the Brushes palette.

3 Choose List View from the Brushes palette menu, and scroll down to see the Pattern brushes. Click a name to select a brush, and apply it to the squiggly shape around the hat. (We selected the Laurel Pattern brush.)

The type of brush (Calligraphic, Scatter, Art, or Pattern) is indicated by an icon to the right of the brush name.

Select the squiggly shape in bottom right rectangle.

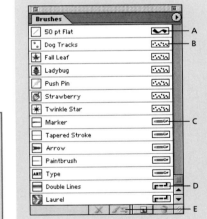

A. Calligraphic B. Scatter C. Art
D. Pattern E. Options of Selected
Object

Apply a Pattern brush.

You can change the size and other characteristics of the pattern after it is applied to the selected object.

4 With the squiggly shape still selected, in the Brushes palette click the Options of Selected Object button (second button from the left) at the bottom of the palette.

5 In the Stroke Options (Pattern Brush) dialog box, select the Preview option to view different settings applied to the artwork without closing the dialog box.

6 Try out different settings to see how they affect the pattern on the squiggly shape, pressing Tab to move between the options. (We entered 75% in the Scale text box.) When you're satisfied with the settings, click OK to apply them to the artwork.

7 Choose File > Save.

8 Close the file.

You've completed painting the hat artwork using a variety of painting tools.

See these topics to learn more on the following painting techniques:

• For information on using brushes, creating your own custom brushes, and using the Brushes palette, see Lesson 5, "Working with Brushes."

• For how to paint objects with colors that blend in multiple directions, see Lesson 11, "Creating Airbrush Effects."

• For how to create other blending effects, see Lesson 8, "Blending Shapes and Colors."

• For more on transparency, styles, appearance attributes, and effects, see Lesson 9, "Using Appearance Attributes, Styles, and Effects".

Review questions

1 Describe three ways to fill an object with color.

2 How can you save a color?

3 How do you name a color?

4 How do you restore the original set of colors in the Swatches palette?

5 How do you paint a shape with a transparent color?

6 How can you desaturate a color?

7 What is a quick way to view all the pattern swatches in the Swatches palette?

8 What are the four types of brushes that you can paint the fill or stroke of objects with?

Review answers

1 To fill an object with color, select it and select the Fill box in the toolbox. Then do one of the following:

• Click a color in the color bar in the Color palette.

• Drag the color sliders or type in values in the text boxes in the Color palette.

• Click a color swatch in the Swatches palette.

• Select the eyedropper tool (✒), and click a color in the artwork.

• Drag and drop an appearance thumbnail onto a shape in the artwork.

• Choose Window > Swatch Libraries to open another color library, and click a color swatch in the color library palette.

2 You can save a color for painting other objects in your artwork by adding it to the Swatches palette. Select the color, and do one of the following:

• Drag it from the Fill box and drop it over the Swatches palette.

• Click the New Swatch button at the bottom of the Swatches palette.

• Choose New Swatch from the Swatches palette menu.

You can also add colors from other color libraries by selecting them in the color library palette and choosing Add to Swatches from the palette menu.

3 To name a color, double-click the color swatch in the Swatches palette or select it and choose Swatch Options from the palette menu. Type the name for the color in the Swatch Options dialog box.

4 To restore the original set of colors in the Swatches palette, choose Window > Swatch Libraries > Default. This palette contains all of the original swatches that appear by default before you customize the Swatches palette.

5 To paint a shape with a transparent color, select the shape and fill it with any color. Then adjust the opacity percentage in the Transparency palette to less than 100%.

6 To desaturate a color, select the color and Shift-drag a slider to the left in the Color palette. Shift-dragging the slider causes the other sliders to move in tandem so the hue won't change.

7 A quick way to view all the pattern swatches in the Swatches palette is to click the Show Pattern Swatches button at the bottom of the palette.

8 The four types of brushes are Calligraphic, Scatter, Art, and Pattern.

Lesson 4

4 Drawing with the Pen Tool

The pen tool is a powerful tool for drawing straight lines, Bézier curves, and complex shapes. Although the pencil tool is
easier for drawing and editing lines, the
pen tool can be more precise. You'll practice drawing with the pen tool by creating
an illustration of a pear.

In this lesson, you'll learn how to do the following:

- Draw straight lines.

- End path segments and split lines.

- Draw curved lines.

- Select curve segments and adjust them.

- Draw different types of curves, smooth and pointed.

- Edit curves, changing from smooth to pointed and vice versa.

Getting started

In this lesson, you'll create an illustration of a pear pierced by an arrow. Before you begin, you'll restore the default preferences for Adobe Illustrator. Then you will open the finished art file for this lesson to see what you'll create.

1 To ensure that the tools and palettes function exactly as described in this lesson, delete or deactivate (by renaming) the Adobe Illustrator 10.0 preferences file. See "Restoring default preferences" on page 4.

2 Start Adobe Illustrator.

3 Choose File > Open, and open the L4end.ai file in the Lesson04 folder, located inside the Lessons folder within the AICIB folder on your hard drive.

4 Choose View > Zoom Out to make the finished artwork smaller and leave it on your screen as you work. (Use the hand tool (🖐) to move the artwork where you want it in the window.) If you don't want to leave the image open, choose File > Close.

For an illustration of the finished artwork in this lesson, see the color section.

Now open the start file to begin the lesson.

5 Choose File > Open, and open the L4start.ai file in the Lesson04 folder, located inside the Lessons folder within the AICIB folder on your hard drive.

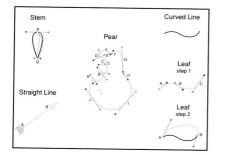

6 Choose File > Save As, name the file **Pear.ai**, and select the Lesson04 folder. Leave the Format option set to Adobe Illustrator® Document, and click Save. In the Illustrator Native Format Options dialog box, select Illustrator 10 Compatibility and click OK.

7 Hold down Shift and press Tab once to hide all of the palettes. (Pressing Shift+Tab toggles between hiding and displaying the palettes. Pressing Tab alone hides or shows the toolbox as well.)

Drawing straight lines

You draw straight lines by using the pen tool to create a starting anchor point and an ending anchor point. You can create straight lines that are vertical, horizontal, or diagonal by holding down Shift as you click with the pen tool. This is called *constraining* the line.

We've created a template layer in this file so you can practice using the pen tool by tracing over the template. (See Lesson 10, "Working with Layers," for information on creating layers.)

You'll begin by drawing the straight line for the arrow.

1 Choose View > Straight Line to zoom into the left corner of the template.

Separate views that show different areas of the template at a higher magnification were created for this document and added to the View menu.

▧ To create a custom view, choose View > New View. For information, see "Viewing artwork" in online Help or Chapter 1 in the Adobe Illustrator User Guide.

2 Choose View > Hide Bounding Box to hide the bounding boxes of selected objects. Select the pen tool ( ) in the toolbox, and move the pointer to the dashed line of the arrow in the artwork. Notice that the pen tool pointer has a small x next to it. This indicates that clicking will begin a new path.

3 Click point A at the left end of the line to create the starting anchor point—a small solid square.

4 Click point B at the right end of the line to create the ending anchor point.

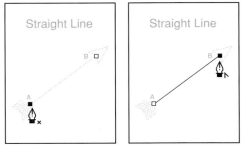

Click once to begin a   Click again to end it.
straight line.

When you click a second time, a caret (^) appears next to the pen tool. The caret indicates that you can split the anchor point to create a direction line for a curve by dragging the pen tool from this anchor point. The caret disappears when you move the pen tool away from the anchor point.

You must end the path before you can draw other lines that aren't connected to the path.

5 End the path using one of the following methods:

• Hold down Ctrl (Windows) or Command (Mac OS) to activate the current selection tool, and click away from the path to deselect it.

• Choose Select > Deselect.

• Click the pen tool in the toolbox.

Now you'll make the straight line thicker by changing its stroke weight.

6 Select the selection tool ( ) in the toolbox, and click the straight line to select it.

7 Choose Window > Stroke to display the Stroke palette.

8 In the Stroke palette, type **3** points in the Weight text box and press Enter or Return to apply the change.

Splitting a path

To continue creating the arrow for this illustration, you'll split the path of the straight line using the scissors tool and adjust the segments.

1 With the straight line still selected, select the scissors tool (✁) in the toolbox and click in the middle of the line to make a cut.

Cuts made with the scissors tool must be on a line or a curve rather than on an endpoint.

Where you click, you see a new selected anchor point. The scissors tool actually creates two anchor points each time you click, but because they are on top of each other, you can see only one.

2 Select the direct-selection tool (▶) in the toolbox, and position it over the cut. The small hollow square on the pointer indicates that it's over the anchor point. Select the new anchor point, and drag it up to widen the gap between the two split segments.

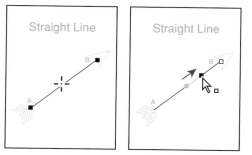

Click with the scissors tool to cut the line.

Drag to separate the new line segments.

Adding arrowheads

Adobe Illustrator lets you add premade arrowheads and tails to open paths by applying a Stylize filter. Now you'll add an arrowhead to the ending point of one line segment and a tail to the starting point of the other line segment.

1 With the top line segment selected, choose Filter > Stylize > Add Arrowheads.

Note: *Choose the top Filter > Stylize command. The second Filter > Stylize command applies painted or impressionistic effects to bitmap images.*

2 In the Add Arrowheads dialog box, leave the Start section set to None. For the end, click an arrow button to select the number 2 style of arrowhead (a thumbnail preview appears in the dialog box), and click OK.

Illustrator adds the arrowhead to the end of the line (the last anchor point created on the uncut line).

3 Using the direct-selection tool ( ), select the bottom line segment, and choose Filter > Add Arrowheads to open the dialog box again. Select the number 18 style of arrowhead from the Start section, select None for the End section, and click OK to add a tail to the starting point of the line.

You can reapply the same arrowhead style to other selected objects by choosing Filter > Apply Add Arrowhead.

4 Choose Select > Deselect to deselect the artwork, and then choose File > Save.

Drawing curves

In this part of the lesson, you'll learn how to draw smooth curved lines with the pen tool. In vector drawing programs such as Adobe Illustrator, you draw a curve, called a Bézier curve, by setting anchor points and dragging to define the shape of the curve. Although drawing curves this way takes some getting used to, it gives you the most control and flexibility in computer graphics.

You'll draw the pear, its stem, and a leaf. You'll examine a single curve and then draw a series of curves together, using the template guidelines to help you.

Selecting a curve

1 Choose View > Curved Line to display a view of a curved line on the template.

2 Using the direct-selection tool ( ), click one of the segments of the curved line to view its anchor points and its direction lines, which extend from the points. The direct-selection tool lets you select and edit individual segments in the curved line.

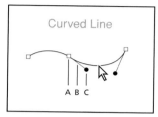

A. *Anchor point* **B.** *Direction line*
C. *Direction point (or handle)*

As their names imply, the anchor points anchor the curved segments, and the direction lines control the direction of the curves. You can drag the direction lines or their endpoints, called *direction points* or *handles*, to adjust the shape of the curve.

Anchor points, direction points, and direction lines are aids to help you draw. They always appear in the current layer color—in this case, red. Anchor points are square, and, when selected, appear filled; unselected, they appear unfilled, like hollow squares. Direction points are round. These lines and points do not print with the artwork.

By selecting the curve, you also select the paint attributes of the curve so that the next line you draw will have the same attributes. For more on paint attributes, see Lesson 3, "Painting."

Drawing the leaf

Now you'll draw the first curve of the leaf.

1 Choose View > Leaf or scroll down to see the guides for Leaf step 1.

Instead of dragging the pen tool to draw a curve, you drag it to set the starting point and the *direction* of the line's curve. When you release the mouse button, the starting point is created and two direction lines are formed. Then you drag the pen tool to end the first curve and to set the starting point and direction of the next curve on the line.

2 Select the pen tool ( ) and position it over point A on the template. Press the mouse button and drag from point A to the red dot. Then release the mouse button.

Next you'll set the second anchor point and its direction lines.

3 Press the mouse button and drag from point B to the next red dot. Then release the mouse button. Illustrator connects the two anchor points with a curve that follows the direction lines you have created. Notice that if you vary the angle of dragging, you change the amount of curve.

If you make a mistake as you draw, you can undo your work by choosing Edit > Undo. Adobe Illustrator by default lets you undo a series of actions—limited only by your computer's memory—by repeatedly choosing Edit > Undo. (To set the minimum number of undos, choose Edit > Preferences > Units & Undo (Windows and Mac OS 9) or Illustrator > Preferences > Units & Undo (Mac OS X).)

4 To complete the curved line, drag the pen tool from point C on the template to the last red dot and release the mouse button.

5 Ctrl-click (Windows) or Command-click (Mac OS) away from the line to indicate the end of the path. (You must indicate when you have finished drawing a path. You can also do this by clicking the pen tool in the toolbox, or by choosing Select > Deselect.)

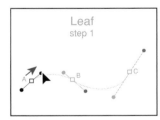
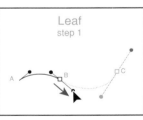
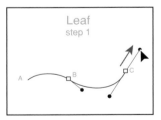

Drag to start the line and set direction of first curve.   *Drag to end first curve and set direction of second curve.*   *Drag to end second curve and adjust its direction.*

Drawing different kinds of curves

Now you'll finish drawing the leaf by adding to an existing curved segment. Even if you end a path, you can return to the curve and add to it later. The Alt key (Windows) or Option key (Mac OS) lets you control the type of curve you draw.

1 Scroll down to the instructions on the template for Leaf step 2.

You'll add a *corner point* to the path. A corner point lets you change the direction of the curve. A *smooth point* lets you draw a continuous curve.

2 Position the pen tool over the end of the line at point A. The slash next to the pen tool indicates that you'll continue the path of the line rather than start a new line.

3 Hold down Alt (Windows) or Option (Mac OS) and notice that the status bar in the lower left corner of the window displays "Pen: Make Corner." Now Alt/Option-drag the pen tool from anchor point A to the red dot. Then release the mouse button.

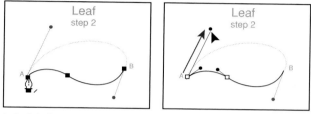

A slash indicates pen tool is aligned with anchor.

Alt/Option-dragging creates corner point.

So far, all of the curves you have drawn have been open paths. Now you'll draw a closed path, in which the final anchor point is drawn on the first anchor point of the path. (Examples of closed paths include ovals and rectangles.) You'll close the path using a smooth point.

4 Position the pointer over anchor point B on the template. A small open circle appears next to the pen tool indicating that clicking will close the path. Press the mouse button and drag from this point to the second red dot.

Notice the direction lines where you close the path. The direction lines on both sides of a smooth point are aligned along the same angle.

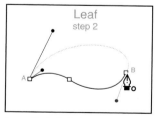
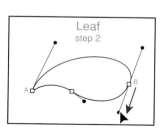

A small circle indicates clicking with pen tool closes the path.

Drag to red dot to lengthen curved line.

5 Ctrl-click (Windows) or Command-click (Mac OS) away from the line, and choose File > Save.

Changing a smooth curve to a corner and vice versa

Now you'll create the stem by adjusting a curved path. You'll convert a smooth point on the curve to a corner point and a corner point to a smooth point.

1 Choose View > Stem to display a magnified view of the stem.

2 Select the direct-selection tool ( ) in the toolbox, position the pointer over point A at the top of the curve to display a hollow square on the pointer, and then click the anchor point to select it and display its red direction lines for the smooth point.

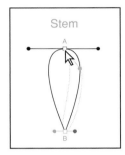

3 Select the convert-anchor-point tool ( ) from the same group as the pen tool in the toolbox.

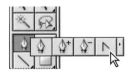

(When the pen tool is the current tool, a shortcut to get the convert-anchor-point tool is to press Alt (Windows) or Option (Mac OS).)

4 Using the convert-anchor-point tool, select the left direction point (on top of the red dot) on the direction line and drag it to the gold dot on the template, and then release the mouse button.

Dragging with the convert-anchor-point tool converts the smooth anchor point to a corner point and adjusts the angle of the left direction line.

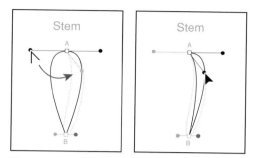

Use convert-anchor-point tool to convert curves to corners.

5 Using the convert-anchor-point tool, select the bottom anchor point and drag from point B to the red dot to convert the corner point to a smooth point, rounding out the curve, and then release the mouse button.

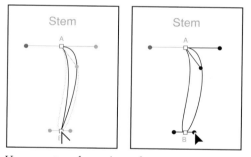

Use convert-anchor-point tool to convert corners to curves.

Two direction lines emerge from the anchor point, indicating that it is now a smooth point.

When using the convert-anchor-point tool, keep these guidelines in mind:

• Drag from the curve's anchor point for a smooth point and continuous curve.

• Click the curve's anchor point or drag a handle (direction point) of the curve for a corner point on a discontinuous curve.

6 Choose File > Save.

Drawing the pear shape

Now you'll draw a single, continuous object that contains smooth points and corner points. Each time you want to change the direction of a curve at a point, you'll hold down Alt (Windows) or Option (Mac OS) to create a corner point.

1 Choose View > Pear to display a magnified view of the pear.

First you'll draw the bite marks on the pear by creating corner points and changing the direction of the curve segments.

2 Select the pen tool ( ) from the same group as the convert-anchor-point tool ( ). Drag the pen tool from point A on the template to the red dot to set the starting anchor point and direction of the first curve. Release the mouse button.

3 Drag the pen tool from point B to the red dot—but don't release the mouse button—and hold down Alt (Windows) or Option (Mac OS) and drag the direction handle from the red dot to the gold dot. Release the mouse button.

4 Continue drawing to points C and D by first dragging from the anchor point to the red dot and then Alt/Option-dragging the direction handle from the red dot to the gold dot.

At the corner points B, C, and D, you first drag to continue the current segment, and then Alt/Option-drag to set the direction of the next curved segment.

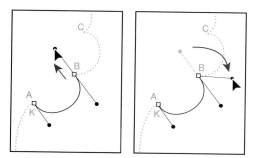

Drag to adjust curve.   Alt/Option-drag
direction point to set
corner point.

Next you'll complete drawing the pear by creating smooth points.

5 Drag from each of the points E through J to their red dots, and then click anchor point K to close the pear shape. Notice that when you hold the pointer over anchor point K, a small open circle appears next to the pen, indicating that the path will close when you click.

6 Hold down Ctrl (Windows) or Command (Mac OS) and click away from the path to deselect it, and choose File > Save.

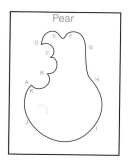

Editing curves

To adjust the curves you've drawn, you can drag the curve's anchor points or its direction lines. You can also edit a curve by moving the line.

1 Select the direct-selection tool ( ), and click the outline of the pear.

Clicking with the direct-selection tool displays the curve's direction lines and lets you adjust the shape of individual curved segments. Clicking with the selection tool selects the entire path.

2 Click the anchor point G at the top right of the pear to select it, and adjust the segment by dragging the top direction handle as shown in the illustration.

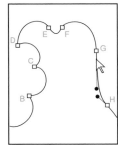
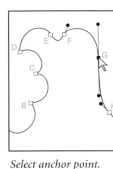
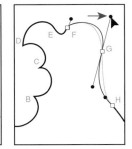

Use direct-selection tool to select individual segments.   *Select anchor point.*   *Adjust anchor point.*

3 In the toolbox, click the Fill box to select it. Then click the None box to change the Fill to None.

4 Now select the pen tool ( ) and drag to draw the small curve on the pear where the arrow will pierce it. (Use the dashed line on the template as a guide.)

Note: If you can't see the dashed, curved line on the template, make sure that the Fill in the toolbox is set to None and that the Stroke is set to black.

5 Choose File > Save.

Tips for drawing curves

Keep the following guidelines in mind to help you draw any kind of curve quickly and easily:

• *Always drag the first direction point in the direction of the bump of the curve, and drag the second direction point in the opposite direction to create a single curve. Dragging both direction points in the same direction creates an S curve.*

• *When drawing a series of continuous curves, draw one curve at a time, placing anchor points at the beginning and end of each curve, not at the tip of the curve. Use as few anchor points as possible, placing them as far apart as possible.*

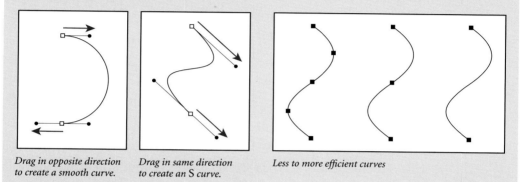

Drag in opposite direction to create a smooth curve.   *Drag in same direction to create an S curve.*   *Less to more efficient curves*

? For information on adding, deleting, and moving anchor points on a path, see "Drawing" in online Help or Chapter 3 in the Adobe Illustrator User Guide.

Finishing the pear illustration

To complete the illustration, you'll assemble the objects together, paint them, and position parts of the arrow to create the illusion of the pear being pierced.

Assembling the parts

1 Double-click the zoom tool (🔍) to zoom to 100%.

2 Choose Window > Layers to display the palette.

3 In the Layers palette, click the template icon (🖹) that's next to the Template layer name to hide the template.

4 Choose View > Show Bounding Box so that you can see the bounding box of selected objects as you transform them.

5 Select the selection tool (⬉) in the toolbox, and Shift-click to select the two single curved lines that you no longer need for the leaf. Press Backspace (Windows) or Delete (Mac OS) to delete them.

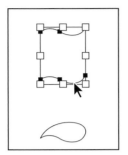

Select and delete extra lines.

Now you'll make the stem and leaf smaller and rotate them slightly using the Transform commands.

6 Select the stem and choose Object > Transform > Scale. Select Uniform and enter **50%** in the Scale text box. Select the Scale Strokes & Effects option, and click OK.

The Scale Strokes & Effects option scales stroke weights and effects automatically. You can also set this option as a preference (choose Edit > General > Preferences).

7 Choose Object > Transform > Rotate. Enter **45** degrees in the Angle text box, and click OK.

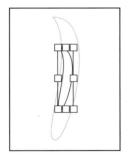
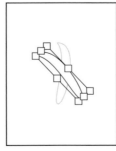

Scale stem 50%.   *Rotate stem 45°.*

Now you'll repeat the scaling and rotation on the leaf.

8 Select the leaf and choose Object > Transform > Scale. Leave the settings as they are, and click OK to scale the leaf by 50%. Then choose Object > Transform > Rotate, and enter **15** degrees in the Angle text box, and click OK.

You can also scale and rotate objects using the scale and rotate tools or the free transform tool to do both. For information, see Lesson 6, "Transforming Objects."

9 Select the selection pointer, and move the stem and the leaf to the top of the pear.

10 Move the parts of the arrow over the pear to make it look as if the arrow is entering the front of the pear and exiting the back.

Objects are arranged in the order in which they are created, with the most recent in front.

11 Select the bottom part of the arrow, and Shift-click to select the curve where the arrow pierces the pear. Then choose Object > Arrange > Bring to Front to arrange them in front of the pear.

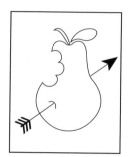

Painting the artwork

Now paint the objects as you like. We removed the stroke on the leaf, the stem, and the pear; and we painted the fills with custom-made gradients called Pear leaf, Pear stem, and Pear body, which are provided in the Swatches palette. We painted the arrow with a dark blue color, and then we added some detail lines to the leaf, the stem, and the round part of the pear using the paintbrush tool and the pen tool. We also stroked the curve where the arrow pierces the pear.

1 Choose Window > Swatches to display the Swatches palette.

2 Select an object, and then select a swatch in the Swatches palette to paint the object with a color, pattern, or gradient.

To learn how to create your own gradients, see Lesson 8, "Blending Shapes and Colors." To learn more about painting options in Illustrator, see Lesson 3, "Painting," and Lesson 11, "Creating Airbrush Effects."

3 In the Color palette, drag the None icon up and drop it on the Stroke box to remove the stroke of a selected object.

4 Choose File > Save to save your work. Choose File > Close to close the file.

You've completed the lesson on drawing straight lines and curves. For additional practice with the pen tool, try tracing over images with it. As you practice more with the pen tool, you'll become more adept at drawing the kinds of curves and shapes you want.

Exploring on your own

Now that you've used the pen tool to draw precise Bézier curves on the pear, try drawing the pear using the pencil tool to create a hand-drawn look. You can edit lines that you draw using the pencil tool to change their shape, and you can use the smooth tool and erase tool to edit the drawing further.

1 Open the L4start.ai file again, and save it as **Pear2.ai**.

2 Select the pencil tool ( ) in the toolbox, and draw the pear in one continuous line without releasing the mouse button. To close the path, hold down Alt (Windows) or Option (Mac OS)—a small circle appears on the pointer—and continue dragging to draw the end of the line connected to the starting point.

Anchor points are set down as you draw with the pencil tool, and you can adjust them once the path is complete. The number of anchor points is determined by the length and complexity of the path and by the tolerance values set in the Pencil Tool Preferences dialog box. (Double-click the tool to display its preferences dialog box.)

Note: You can draw and edit brushed paths with the paintbrush tool by using the same methods as for paths drawn with the pencil tool. (See Lesson 5, "Working with Brushes.")

3 Use the pencil tool (✐) to edit the shape of the pear by redrawing segments on the path.

To change a path with the pencil tool:

1. *If the path you want to change is not selected, select it with the selection tool. Or Ctrl-click (Windows) or Command-click (Mac OS) the path to select it.*

2. *Position the pencil tool on or near the path to redraw, and drag the tool until the path is the desired shape.*

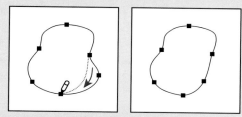

Using the pencil tool to edit a closed shape

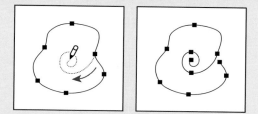

Using the pencil tool to create an open shape

Depending on where you begin to redraw the path and in which direction you drag, you may get unexpected results. For example, you may unintentionally change a closed path to an open path, change an open path to a closed path, or lose a portion of a shape.

— From the Adobe Illustrator User Guide, Chapter 3

---

4 Use the smooth tool (✐), in the same group as the pencil tool (✐) in the toolbox, to round out the shape of a curved segment (deleting anchor points if necessary).

The number of anchor points is determined by the length and complexity of the new path and by the tolerance values set in the Smooth Tool Preferences dialog box.

Smoothing the path with the smooth tool

The smooth tool lets you smooth out an existing stroke or section of a path. The smooth tool retains the original shape of the path as much as possible.

Stroke before and after using the smooth tool

To use the smooth tool:

1. *If the path to smooth is not selected, select it with the selection tool. Or Ctrl-click (Windows) or Command-click (Mac OS) the path to select it.*

2. *Do one of the following:*

• *Select the smooth tool ( ) in the same group as the pencil tool ( ) in the toolbox.*

• *When the pencil or paintbrush tool is selected, hold down Alt (Windows) or Option (Mac OS) to change the pencil to the smooth tool.*

3. *Drag the tool along the length of the path segment you want to smooth out. The modified stroke or path may have fewer anchor points than the original.*

4. *Continue smoothing until the stroke or path is the desired smoothness.*

–From online Help and the Adobe Illustrator User Guide, Chapter 3

5 Use the erase tool (), in the same group as the pencil tool ()in the toolbox, to erase segments on the path of the pear; then redraw them using the pencil tool ().

Erasing the path with the erase tool

The erase tool lets you remove a portion of an existing path or stroke. You can use the erase tool on paths (including brushed paths), but not on text or meshes.

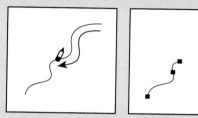
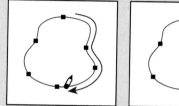

Strokes before and after using the erase tool

To use the erase tool:

1. *Select the erase tool ( ) in the same group as the pencil tool ()in the toolbox.*

2. *Drag the tool along the length of the path segment you want to erase (not across the path). For best results, use a single, smooth, dragging motion.*

Anchor points are added to the ends of the new paths.

–From online Help and the Adobe Illustrator User Guide, Chapter 3

Review questions

1 Describe how to draw straight vertical, horizontal, or diagonal lines using the pen tool.

2 How do you draw a curved line using the pen tool?

3 How do you draw a corner point on a curved line?

4 How do you change a smooth point on a curve to a corner point?

5 What tool do you use to edit a segment on a curved line?

Review answers

1 To draw a straight line, you click twice with the pen tool—the first click sets the starting anchor point, and the second click sets the ending anchor point of the line. To constrain the straight line vertically, horizontally, or along a 45° diagonal, hold down Shift as you click with the pen tool.

2 To draw a curved line using the pen tool, you hold down the mouse button and drag to create the starting anchor point and set the direction of the curve, and then you click to end the curve.

3 To draw a corner point on a curved line, hold down Alt (Windows) or Option (Mac OS) and drag the direction handle on the endpoint of the curve to change the direction of the path, and then continue dragging to draw the next curved segment on the path.

4 Use the direct-selection tool (⮠) to select the anchor point, and then use the convert-anchor-point tool (⌐) to drag a direction handle to change the direction.

5 To edit a segment on a curved line, select the direct-selection tool (⮠) and drag the segment to move it, or drag a direction handle on an anchor point to adjust the length and shape of the segment.

Lesson 5

5 | **Working with Brushes**

The variety of brush types in Adobe Illustrator lets you create myriad effects simply by painting or drawing on paths. You can choose from the provided Art, Calligraphic, Pattern, and Scatter, brushes, or create new ones from your Illustrator artwork. You can use the paintbrush tool or the drawing tools to apply brushes to artwork. Alternatively, you can use symbols to create repeating designs from instances of the symbol.

In this lesson, you'll learn how to do the following:

• Draw with each of the four brush types—Art, Calligraphic, Pattern, and Scatter—using the paintbrush tool.

• Change brush color and adjust brush settings before and after applying brushes to artwork.

• Create new brushes from Adobe Illustrator artwork.

• Apply brushes to paths created with drawing tools.

• Create symbols from an object or group of objects in the artwork.

• Create repeating designs in your artwork.

Applying brushes to paths

Adobe Illustrator brushes let you apply artwork to paths to decorate paths with patterns, figures, textures, or angled strokes. You can modify the brushes provided with Illustrator, and you can create your own brushes. Brushes appear in the Brushes palette.

You apply brushes to paths using the paintbrush tool or the drawing tools. To apply brushes using the paintbrush tool, you choose a brush from the Brushes palette and draw in the artwork. The brush is applied directly to the paths as you draw. To apply brushes using a drawing tool, you draw in the artwork, select a path in the artwork, and then choose a brush in the Brushes palette. The brush is applied to the selected path.

You can change the color, size, and other features of a brush. You can also edit paths after brushes are applied.

Getting started

In this lesson, you'll learn to use the four brush types in the Brushes palette, including how to change brush options and how to create your own brushes. Before you begin, you'll need to restore the default preferences for Adobe Illustrator. Then you'll open the finished art file for this lesson to see what you'll create.

1 To ensure that the tools and palettes function exactly as described in this lesson, delete or deactivate (by renaming) the Adobe Illustrator 10.0 preferences file. See "Restoring default preferences" on page 4.

2 Start Adobe Illustrator.

3 Choose File > Open, and open the L5end.ai file in the Lesson05 folder, located inside the Lessons folder in the AICIB folder on your hard drive.

4 If you like, choose View > Zoom Out to make the finished artwork smaller, adjust the window size, and leave it on your screen as you work. (Use the hand tool (🖐) to move the artwork where you want it in the window.) If you don't want to leave the image open, choose File > Close.

🌑 For an illustration of the finished artwork in this lesson, see the color section.

To begin working, you'll open an existing art file set up with guides to draw the artwork.

5 Choose File > Open to open the L5start.ai file in the Lesson05 folder inside the AICIB folder on your hard drive.

6 Choose File > Save As, name the file **Brushes.ai**, and select the Lesson05 folder. Leave the Format option set to Adobe Illustrator® Document, and click Save. In the Illustrator Native Format Options dialog box, select Illustrator 10 Compatibility and click OK.

Using Art brushes

Art brushes stretch artwork evenly along a path. Art brushes include strokes resembling various graphic media, such as the Charcoal and Marker brushes. Art brushes also include images, such as the Arrow brush, and text, such as the Type brush, which paints the characters *A-R-T* along a path. In this section, you'll use the Charcoal brush to draw the trunk and limbs of a tree.

The start file has been created with *guides* that you can use to create and align your artwork for the lesson. Guides are paths that have been converted using the View > Make Guides command. The guides are locked and cannot be selected, moved, modified, or printed (unless they are unlocked).

For more information on guides, see "Using guides and grids" in online Help or Chapter 4 in the Adobe Illustrator User Guide.

Drawing with the paintbrush tool

Now you'll use the paintbrush tool to apply a brush to the artwork.

1 In the toolbox, click the paintbrush tool ( ) to select it.

You select a brush in the Brushes palette to be applied to the artwork.

2 Click the Brushes tab to bring the Brushes palette to the front. (If the palette isn't visible on-screen, choose Window > Brushes.)

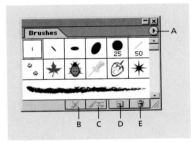

A. Displays Brushes palette menu
B. Remove Brush Stroke
C. Options of Selected Object
D. New Brush   E. Delete Brush

Brushes are arranged according to brush type, in the following order: Calligraphic, Scatter, Art, and Pattern.

By default, brushes appear as icons. You can also view brushes by name. When viewed by name, a small icon to the right of the brush name indicates the brush type.

3 In the Brushes palette, position the mouse button over the triangle in the top right corner of the Brushes palette, press the mouse button to display the palette menu, and choose List View.

You can choose which types of brushes are displayed in the Brushes palette to reduce the palette size and make it easier to find the brushes you want to use.

4 Choose Show Calligraphic Brushes from the palette menu. Then repeat the step to choose Show Scatter Brushes and Show Pattern Brushes and deselect those options, leaving only Art brushes visible in the palette. A check mark next to the brush type in the Brushes palette menu indicates that the brush type is visible in the palette.

Showing and hiding brush types

5 Select the Charcoal art brush in the Brushes palette.

Brushes are applied to paths as a stroke color. If you have a fill color selected when you apply a brush to a path, the path will be stroked with the brush and filled with the fill color. Use a fill of None when applying brushes to prevent the brushed paths from being filled. Later in this lesson you'll use a fill color with a brush. For more information on stroke and fill color, see Lesson 3, "Painting."

6 In the toolbox, click the Fill box and click the None box.

7 Use the paintbrush tool to draw a long, upward stroke to create the left side of the tree trunk, tracing over the guides as you draw. Don't worry if your stroke doesn't follow the guide exactly. You'll remove the guides at the end of the lesson, so that they won't show through the finished artwork.

8 Draw a second upward stroke to create the right side of the tree trunk, using the guide to place your drawing.

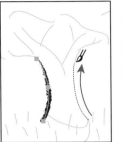

Draw with the   *Last path drawn remains*
paintbrush tool.   *selected.*

Each path remains selected after you draw it, until you draw another path.

9 Choose File > Save to save your work.

Editing paths with the paintbrush tool

When you draw with the paintbrush tool, the last path you draw remains selected by default. This feature makes it easy to edit paths as you draw. If you draw over the selected path with the paintbrush tool, the part of the selected path that you drew over is edited. You can disable or set a tolerance for path editing in the Paintbrush Tool Preferences dialog box.

Now you'll use the paintbrush tool to edit the selected path.

1 Place the paintbrush tool (✐) near the top of the selected path (the right side of the tree trunk) and draw upward.

The selected path is edited from the point where you began drawing over it. The new path is added to the selected path (instead of becoming a separate path).

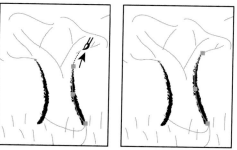

Draw over selected path   *Selected path is edited.*
to edit it.

When drawing with the paintbrush tool, you may want paths to remain unselected so that you can draw over paths without altering them and create layered or overlapping strokes. You can change the paintbrush tool preferences to keep paths unselected as you draw.

2 Choose Select > Deselect.

3 In the toolbox, double-click the paintbrush tool to display the Paintbrush Tool Preferences dialog box. You use this dialog box to change the way the paintbrush tool functions.

4 Click the Keep Selected option to deselect it, and click OK. Now paths will remain unselected as you draw, and you can draw overlapping paths without altering the earlier paths.

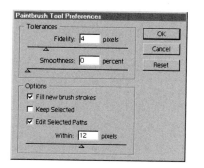

You'll draw the limbs of the tree.

5 Draw shorter strokes to create the limbs of the tree.

When the Keep Selected option is turned off, you can edit a path with the paintbrush tool by selecting the path with the selection tool (or selecting a segment or point on the path with the direct-selection tool) and then redrawing the path with the paintbrush tool.

6 Press Ctrl (Windows) or Command (Mac OS) to toggle to the selection tool (➤), and select a branch in the artwork that you want to redraw.

Pressing Ctrl/Command temporarily selects the selection tool (or the direct-selection or group-selection tool, whichever was used last) when another tool is selected.

Draw with the   *Path remains unselected.*   *Select path to edit it.*
paintbrush tool.

7 Use the paintbrush tool to draw over the selected path.

You can also edit paths using the smooth tool and the erase tool (located under the pencil tool in the toolbox) to redraw or remove parts of a path drawn with the paintbrush tool. For information on using the smooth and erase tools, see "Exploring on your own" on page 132 in Lesson 4, "Drawing with the Pen Tool."

After you apply a brush to an object, it's easy to apply another brush to the paths to change the appearance of the object.

8 Select the selection tool (➤) and drag a marquee to select the tree trunk and branches.

9 In the Brushes palette, click the Marker brush. The new brush is applied to the selected paths in the artwork.

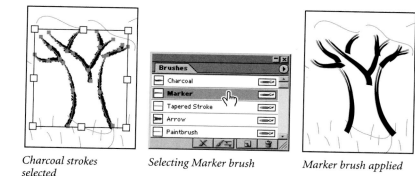

Charcoal strokes selected　　　*Selecting Marker brush*　　　*Marker brush applied*

10 Click outside the artwork to deselect it and view the tree without selection highlights.

11 Drag a selection marquee to select the tree again.

12 Click several other brushes in the Brushes palette to see the effects of those brushes in the artwork. When you have finished, click the Charcoal brush again to reapply that brush.

13 Click outside the artwork to deselect it.

14 Choose File > Save to save your work.

As you complete the rest of this lesson, use the methods you learned in this section to edit paths as you draw with the paintbrush tool. You can use the brushes, editing paths with the Keep Selected option if you want strokes to remain selected as you draw, or use the selection tool to select strokes to be edited.

Using Scatter brushes

Scatter brushes randomly spread an object, such as a leaf, a ladybug, or a strawberry, along a path. In this section, you'll use the Fall Leaf Scatter brush to create leaves on the tree. You'll start by adjusting options for the brush to change its appearance in the artwork.

Changing brush options

You change the appearance of a brush by adjusting its settings in the Brush Options dialog box, either before or after brushes have been applied to artwork. The changes you make appear when you apply the brush to artwork, but do not appear in the brush icon in the Brushes palette.

1 In the Brushes palette, choose Show Scatter Brushes from the palette menu to select that option. Then choose Show Art Brushes to deselect that option.

2 Double-click the Fall Leaf brush to open the Scatter Brush Options dialog box.

Brush options vary according to the type brush. For Scatter brushes, you can set either fixed values or a range (random) of values for the brush size, spacing, scatter, and rotation. If you have a pressure-sensitive drawing tablet attached to your computer, you can also set the pressure of the stylus using the Pressure option.

3 Set the following values, either dragging the slider or entering values, and pressing Tab to move between the text boxes:

• For Size, set the size of the brush object relative to the default (100%) by choosing Random and entering **40**% and **60**%.

• For Spacing, set the distance between brush objects on a path relative to 100% (objects touching but not overlapping) by choosing Random and entering **10**% and **30**%.

• For Scatter, indicate how far objects will deviate from either side of the path, where 0% is aligned on the path, by choosing Random and entering **–40**% and **40**%.

- For Rotation relative to the page or path, enter **–180°** and **180°**; then choose Rotation Relative to Page.

Select Fall Leaf brush.

Set brush options.

4 Click OK.

In addition to the features you adjusted in this section, you can change the color of a brush. You'll change the color of the Fall Leaf brush and another brush later in this lesson.

Applying a scatter brush to paths

Now you'll use the Fall Leaf brush with its adjusted settings to draw leaves on the tree in the artwork. First you'll select and lock the tree. Locking an object prevents it from being altered while you work on other objects in the artwork.

1 Use the selection tool ( ) to drag a marquee around all parts of the tree to select them.

2 Choose Object > Lock > Selection.

The selection highlights and bounding box around the tree disappear, and the tree is locked.

3 Select the Fall Leaf scatter brush.

4 Use the paintbrush tool (✐) to draw strokes with the Fall Leaf brush above the tree branches, using the guides to help place your paths. Remember that if you want to edit paths as you draw, you can use the Keep Selected option for the paintbrush tool or select paths with the selection tool.

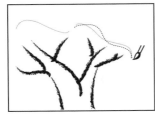
Drawing with paintbrush tool

Fall Leaf brush applied to artwork

5 Choose File > Save.

Changing the color attributes of brushes

You'll change the color of the Fall Leaf brush in the artwork.

Before you change the brush color, it's helpful to understand how Illustrator applies color to brushes.

To change the color of Art, Pattern, and Scatter brushes, you use one of three *colorization methods*—models for applying color to the artwork in a brush. To change the color of Calligraphic brushes, you simply select the brush and choose a stroke color. (See Lesson 3, "Painting," for information on choosing a stroke color.) You can change the color attributes of a brush before and after you apply the brush to artwork.

When you apply a brush to artwork, Illustrator uses the current stroke color for the brush only if a colorization method is chosen. Selecting brush strokes and choosing a new stroke color applies that new color to the brush. If no colorization method is set, Illustrator uses the brush's default color. For example, the Fall Leaf brush was applied with its default color of red (not the current stroke of black) because its colorization method was set to None.

For an illustration of brush colorization methods, see figure 5-1 in the color section.

To colorize Art, Pattern, and Scatter brushes, you choose from three colorization methods—Tints, Tints and Shades, and Hue Shift:

- Tints displays the brush stroke in tints of the stroke color. Portions of the art that are black become the stroke color, portions that aren't black become tints of the stroke color, and white remains white. If you use a spot color as the stroke, Tints generates tints of the spot color. Choose Tints for brushes that are in black and white, or when you want to paint a brush stroke with a spot color.

- Tints and Shades displays the brush stroke in tints and shades of the stroke color. Tints and Shades maintains black and white, and everything between becomes a blend from black to white through the stroke color. Because black is added, you may not be able to print to a single plate when using Tints and Shades with a spot color. Choose Tints and Shades for brushes that are in grayscale.

- Hue Shift uses the key color in the brush artwork, by default the most prominent color in the art. Everything in the brush artwork that is the key color becomes the stroke color. Other colors in the brush artwork become colors related to the stroke color (the complement on the color wheel). Hue Shift maintains black, white, and gray. Choose Hue Shift for brushes that use multiple colors. You can change the key color. (If the original brush has only one color, the Hue Shift colorized brush also will contain only one color.)

Note: Brushes colorized with a stroke color of white may appear entirely white. Brushes colorized with a stroke color of black may appear entirely black. Results depend on the original brush colors.

Changing the brush color using Hue Shift colorization

Now you'll change the color of the Fall Leaf brush using the Hue Shift colorization method.

1 Select the selection tool ( ), and drag a selection marquee to select the Fall Leaf strokes in the artwork.

2 Click the Color palette tab to bring the palette to the front. (If the Color palette isn't visible on-screen, choose Window > Color.)

3 Select the Stroke box in the Color palette to bring it to the front. Then click in the color bar to select a color for the Fall Leaf brush. (We chose a lavender color.)

4 In the Brushes palette, double-click the Fall Leaf brush to view the Scatter Brush Options dialog box for the brush. Move the dialog box off to the side so that you can see your artwork as you work.

You'll select a colorization method for the brush. For brushes set to a default colorization method of None, you must choose a colorization method before you can change the brush color. Brushes set to the Tints, Tints and Shades, or Hue Shift colorization method by default automatically apply the current stroke color to the brush when you use it in the artwork.

Note: To find a brush's default colorization setting, double-click the brush in the Brushes palette to view the Brush Options dialog box, and then select the setting in the Method pop-up menu in the Colorization section.

5 In the Colorization section in the dialog box, choose Hue Shift from the Method pop-up menu.

Select brush color.   *Set colorization method.*

The Key Color swatch in the Colorization section indicates the brush color that will shift to the new stroke color. The Key Color box displays the default key color (in this case, the leaf's red color) or the key color you select. For this lesson, you'll use the default key color.

It can be useful to select a new key color if a brush contains several colors and you want to shift different colors in the brush. To select a different key color, you click the Key Color eyedropper in the dialog box and position the eyedropper on the desired color in the preview (such as one of the black veins in the leaf), and click. The new key color shifts to the stroke color when you use the brush in the artwork (and other colors in the brush will shift correspondingly).

6 Click Preview to preview the color to be applied by the colorization method.

The selected Fall Leaf strokes are colorized with the current stroke color (the color you selected in step 3). This color will appear when you apply the Hue Shift colorization method.

7 If desired, choose the Tints or Tints and Shades colorization method from the pop-up menu to preview the change. Then return to the Hue Shift method.

8 Click OK. At the alert message, click Apply To Strokes to apply the colorization change to the strokes in the artwork. You can also choose to change only subsequent brush strokes and leave existing strokes unchanged.

Once you select a colorization method for a brush, the new stroke color applies to selected brush strokes and to new paths painted with the brush.

9 In the Color palette, click the color bar in several different places to try other stroke colors for the selected brush strokes.

10 When you are satisfied with the color of the Fall Leaf brush strokes, click away from the artwork to deselect it.

11 Choose File > Save.

Changing the brush color using Tints colorization

Now you'll apply a new color to the Marker brush in the Art Brushes section of the Brushes palette, and use the brush to draw blades of grass in the artwork.

You'll begin by selecting the brush in the Brushes palette.

1 In the Brushes palette menu, choose Show Art Brushes. Then choose Show Scatter brushes to hide those brushes.

You'll display the Brush Options dialog box for the Marker brush to see the default colorization settings for the brush and change the brush size.

2 In the Brushes palette, double-click the Marker brush. The brush's original color is black.

3 In the Art Brush Options dialog box, note that the Marker brush is set by default to the Tints colorization method.

The Tints colorization method replaces black with the stroke color. Neither the Tints and Shades nor the Hue Shift colorization method works with black brushes; both methods replace the original black color with black, leaving the brush unchanged.

4 In the Size section of the dialog box, enter **50%** for Width to change the size to a more appropriate scale for drawing in the artwork.

Marker brush selected   *Marker brush with default Tints colorization method*

5 Click OK to accept the settings and close the dialog box.

Now you'll select a color for the grass, and draw the grass with the Marker brush.

6 In the Color palette, click in the color bar to select a color for the grass. (We chose a bright green.)

7 Use the paintbrush tool ( ) to draw short, upward strokes around the base of the tree, applying the stroke color you selected in step 6. Use the guides to place your drawing. Don't paint the grass around the canoe; you'll paint this later in the lesson.

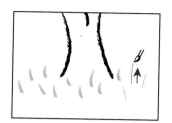

Because the Marker brush is all one color, the Tints colorization method applies the new stroke color as one color (rather than varied tints of the color). When the original brush contains several colors, the Tints colorization method applies a different tint for each color in the brush.

Using a fill color with brushes

When you apply a brush to an object's stroke, you can also apply a fill color to paint the interior of the object with a color. When you use a fill color with a brush, the brush objects appear on top of the fill color in places where the fill and the brush objects overlap.

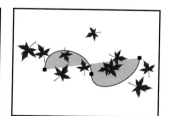

Choose fill color.   *Draw with paintbrush.*   *Brush objects appear on top of fill.*

Now you'll use the paintbrush tool to draw a canoe at the edge of the grass with an Art brush. You'll begin by selecting the brush in the Brushes palette.

1 In the Brushes palette, select the Tapered Stroke brush.

The Tapered Stroke brush uses the Tints colorization method by default. To change the color of the Tapered Stroke brush, you'll simply select a stroke color.

2 In the Color palette, make sure that the Stroke box is selected. Then click in the color bar to select a color for the edges of the canoe. (We chose a dark orange.)

Now you'll use the paintbrush tool to draw the edges of the canoe. Use the guides to align your drawing.

3 Use the paintbrush tool ( ) to draw a crescent shape to make the side and bottom of the canoe:

• Draw a long stroke from left to right to make the side edge of the canoe. Do not release the mouse button.

• While still holding down the mouse button, draw a second long stroke beneath the first, from right to left, connecting the two strokes at the right endpoint of the object, to make a crescent shape. When you have drawn the second stroke, release the mouse button.

You may have to draw the crescent shape more than once to create a shape with a single path. Remember that you can edit paths as you draw. Use the direct-selection tool to select a segment of the path that you want to redraw.

Don't worry if your drawing doesn't match the guides exactly. What's important is drawing the shape as one path, without releasing the mouse button, so that you can fill the object correctly. (If a shape is made of separate paths, the fill color is applied to each path separately, yielding unpredictable results.)

4 Draw a third long stroke for the top side of the canoe. Then draw two shorter strokes for the crossbars. (Draw the top side and crossbars as separate paths, releasing the mouse button after each one.)

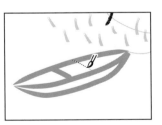

Draw crescent as one path.   *Add top.*   *Add crossbars.*

Now you'll fill the side of the canoe with a color.

5 Select the selection tool ( ), and select the crescent shape you drew for the lower side and bottom of the canoe.

6 In the Color palette, select the Fill box. Then click in the color bar to select a fill color for the canoe. (We chose a yellowish orange.)

Selected shape is filled.

7 Click outside the artwork to deselect it.

8 Choose File > Save.

Using Calligraphic brushes

Calligraphic brushes resemble strokes drawn with the angled point of a calligraphic pen. Calligraphic brushes are defined by an elliptical shape whose center follows the path. Use these brushes to create the appearance of hand-drawn strokes made with a flat, angled pen tip.

You'll use a Calligraphic pen to draw water in front of the canoe. You'll begin by selecting the brush, and then choose a color for the brush.

1 In the Brushes palette, choose Show Calligraphic Brushes from the palette menu to select that option. Then choose Show Art Brushes from the menu to deselect that option.

2 In the Brushes palette, select the 12 pt Oval brush.

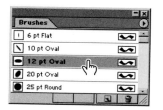

3 In the Color palette, click the Stroke box. Then click in the color bar to select a new color for the water. (We chose a light blue.)

Calligraphic brushes use the current stroke color when you apply the brushes to artwork. You do not use colorization methods with Calligraphic brushes.

4 In the Color palette, click the Fill box and then click the None box. A fill of None with brushes prevents paths from being filled when you apply the brush.

5 Select the paintbrush tool ( ), and draw wavy lines for the water surface. The paths you draw use the stroke color you selected in step 3.

Now you'll change the shape of the 12 pt Oval brush in the Brush Options dialog box to change the appearance of the strokes made with the brush.

6 In the Brushes palette, double-click the 12 pt Oval brush to display the Calligraphic Brush Options dialog box.

You can change the angle of the brush (relative to a horizontal line), the roundness (from a flat line to a full circle), and the diameter (from 0 to 1296 points) to change the shape that defines the brush's tip, and change the appearance of the stroke that the brush makes. Now you'll change the diameter of the brush.

7 Enter **8 pt** for Diameter. In the Name text box, enter **8 pt Oval**. Notice that the weight of the Calligraphic brush strokes in the artwork decreases.

The Preview window in the dialog box shows changes you make to the brush.

8 Click OK. At the alert message, click Apply To Strokes to apply the change to the strokes in the artwork.

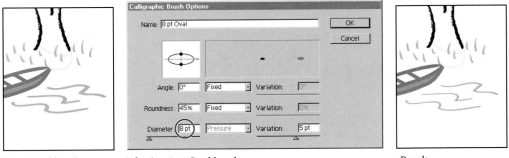

12 pt Oval brush   *Selecting 8 pt Oval brush*   *Result*

9 Ctrl/Command-click outside the artwork or choose Select > Deselect to deselect it.

10 Choose File > Save.

Using Pattern brushes

Pattern brushes paint a pattern made up of separate sections, or *tiles*, for the sides (middle sections), ends, and corners of the path. When you apply a Pattern brush to artwork, the brush applies different tiles from the pattern to different sections of the path, depending on where the section falls on the path (at an end, in the middle, or at a corner). You'll use the Rope Pattern brush to draw a rope from the canoe to the tree, with different tiles used for the rope's middle and end sections.

1 In the Brushes palette, choose Show Pattern Brushes from the palette menu to select that option. Then choose Show Calligraphic Brushes from the menu to deselect that option.

2 Double-click the Rope brush to display the Pattern Brush Options dialog box for the brush.

The Brush Options dialog box displays the tiles in the Rope brush. The first tile on the left is the Side tile, used to paint the middle sections of a path. The second tile on the right is the Start tile, used to paint the beginning section of a path. The last tile on the right is the End tile, used to paint the end of a path.

Pattern brushes can have up to five tiles—the Side, Start, and End tiles, plus an Outer Corner tile and an Inner Corner tile to paint sharp corners on a path. The Rope brush has no corner tiles because the brush is designed for curved paths, not sharp corners (just as a real rope creates loops or coils, not sharp angles). In the next part of this lesson, you'll create a Pattern brush that uses corner tiles.

Now you'll change the scale of the Pattern brush so that the brush is in scale with the rest of the artwork when you apply it.

3 In the Pattern Brush Options dialog box, enter **20%** in the Scale text box, and click OK.

Rope brush   *Rope brush with Side, Start, and End tiles scaled 20%*

4 Select the paintbrush tool (   ), and draw a path that loops around the base of the tree. Then draw a second path that leads from the loop around the tree to the canoe.

Draw the rope as two separate paths, rather than one path, to avoid creating a path with a sharp angle. (Because the Rope brush does not include corner tiles, the brush uses Side tiles to paint sharp angles. The Side tiles appear severed at sharp corners, and the rope appears to be cut.)

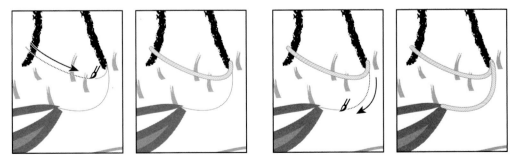

Apply Rope brush as two separate paths.

Now you'll select a blade of grass you created earlier in the lesson and move it in front of the rope to make the rope appear to lie behind the grass.

5 Select the selection tool (▶), and then select a grass blade lying along the path of the rope. (Be careful not to select the rope along with the grass.)

If you like, you can Shift-click to select additional grass blades along the path of the rope.

6 Choose Object > Arrange > Bring to Front.

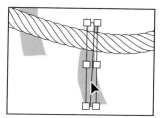

Selecting grass blade   *Bring grass to front.*

7 Choose File > Save.

Tips for using brushes

When you work with brushes, keep the following points in mind:

• *You can often use Scatter brushes and Pattern brushes to achieve the same effect. However, one way in which they differ is that Pattern brushes follow the path exactly, whereas Scatter brushes do not.*

• *If you apply a brush to a closed path and want to control the placement of the end of the path, select the scissors tool and split the path. To change again, select the endpoints, choose Object > Path > Join, and use the scissors again.*

• *To select all brushstroke paths in the current artwork, choose Select > Object > Brush Strokes.*

• *For better performance when creating a brush from art that contains multiple overlapping paths filled with the same color and with no stroke, select the paths and click the Unite button in the Pathfinder palette before you create the brush.*

–From online Help and the Adobe Illustrator User Guide, Chapter 3

Painting with symbols

You can also paint using symbols. A symbol is an art object that you store in the Symbols palette and reuse in a document. In this part of the lesson, you'll create a symbol from a selection of grass. Each symbol instance is linked to the symbol in the palette. If you use the same artwork multiple times within a document, symbols can save time and greatly reduce file size.

For the symbol, you'll use three blades of grass that you created earlier.

1 Click the Symbols palette tab or choose Window > Symbols to display the palette.

2 Select the selection tool ( ), and drag a selection marquee to select the three blades of grass off to the right of the trunk.

3 In the Symbols palette, click the New Symbol button at the bottom of the Symbols palette.

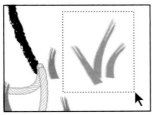
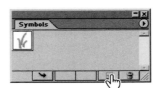

Select grass blades.   *Click New Symbol button.*

4 Double-click the symbol, and name it **Grass**. Click OK.

Now you'll place an instance of the symbol in your artwork using the Symbols palette.

5 Select the grass symbol in the Symbols palette, and drag the symbol to the artwork to place a single instance of this symbol. Use the guides provided to position the symbol next to the canoe.

Symbol instances placed using the Symbols palette are exact replicas of the original. When selected in the artboard, symbol instances have a bounding box around them, similar to grouped artwork.

You can also place symbol instances in your document using the symbol sprayer tool to create multiple symbol instances as a set. When you use the symbol sprayer, all of the symbols that appear from each spray become one instance set that you manipulate and edit as a whole.

[?] For more information on the symbol sprayer tool, see "Using symbolism tools" in online Help or in Chapter 3 of the Adobe Illustrator User Guide.

6 Select the symbol instance in the artwork, and Alt-drag (Windows) or Option-drag (Mac OS) the instance on the left side of the canoe to duplicate the instance.

Note: You can move, scale, rotate, shear (or skew), or reflect a symbol instance using commands in the Object menu or in the Transform or Align palettes. You can also perform any operation from the Transparency, Appearance, and Styles palettes and apply any effect from the Effect menu.

Painting with symbols is similar to painting with a Scatter brush, with an important exception. Symbol instances are linked to the symbol in the palette; when you paint with a symbol, you're actually using the same artwork multiple times in a document. So the file size does not increase. Brushstrokes made with the Scatter brush are separate objects, and painting with them affects the file size.

Next you'll create a mirror copy of a symbol instance and position it next to the canoe.

7 In the artwork, select one of the symbol instances.

8 Select the reflect tool (🖾) under the rotate tool (🖸) in the toolbox. Alt/Option-click in the artwork to display the Reflect Options dialog box. Select Vertical and click Copy. (Do not click OK.)

9 If desired, press Ctrl (Windows) or Command (Mac OS) to get the selection tool, and drag the copy of the grass to reposition it.

10 Choose Select > Deselect to deselect your work.

11 Choose File > Save.

Creating brushes

You can create new brushes of all four brush types, using artwork in an Illustrator file as the basis for the brush. In this section, you'll use artwork provided with the lesson to create a new Pattern brush with three tiles—a cloud for the Side tile, and a sun for the Outer Corner tile and Inner Corner tile.

Creating swatches for a Pattern brush

You create Pattern brushes by first creating swatches in the Swatches palette with the artwork that will be used for the Pattern brush tiles. In this section, you'll use the cloud and sun drawings included with the artwork file to create swatches.

1 Use the scroll bars, the hand tool, or the Navigator palette to display the scratch area to the right of the artboard to view the cloud and sun drawings located there.

For information on moving to different areas of the document window, see Lesson 1, "Getting to Know the Work Area."

The cloud and sun were created using the Marker brush. (You can use any drawing tool to create artwork for new brushes.) Each piece was then expanded using the Object > Expand Appearance command. If you used a brush to create art for the swatch, you must first expand the art before you can create a swatch in the Swatches palette.

You'll unlock the sun and cloud artwork, and then use the artwork to create swatches. The objects were locked to prevent them from being altered while you completed the earlier sections of the lesson.

2 Choose Object > Unlock All.

Bounding boxes and selection highlights appear around the sun and cloud, indicating that the objects are unlocked and selected. The tree, which you locked earlier in the lesson, is also unlocked and selected. (The tree can be unlocked, because you've finished drawing in the area of the tree.)

3 Click outside the artwork to deselect the objects.

4 Click the Swatches palette tab to view the Swatches palette. (If the palette isn't visible on-screen, choose Window > Swatches.)

Now you'll create a pattern swatch.

5 Select the selection tool ( ), and drag the cloud onto the Swatches palette. The new swatch appears in the pattern swatches group.

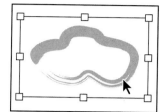
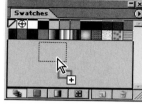
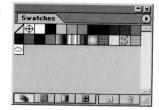

Select cloud.   *Drag it onto Swatches palette.*   *Cloud swatch is added to palette.*

6 Click away from the artwork to deselect the cloud.

7 In the Swatches palette, double-click the cloud swatch. Double-clicking the cloud swatch changes the current fill or stroke box to that swatch and opens the Swatch Options dialog box.

8 Name the swatch **Cloud**, and then click OK.

9 Now repeat steps 5 through 8 to create a pattern swatch of the sun art:

• Use the selection tool to drag the sun onto the Swatches palette. The new swatch appears in the pattern swatches group.

• Click away from the artwork to deselect the sun.

• In the Swatches palette, double-click the sun swatch.

• Name the swatch **Sun**, and then click OK.

🔲 For more information on creating pattern swatches, see "Creating and working with patterns" in online Help or Chapter 8 in the Adobe Illustrator User Guide.

Creating a Pattern brush from swatches

To create a new Pattern brush, you apply swatches from the Swatches palette to tiles in the Brush Options dialog box. Now you'll apply the Cloud and Sun swatches to tiles for a new Pattern brush.

First you'll open a Brush Options dialog box for a new Pattern brush.

1 Click the Brushes palette tab to view the palette.

2 In the Brushes palette, click the New Brush button.

3 Select New Pattern Brush and click OK.

Create new brush.   *Select brush type.*

You'll apply the Cloud swatch to the Side tile for the new Pattern brush.

4 In the Pattern Brush Options dialog box, select the Side tile box (the far left tile box).

5 In the pattern swatches scroll list, select the Cloud swatch. The Cloud swatch appears in the Side tile box.

Next you'll apply the Sun swatch to the Outer Corner tile and Inner Corner tile for the new Pattern brush.

6 In the Pattern Brush Options dialog box, select the Outer Corner tile box (the second tile box from the left). In the pattern swatches scroll list, select the Sun swatch. The Sun swatch appears in the Outer Corner tile box.

7 In the Pattern Brush Options dialog box, select the Inner Corner tile box (the middle tile box). In the pattern swatches scroll list, select the Sun swatch. The Sun swatch appears in the Inner Corner tile box.

You won't create a Start tile or End tile for the new brush. (You'll apply the new brush to a closed path in the artwork later in the lesson, so you won't need Start or End tiles this time. When you want to create a Pattern brush that includes Start and End tiles, you add those tiles the same way as you did the Side and Corner tiles.)

8 In the Name text box, name the brush **Clouds and Sun**. Then click OK.

The Clouds and Sun brush appears in the Pattern brush section in the Brushes palette.

Note: When you create a new brush, the brush appears in the Brushes palette of the current artwork only. If you open another file in Illustrator, the Clouds and Sun brush won't appear in that file's Brushes palette.

[?] To save a brush and reuse it in another file, you can create a brush library with the brushes you want to use. For more information, see "Using the brush libraries" in online Help or Chapter 3 of the Adobe Illustrator User Guide.

Painting with the Pattern brush

So far in this lesson you've used the paintbrush tool to apply brushes to paths. You can also apply brushes to paths created with any drawing tool—including the pen, pencil, ellipse, and rectangle tools—and the other basic shapes tools. In this section, you'll use the rectangle tool to apply the Clouds and Sun brush to a rectangular border around the artwork.

When you use drawing tools to apply brushes to artwork, you first draw the path with the tool and then select the brush in the Brushes palette to apply the brush to the path.

First you'll set the fill color to None.

1 In the toolbox, click the Fill box and click the None box.

2 Use the Navigator palette or the zoom tool (🔍) to reduce the view of the artwork.

Now you'll draw a border with the rectangle tool, and apply the brush to the path.

3 Select the rectangle tool (▱). Drag to draw a rectangle on the artboard, about 1/2-inch inside the imageable area on each side, as indicated by the guide.

4 In the Brushes palette, click the Clouds and Sun brush.

The rectangle path is painted with the Clouds and Sun brush, with the Cloud tile on the sides and the Sun tile on the corners.

Draw rectangle.   Select Pattern brush.   Brush is applied to
rectangle path.

5 Ctrl-click (Windows) or Command-click (Mac OS) outside the artwork to deselect it.

Now you'll draw a curved path using the Clouds and Sun brush.

6 In the Brushes palette, double-click the Clouds and Sun Pattern brush to view the Brush Options dialog box for the brush.

You'll change the scale and spacing of the brush for a different look.

7 Under Size, enter **250%** for Scale and **30%** for Spacing. Click OK.

Select Clouds and Sun Pattern brush.   *Change scale and spacing.*

8 At the Brush Change alert message, click Leave Strokes to keep the border brush strokes as they are.

The Leave Strokes option preserves paths in the artwork that are already painted with the brush. The changes you made to the brush will apply to subsequent uses of the brush. Now you'll use the brush to paint a curved path in the artwork.

9 Select the paintbrush tool (✎) and draw a smooth curve over the tree. Use the guides for placement.

Apply Pattern brush to path with paintbrush.   *Result*

The path is painted with the clouds from the Clouds and Sun brush (the Side tile in the brush). Because the path does not include sharp corners, the Outer Corner tile and Inner Corner tile (the Sun tiles) are not applied to the path.

You've completed the artwork for the lesson. Now you'll remove the guides so you can view the artwork in its finished form.

When working with guides, you can temporarily hide guides by choosing View > Guides > Hide Guides. The guides disappear but are preserved in the artwork. You can display hidden guides by choosing View > Guides > Show Guides. You won't need the guides again in this lesson, so you'll delete them using the Clear Guides command.

10 Choose View > Guides > Clear Guides. The guides are deleted from the artwork.

11 Choose File > Save to save your work. Choose File > Close to close the file.

Exploring on your own

Here are some ideas you can try on your own.

Applying brushes to paths

Practice applying brushes to paths you create with drawing tools (just as you applied the Clouds and Sun Pattern brush to a path drawn with the rectangle tool in the final section of the lesson).

1 In the Brushes palette menu, make sure that Show Scatter Brushes is selected (indicated by a check mark next to the option).

2 Use the drawing tools (the pen or pencil tool, and any of the basic shapes tools) to draw objects. Use the default fill and stroke colors when you draw.

3 With one of the objects selected, click a brush in the Brushes palette to apply the brush to the object's path.

4 Repeat step 3 for each object you drew.

5 Display the Brush Options dialog box for one of the brushes you used in step 3, and change the color, size, or other features of the brush. After you close the dialog box, click Apply To Strokes to apply your changes to the brush in the artwork.

Creating brushes

Use one of the basic shapes tools to create artwork to use as a new Scatter brush.

1 Select a basic shape tool in the toolbox, and draw an object, keeping it selected.

2 Click the New Brush button at the bottom of the Brushes palette.

Note: You can use more than one object to create the new brush. All selected objects in the artwork will be included in the brush. If you use a brush to create artwork for a new brush, remember to expand the brush strokes before creating the new brush.

3 In the New Brush dialog box, select New Scatter Brush and click OK.

The Brush Options dialog box for the new brush appears, with the selected objects displayed in the brush example. The new brush is named Scatter Brush 1 by default.

4 Enter a name for the brush. Then click OK to accept the settings for the brush.

5 Select the paintbrush tool and draw a path. The new brush is applied to the path.

6 Double-click the new brush to display the Brush Options dialog box. Change the brush settings to try out different versions of the brush. When you have finished, click OK.

Using a brush library

Try out some of the brushes included in the brush libraries in Illustrator.

1 To open a brush library, choose Window > Brush Libraries.

2 Choose a library from the submenu. Illustrator includes nine brush libraries in addition to the default brush library that appears when you start the program.

You can also create your own brush libraries. See "Using the Brush Libraries" in online Help or Chapter 3 in the Adobe Illustrator User Guide.

Using the symbol sprayer

Try out some of the symbols in Illustrator's symbol libraries using the symbol sprayer.

1 To open a symbol library, choose Window > Symbol Libraries.

2 Choose Nature from the submenu. Illustrator includes six symbol libraries.

3 Select the grass symbol in the Symbols palette, or try out other symbols in the palette.

4 Select the symbol sprayer tool ( ) in the toolbox, and drag the tool in your artwork to add to your composition.

Review questions

1 Describe each of the four brush types—Art, Calligraphic, Pattern, and Scatter.

2 What is the difference between applying a brush to artwork using the paintbrush tool and applying a brush to artwork using one of the drawing tools?

3 Describe how to edit paths with the paintbrush tool as you draw. How does the Keep Selected option affect the paintbrush tool?

4 How do you change the colorization method for an Art, Pattern, or Scatter brush? (Remember you don't use colorization methods with Calligraphic brushes.)

Review answers

1 The following are the four brush types:

• Art brushes stretch artwork evenly along a path. Art brushes include strokes that resemble graphic media (such as the Charcoal brush used to create the tree, or the Marker brush used to create the grass). Art brushes also include objects, such as the Arrow brush.

• Calligraphic brushes are defined by an elliptical shape whose center follows the path. They create strokes that resemble hand-drawn lines made with a flat, angled calligraphic pen tip.

• Pattern brushes paint a pattern made up of separate sections, or tiles, for the sides (middle sections), ends, and corners of the path. When you apply a Pattern brush to artwork, the brush applies different tiles from the pattern to different sections of the path, depending on where the section falls on the path (at an end, in the middle, or at a corner).

• Scatter brushes scatter an object, such as a leaf, along a path. You can adjust the Size, Spacing, Scatter, and Rotation options for a Scatter brush to change the brush's appearance.

2 To apply brushes using the paintbrush tool, you select the tool, choose a brush from the Brushes palette, and draw in the artwork. The brush is applied directly to the paths as you draw. To apply brushes using a drawing tool, you select the tool and draw in the artwork; then you select a path in the artwork and choose a brush in the Brushes palette. The brush is applied to the selected path.

3 To edit a path with the paintbrush tool, simply drag over a selected path to redraw it. The Keep Selected option keeps the last path selected as you draw with the paintbrush tool. Leave the Keep Selected option turned on (the default setting) when you want to easily edit the previous path as you draw. Turn off the Keep Selected option when you want to draw layered paths with the paintbrush without altering previous paths. When the Keep Selected option is turned off, you can use the selection tool to select a path and then edit the path.

4 To change the colorization method of a brush, double-click the brush in the Brushes palette to view the Brush Options dialog box. Use the Method pop-up menu in the Colorization section to select another method. If you choose Hue Shift, you can use the default color displayed in the dialog box preview; or you can change the key color (the new color that will appear) by clicking the Key Color eyedropper, and clicking a color in the preview. Click OK to accept the settings and close the Brush Options dialog box. Click Apply to Strokes at the alert message if you want to apply the changes to existing strokes in the artwork.

Existing brush strokes are colorized with the stroke color that was selected when the strokes were applied to the artwork. New brush strokes are colorized with the current stroke color. To change the color of existing strokes after applying a different colorization method, select the strokes and select a new stroke color.

Lesson 6

6 Transforming Objects

You can modify objects in many ways as you create your artwork—and quickly and precisely control their size, shape, and orientation. In this lesson, you'll explore the various transform tools, commands, and palettes as you create three pieces of artwork.

In this lesson, you'll learn how to do the following:

• Select individual objects, objects in a group, and parts of an object.

• Move, scale, and rotate objects using a variety of methods.

• Reflect, shear, and distort objects.

• Adjust the perspective of an object.

• Create symbols for artwork that you'll reuse.

• Repeat transformations quickly and easily.

• Explore using variables to create different versions of a design.

Getting started

In this lesson, you'll transform parts of a logo to use in three pieces of artwork to create a letterhead design, an envelope, and business cards. Before you begin, you'll restore the default preferences for Adobe Illustrator; then you'll open a file containing a composite of the finished artwork to see what you'll create.

1 To ensure that the tools and palettes function exactly as described in this lesson, delete or deactivate (by renaming) the Adobe Illustrator 10.0 preferences file. See "Restoring default preferences" on page 4.

2 Start Adobe Illustrator.

3 Choose File > Open, and open the L6comp.ai file in the Lesson06 folder, located inside the Lessons folder within the AICIB folder on your hard drive.

This file contains a composite of the three pieces of finished artwork. The Citrus Bath & Soap logo in the top left corner of the letterhead is the basis for all the modified objects. The logo has been resized for the letterhead, envelope, and business card.

Note: You can also view the individual pieces of finished artwork by opening the files L6end1.ai, L6end2.ai, and L6end3.ai in the Lesson06 folder.

4 If you like, choose View > Zoom Out to reduce the view of the finished artwork, adjust the window size, and leave it on your screen as you work. (Use the hand tool ( ) to move the artwork where you want it in the window.) If you don't want to leave the image open, choose File > Close.

 For an illustration of the finished artwork in this lesson, see the color section.

To begin working, you'll open an existing art file set up for the letterhead artwork.

5 Choose File > Open to open the L6start1.ai file in the Lesson06 folder, located inside the Lessons folder within the AICIB folder on your hard drive.

This start file has been saved with the rulers showing, custom swatches added to the Swatches palette, and blue guidelines for scaling the logo and objects on the letterhead.

6 Choose File > Save As, name the file **Letterhd.ai**, and select the Lesson06 folder. Leave the Format option set to Adobe Illustrator® Document, and click Save. In the Illustrator Native Format Options dialog box, select Illustrator 10 Compatibility and click OK.

Scaling objects

You scale objects by enlarging or reducing them horizontally (along the x axis) and vertically (along the y axis) relative to a fixed point of origin that you designate. If you don't designate an origin, the objects are scaled from their center points. You'll use three methods to scale the logo and two objects copied from the logo.

First you'll use the Transform palette to scale down the logo by entering new dimensions and designating the point of origin from which the logo will scale.

1 Using the selection tool (▶) in the toolbox, click the logo to select the group of objects (type, background, lemon, orange slice, lime slice) that make up the logo.

2 Choose Window > Transform to display the Transform palette. (A check mark indicates that the palette is displayed on-screen.)

The Transform palette contains a small grid of squares or *reference points* that represent points on the selection's bounding box. All values in the palette refer to the bounding boxes of the objects.

3 Click the reference point in the top left corner of the grid (as shown in the illustration) to set the point of origin from which the objects will scale. Type **83.75** in the W text box, and then press Tab and type **88.5** in the H text box. Then press Enter or Return to scale down the logo to fit in the blue guideline.

By default, the ruler units of measure are set to points.

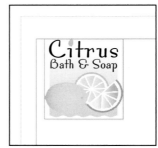

Set reference point, width,   Result
and height.

Next you'll copy the background object in the logo and scale the new object by dragging its bounding box to fit the background of the letterhead.

4 With the logo still selected, choose Object > Ungroup to ungroup the larger group in the logo. (Smaller subgroups remain grouped.)

Ungrouping the background object from the other objects lets you make copies that are separate from the group.

5 If desired, use the zoom tool (🔍) to zoom in on the logo.

6 Using the selection tool (▶), click away from the logo to deselect it, and then click below the word *Bath* to select the light-blue background object in the logo. Hold down Alt (Windows) or Option (Mac OS) and drag from the center of the object down to copy the object and move it to the bottom left corner of the page, aligning it with the guides. You can press the arrow keys to nudge the object into place.

Holding down Alt/Option as you drag an object duplicates it.

Next you'll make this background object the background for the page.

7 Drag the top right corner of the new object's bounding box up to the top right side of the blue letterhead guide, to just below the return address.

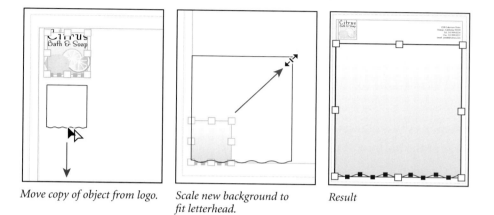

Move copy of object from logo.   Scale new background to fit letterhead.   Result

You'll use the Swatches palette to paint the background with a lighter gradient that we provided. To learn how to create your own gradients, see Lesson 8, "Blending Shapes and Colors."

8 Click the Swatches tab to bring the palette to the front of its group. With the background selected, hold the pointer over the swatches in the Swatches palette until you see their names. Then click the New Background swatch in the third row to paint the object with a lighter gradient.

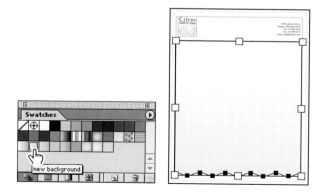

9 With the background object still selected, choose Object > Lock > Selection to lock the object and deselect it. Locking the background object makes it easier to select other objects you'll add to the artwork.

You can also lock all artwork above the selected object—for example, if you want to edit an object in the background that has objects on top of it—or all objects on other layers. In addition, you can use the Layers palette to lock objects. Once objects are locked, they cannot be selected or edited. You can quickly lock multiple objects, groups of objects, and sublayers by locking the parent layer.

The lemon is two objects grouped together in the logo. Now you'll copy the lemon and place it at the bottom of the letterhead.

10 Select the lemon in the logo, and Alt-drag (Windows) or Option-drag (Mac OS) to copy and move the new lemon to the bottom right corner of the letterhead guide.

You'll use the scale tool to resize the new lemon and set a fixed point for the scaling.

11 Select the scale tool in the toolbox, hold down Alt (Windows) or Option (Mac OS), and click the bottom right corner point of the letterhead guide.

Clicking the corner point of the guide sets the point of origin from which the lemon will scale. Holding down Alt/Option as you click displays the Scale dialog box.

12 In the Scale dialog box, type **300%** in the Scale text box and click OK to make the lemon three times as large.

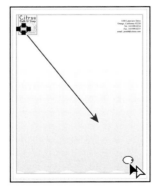

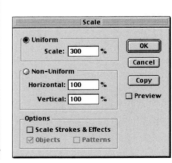

Move copy of lemon.   *Set point of origin.*   *Scale dialog box*

Rotating objects

Objects are rotated by turning them around a designated point of origin. You can rotate objects by displaying their bounding boxes and moving the pointer to an outside corner. Once the rotate pointer appears, just click to rotate the object around its center point. You can rotate objects using the Transform palette to set a point of origin and rotation angle. You can also rotate objects using the rotate tool to drag the object or set its rotation angle.

You'll rotate the lemon 30° around its center point using the rotate tool.

1 With the lemon selected, select the rotate tool (⟳) in the toolbox.

Notice that the lemon's point of origin is still at the bottom right corner of the letterhead.

2 Begin dragging the selected lemon. Notice how the movement is constrained to a circle rotating around the point of origin. Continue dragging until the lemon is in its original position on the letterhead, and then release the mouse button. You can also choose Edit > Undo Rotate.

3 Now, with the lemon still selected, double-click the rotate tool in the toolbox.

When an object is selected and you double-click the rotate tool in the toolbox, the object is rotated exactly from the center of the object. (This also applies to the scale tool.)

4 In the Rotate dialog box, type **30** in the Angle text box, and click OK to rotate the lemon 30° around its center point.

Rotating around different points of origin

Now you'll select one of the objects within the lemon without ungrouping the lemon so that you can paint it a lighter color.

5 Select the group-selection tool (⟨⃕⟩) in the same group as the direct-selection tool (⟨⃔⟩) in the toolbox. Hold down Shift and click the stem's core (not the lemon body) to deselect it. The group-selection tool lets you select individual objects or subgroups within a group.

6 With the lemon body selected, click a color in the Color palette or a swatch in the Swatches palette to paint the lemon a lighter gradient. (We used the Pale Yellow gradient.)

7 Choose File > Save.

Distorting objects

Various tools and filters let you distort the original shape of objects in different ways. For example, the wavy line on the bottom of the background object in the logo and on the letterhead was created by applying the Zig Zag distort filter to the straight edge.

Converting straight lines to zigzags

The Zig Zag filter adds anchor points to an existing line and then moves some of the points to the left of (or upward from) the line and some to the right of (or downward from) the line. You can specify the number of anchor points to create and the distance to move them. You can also choose whether to create smooth anchor points for a wavy line effect, or corner anchor points for a jagged line effect.

Original line, four corner ridges applied, and four smooth ridges applied

To convert straight lines to zigzags:

1. Do one of the following:

• To apply the distortion permanently, use any selection tool to select the line you want to convert. Then choose Filter > Distort > Zig Zag.

• To apply the distortion as an effect that can be removed, select an object or group, or target a group or layer in the Layers palette. (For more on targeting, see Lesson 10, "Working with Layers.") Then choose Effect > Distort & Transform > Zig Zag.

2. Select how to move points: Relative by a percentage of the object's size, or Absolute by a specific amount.

3. For Size, enter the distance you want to move points on the line, or drag the slider.

4. For Ridges per Segment, enter the number of ridges per line segment you want, or drag the slider.

5. Select the type of line to create: Smooth to create smooth points for a wavy line, or Corner to create corner points for a jagged line.

6. Click Preview to preview the line.

7. Click OK.

Now you'll create a flower using the twist tool to twirl the shape of a star and the Pucker & Bloat distort filter to transform another star in front of it.

To begin, you'll draw a star for part of the flower and use the twirl tool and Info palette to distort it.

1 Select the star tool (⭐) from the same group as the rectangle tool (▭) in the toolbox, and position the pointer in the artwork next to the lemon. Drag the tool to draw a five-pointed star that's about the same size as the lemon.

The star is painted with the paint attributes of the last selected object (in this case, the lemon).

2 With the star still selected, click a color swatch in the Swatches palette to paint the star with that color. (We selected the Lime Green swatch in the Swatches palette.) Leave the stroke unpainted.

3 Click the Info tab behind the Navigator palette or choose Window > Info to display the Info palette.

The Info palette displays information about the size and position of the selected object's bounding box.

4 Select the twist tool (🌀) from the same group as the rotate tool (🔄) in the toolbox and select a point on the star (don't release the mouse button). Referring to the Info palette, begin dragging the star's point to the right (in a clockwise direction) until the Info palette displays about 72°, and then release the mouse button.

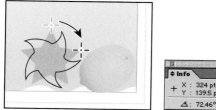

Twist star using Info palette as guide.

Now you'll draw another star that's centered on top of the first star.

5 With the star selected, click the Attributes tab behind the Color palette or choose Window > Attributes to display the Attributes palette. Then click the Show Center button (▫) to display the star's center point.

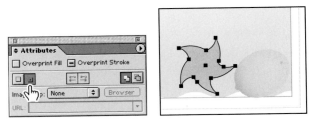

Display center point of star.

6 Select the star tool again, hold down Alt (Windows) or Option (Mac OS), and drag from the center point to draw another star over the center of the first one. Before you release the mouse button, drag the star in an arc to rotate it so the points appear between the points of the star behind it. Keep the star selected.

7 In the Attributes palette, click the Show Center button (▫) to display the second star's center point.

8 Click the Color tab behind the Attributes palette to bring the Color palette to the front. Click the White color box at the right end of the color bar to paint the star's fill with white. Then click the Stroke box to select the star's stroke, and click a color in the color bar or in the Swatches palette to paint the star's stroke. (We selected the Yellow color swatch.)

Now you'll distort the star using the Pucker & Bloat filter. This filter distorts objects inward and outward from their anchor points.

9 With the white star selected, choose Effect > Distort & Transform > Pucker & Bloat.

The Pucker & Bloat distortion can be applied to objects two ways. Applying it as a filter permanently distorts the object. Applying it as an effect maintains the original shape and lets you remove or edit the effect at any time.

10 In the Pucker & Bloat dialog box, select the Preview option, and drag the slider to distort the star (we selected 50%). Click OK.

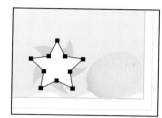
Draw star shape.

Apply Pucker & Bloat effect.

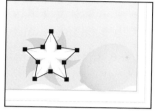
Result

11 Keep the artwork selected, and choose File > Save.

Shearing objects

Now you'll complete the flower with an orange center, scale it, and shear it. Shearing an object slants, or skews, the sides of the object along the axis you specify, keeping opposite sides parallel and making the object nonsymmetrical.

1 Click the Appearance tab behind the Info palette to bring the Appearance palette to the front of its group. (If the Appearance palette isn't visible on-screen, choose Window > Appearance to display it.)

The Appearance palette displays the fill, stroke, effects, and transparency of the last object created. By default the next shape you create will retain all of these attributes. Because the next shape will have different attributes, you will change this default setting.

2 Click the New Art Maintains Appearance button at the bottom of the Appearance palette.

The next shape will maintain only the stroke and fill attributes of the last shape.

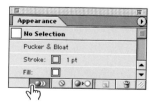
Clicking New Art Maintains Appearance button

3 Select the ellipse tool (◯) from the same group as the star tool (☆) in the toolbox.

4 With the stars still selected and their center points visible, press Alt (Windows) or Option (Mac OS), position the ellipse tool's cross hairs over the stars' center points, and drag to draw an oval from the center.

5 Click the Fill box in the toolbox to select the object's fill. In the Swatches palette, click the Orange swatch to paint the oval a light orange color.

6 In the Color palette, drag the None icon, and drop it on the Stroke box to remove the stroke.

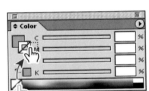

Draw oval shape and paint fill.   Drag and drop None button over Stroke box.

Now, you'll group and then shear the flower.

7 Select the selection tool (▶), Shift-click to select the three parts of the flower, and choose Object > Group to group them together.

8 In the Transform palette, type **10°** degrees in the Shear text box, and press Enter or Return to apply the shearing effect on the flower.

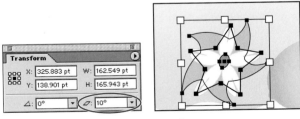

Enter 10° shear angle.   Result

9 Type **0.75 in** in the W text box and **0.75 in** in the H text box to scale the flower down to three-quarters of an inch.

Although the default unit of measure is set to points, when you type *inches* or *in* in the text boxes, Illustrator calculates the equivalent measurement in points.

You can have Illustrator convert unit values and perform mathematical operations in any text box that accepts numeric values. To automatically multiply or divide the size of an object by a number you specify, enter an asterisk (*) or a slash (/) and a number after the value in either the W or the H text box, and press Enter or Return to scale the object. For example, enter /2 after the values in the W and H text boxes to scale the object by 50%.

10 Using the selection tool, drag the flower next to the lemon in the bottom right corner of the page.

11 Choose Select > Deselect to deselect the artwork, and then choose File > Save.

You've completed the letterhead artwork. You'll keep the file open, so that you can use its artwork later in the lesson.

Positioning objects precisely

You can use the Transform palette to move objects to exact coordinates on the *x* and *y* axes of the page and to control the position of objects in relation to the trim edge.

To learn how to produce crop marks for the trim edge, see "Setting crop marks and trim marks" in online Help or Chapter 15 in the Adobe Illustrator User Guide.

You'll create the envelope by first pasting a copy of the logo into the envelope artwork, and then specifying the exact coordinates on the envelope where the pasted logo will go.

1 Double-click the hand tool ( ) in the toolbox to fit the artwork in the window.

2 Using the selection tool ( ), draw a marquee around the logo so that all of the objects in it are selected.

3 Choose Edit > Copy to copy the logo to the Clipboard.

Now you'll open the start file for the envelope artwork.

4 Choose File > Open to open the L6start2.ai file in the Lesson06 folder, located inside the Lessons folder within the AICIB folder on your hard drive.

5 Choose File > Save As, name the file **Envelope.ai**, and select the Lesson06 folder. Leave the Format option set to Adobe Illustrator® Document, and click Save. In the Illustrator Native Format Options dialog box, select Illustrator 10 Compatibility and click OK.

6 Choose Edit > Paste.

You'll move the pasted logo to within 1/4-inch of the top left corner of the envelope by specifying the *x* and *y* coordinates in relation to the *ruler origin*. The ruler origin is the point where 0 appears on each ruler. We changed the ruler origin in this file to begin at the top left corner of the envelope and the ruler units to inches.

For more information, see "Defining ruler units" and "Changing the ruler origin" in online Help or Chapter 4 in the Adobe Illustrator User Guide.

7 In the Transform palette, click the top left reference point and then type **0.25 in** (18 pt) in the X text box and **–0.25 in** (a negative coordinate) in the Y text box. Press Enter or Return to apply the last setting you typed.

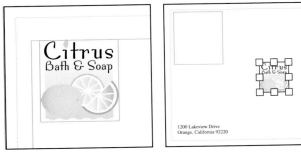
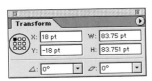

Copy the logo from the letterhead.   *Paste into the envelope.*   *Select top left reference point and enter* X *and* Y *coordinates.*

Note: *You can also move selected objects to exact* x *and* y *coordinates by choosing Object > Transform > Move and entering coordinates in the Move dialog box.*

8 With the logo still selected, drag the bottom right corner of the bounding box to scale the logo and make it fit within the blue square guideline.

9 Click away from the artwork to deselect it, and then choose File > Save.

Reflecting objects

Objects are reflected by flipping them across an invisible vertical or horizontal axis. Copying objects while reflecting creates a mirror image of the objects. Similar to scaling and rotating, you designate the point of origin from which an object will reflect or use the object's center point by default.

Now you'll use the reflect tool to make a mirror image of the orange slice in the logo.

1 Use the selection tool (▶) to select the orange slice in the logo.

2 Zoom in, if necessary.

3 Select the reflect tool (⬚) under the twist tool (⑤) in the toolbox, hold down Alt (Windows) or Option (Mac OS), and click the right edge of the orange slice.

Clicking the edge of the object designates the point of origin. Holding down Alt/Option as you click displays the Reflect dialog box.

4 In the Reflect dialog box, make sure that the Vertical option is selected and **90°** is entered in the Angle text box. Then click Copy (don't click OK).

Note: You can also use the Transform palette to reflect selected objects by choosing Flip Horizontal or Flip Vertical from the palette menu.

5 Click the selection tool to select the bounding box of the new orange slice and move the object down below the logo, Shift-dragging the selection to constrain the move. Then Shift-drag the bounding box to scale the orange slice and make it bigger (as it is in the illustration).

Move reflected copy down and rescale it.

Changing the perspective

Now you'll use the free transform tool to change the perspective of the orange slice.

1 With the orange slice selected, select the free transform tool (⌖) in the toolbox.

2 Position the double-headed arrow pointer over the bottom left corner of the object's bounding box, and select the bottom left corner handle (don't release the mouse button). Hold down Shift+Alt+Ctrl (Windows) or Shift+Option+Command (Mac OS), and slowly drag up to change the perspective of the object.

Holding down Shift as you drag scales the objects proportionally, holding down Alt/Option scales from the center point, and holding down Ctrl/Command as you drag distorts the object from the anchor point or bounding box handle that you're dragging.

3 Select the group-selection tool (⇗) in the toolbox, and click away from the orange slice to deselect it. Then Shift-click to select the segments of the orange slice and its rind. (Don't select the inner white pith of the rind.)

4 In the Swatches palette, select the Pale Orange gradient swatch to paint the selected objects with a lighter gradient.

Change perspective.

Select colored parts.

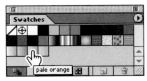

Paint with lighter gradient.

5 Choose Select > Deselect.

Choose File > Save. You can leave the file open on your desktop and minimize it; or close the file. You'll use the file later in this lesson.

Using the free transform tool

The free transform tool is a multipurpose tool that, besides letting you change the perspective of an object, combines the functions of scaling, shearing, reflecting, and rotating.

Now you'll use the free transform tool to transform objects copied from the logo into a business card.

1 Choose File > Open, and open the L6start3.ai file in the Lesson06 folder, located inside the Lessons folder within the AICIB folder on your hard drive.

2 Choose File > Save As, name the file **Buscards.ai**, and select the Lesson06 folder. Leave the Format option set to Adobe Illustrator® Document, and click Save. In the Illustrator Native Format Options dialog box, select Illustrator 10 Compatibility and click OK.

3 Click the Navigator tab behind the Info palette to bring the Navigator palette to the front of its group. (If the Navigator palette isn't visible on-screen, choose Window > Navigator to display it.) In the Navigator palette, click the Zoom In button (⌂) a few times to zoom to 200%, and then move the red view box over the top left corner of the artwork.

4 Choose the selection tool (▶), and click to select the lime slice in the logo. Then, Alt-drag (Windows) or Option-drag (Mac OS) to make a copy of the object. Position the new lime slice below and slightly to the right of the logo.

Now you'll use the free transform tool to scale, distort, and rotate the new lime slice.

5 With the lime slice still selected, select the free transform tool (⬚) in the toolbox. Hold down Shift+Alt (Windows) or Shift+Option (Mac OS), and drag the bottom right corner down to scale the object from its center and make the lime slice bigger.

Make copy of lime slice.   *Use free transform tool to scale object.*

Although you can scale objects using the selection tool, scaling with the free transform tool lets you perform other transformations without switching tools.

6 To distort the lime slice using the free transform tool, select the bottom right corner of the object's bounding box—don't release the mouse button. Begin dragging, and then hold down Ctrl (Windows) or Command (Mac OS), and slowly drag toward the opposite corner of the object.

(You can use the free transform tool to shear an object by dragging a side handle rather than a corner handle of the bounding box.)

7 To slightly rotate the lime slice, position the free transform tool just outside of the bottom right corner of the object's bounding box until you see the rotate pointer, and then drag to rotate the object.

Distort object using free   *Rotate object using free*
transform tool.   *transform tool.*

8 With the lime slice selected, select the group-selection tool (✥) in the toolbox and Shift-click the inner white pith of the rind to deselect it. In the Swatches palette, select the Pale Green gradient swatch to paint the lime slice with a lighter gradient.

9 Select the selection tool (▶), and drag a marquee to select all of the slice (including the inner white pith of the rind). Then choose Object > Arrange > Send to Back, and move the slice to tuck it under the logo.

Now you'll explore a slightly different way of distorting objects. Free Distort lets you distort a selection by moving any of its four corner points. It can be used either as a filter to apply a permanent change, or as an effect to apply a change that can be removed.

10 With the lime slice still selected, choose Filter > Distort > Free Distort.

Note: Choose the top Filter > Distort command. The bottom Filter > Distort commands work only on bitmap images).

11 Turn on the Preview option and drag one or more of the handles to distort the selection. Click OK.

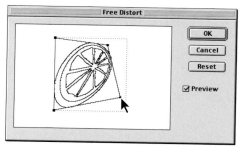

Previewing a free distortion

12 Click outside of the artwork to deselect it, and choose File > Save.

Working with symbols

You'll complete the logo design by adding the flower artwork you created earlier in the lesson, and then convert the logo into a symbol. Symbols save you time and greatly reduce file size by letting you use the same artwork multiple times in a document.

1 Make the Letterhd.ai file active; or if you closed the file, choose File > Open, and open the Letterhd.ai file in the Lesson06 folder.

2 Using the selection tool, select the flower artwork you created. Then choose Edit > Copy.

3 Make the Buscards.ai file active. Choose File > Paste to paste the flower artwork into the file. Use the selection tool to position the artwork below and to the right of the lime artwork that you just distorted.

You'll convert the Citrus Bath and Soap logo, and the lime and flower artwork into a symbol.

4 Press Shift+Tab to hide the palettes and make your window less cluttered.

5 Choose Window > Symbols to display the Symbols palette.

You use the Symbols palette to create, store, and place symbols. A symbol is an art object—like the logo—that you store in the Symbols palette and reuse one or more times in a document. You can then add *instances* of that symbol as many times as you want to your artwork without actually adding the complex art multiple times.

6 Choose Select > All to select all of the objects on the business card. Then Shift-click to deselect the type and the border of the business card. Just the logo artwork should be selected.

7 At the bottom of the Symbols palette, click the New Symbol button. The logo selection appears in the Symbols palette, outlined to indicate that it's selected.

Symbols palette   *Selected artwork*   *New symbol from selection*

You can create symbols from any Illustrator art object, including paths, compound paths, text, raster images, gradient meshes, and groups of objects. (You can't use nonembedded placed art as a symbol.) If you include active objects, such as brush strokes, blends, effects, or other symbol instances in a symbol, Illustrator automatically expands the objects when the symbol is created, and you can no longer edit those objects independently.

Now you'll add the instance to your artwork and then delete your original artwork. You've finished revising the artwork, and no longer need the original.

8 In the Symbols palette, click the Place Symbol Instance at the bottom of the Symbols palette.

The symbol instance appears in the center of the document window. You can also place an instance by dragging it from the Symbols palette to your artwork.

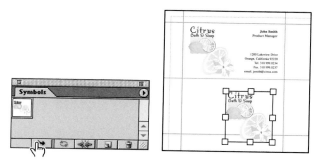

Click Place Symbol Instance button.

Symbol instance is pasted in center of document window.

The symbol instance is selected and has a bounding box around it, similar to grouped artwork. Symbol instances placed using the Symbols palette are exact replicas of the original.

9 Choose Select > Deselect.

10 Using the selection tool, click the symbol instance of the logo again to select it. Use the pointer to try moving some of the logo elements.

The artwork is one unit; selecting the symbol instance is similar to selecting grouped artwork. Each symbol instance is linked to the symbol in the Symbols palette.

You've finished revising the logo artwork, so you no longer need the original. Now you'll replace your original logo artwork with its symbol.

11 Using the selection tool, drag a marquee to select the original logo artwork in the upper left corner. (If necessary, Shift-click to deselect the business card border). Press Delete to delete the logo.

Although you've deleted the original artwork, you can retrieve it by breaking the link to the symbol.

💡 *To make the selected artwork an instance of the newly created symbol, press Shift as you drag the selected artwork to the Symbols palette.*

You'll use the Transform palette to place the symbol instance precisely at 1/4-inch from the top corner of the artwork.

12 In your artwork, select the symbol instance.

Selecting symbol instance

13 Choose Window > Transform to display the Transform palette.

14 In the Transform palette, click the top left reference point and then type **62** pt in the X text box and **745** pt in the Y text box. Press Enter or Return.

15 Save your work.

Once you've created symbol instances, you can edit the symbol instances on the artboard and automatically update the original symbol art with your edits. You can also redefine the original symbol with the edit. To create new symbols from existing symbols, duplicate a symbol and edit it.

Another way to add symbols to your artwork is with the symbolism tools. These tools let you add and manipulate multiple symbol instances at once. For more practice creating and using symbols, see Lesson 15, "Creating a Web Publication."

📓 For information on using symbolism tools with symbols, see "Using symbolism tools" in online Help or Chapter 3 of the Adobe Illustrator User Guide.

Creating and working with symbols

A symbol is an art object that you store in the Symbols palette and reuse in a document. For example, if you create a symbol from a flower, you can then add instances of that symbol multiple times to your artwork without actually adding the complex art multiple times. Each symbol instance is linked to the symbol in the palette. If you use the same artwork multiple times within a document, symbols can save time and greatly reduce file size. Symbols also provide excellent support for SWF and SVG export.

After you create a symbol, you can edit the symbol's instances on the artboard and, if you want, redefine the original symbol with the edits. Symbolism tools let you add and manipulate multiple symbol instances at once.

You can create symbols from any Illustrator art object, including paths, compound paths, text, raster images, mesh objects, and groups of objects. (However, you cannot use nonembedded placed art as a symbol, nor can you use some groups, such as groups of graphs.) Symbols may also include active objects, such as brush strokes, blends, effects, or other symbol instances in a symbol. You can use the Symbols palette as a database for your artwork—to recover the original definition with all of its active elements, simply expand a symbol instance.

You can modify the symbol instances and automatically update the original symbol art with your edits. To create new symbols from existing symbols, duplicate a symbol and edit it.

To duplicate a symbol in the Symbols palette:

In the Symbols palette, do one of the following:

* *Drag a symbol to the New Symbol button.*

* *Select a symbol, and choose Duplicate Symbol from the Symbols palette menu.*

Making multiple transformations

Now you'll create multiple copies of the business card and replicate the symbol instances in a few easy steps.

1 Double-click the hand tool (🖑) in the toolbox to zoom out and fit the artwork in the window.

2 Choose Select > All to select all of the objects on the business card.

3 Choose Object > Transform > Transform Each.

The Move options in the Transform Each dialog box let you move objects in a specified or random direction. Now you'll move a copy of the selected objects down 2 inches from the original objects.

4 In the Transform Each dialog box, enter **–2 in** in the Move Vertical text box, leave the other settings as they are, and click Copy (don't click OK).

Move object down 2 inches and copy it.

5 Choose Object > Transform > Transform Again to create another copy.

Now you'll use the keyboard shortcut to repeat the transformations.

6 Press Ctrl+D (Windows) or Command+D (Mac OS) twice to transform again two more times, creating a total of five cards in the column.

Note: *You can also apply multiple transformations as an effect, including scaling, moving, rotating, and reflecting an object. After selecting the objects, choose Effect > Distort & Transform > Transform. The dialog box looks the same as the Transform Each dialog box. Transforming as an effect has the advantage of letting you change or remove the transformation at any time.*

Next you'll use some shortcuts to make a copy of the column.

7 Press Ctrl+A (Windows) or Command+A (Mac OS) to select everything on the five business cards, and right-click (Windows) or Ctrl-click (Mac OS) in the window to display a shortcut menu. Choose Transform > Transform Each from the shortcut menu.

8 This time in the Transform Each dialog box, enter **3.5 in** in the Move Horizontal text box and **0** inches in the Move Vertical text box. Leave the other settings as they are, and click Copy (don't click OK).

9 To clear the window so that you can view the finished artwork, press Ctrl (Windows) or Command (Mac OS) and click outside the artwork to deselect it. Then choose View > Guides > Hide Guides to hide the blue guidelines, and press Tab to close the toolbox and palettes.

Pressing Tab toggles between hiding and showing the toolbox and all of the palettes. Pressing Shift+Tab hides or shows only the palettes.

10 Choose Select > Deselect and choose File > Save.

Modifying and redefining a symbol

Using symbols lets you globally update your artwork quickly. As a final step, you'll update the business card artwork.

1 In your artwork, select an instance of the symbol.

2 In the Symbols palette, click the Break Link to Symbol button.

Select symbol instance.   *Click Break Link to Symbol button.*

You've converted the symbol instance to editable artwork. The artwork is grouped.

3 In the artwork, use the group-selection tool (⭢⁺) to select the large lime in the center of the logo. Shift-click to deselect the white pith of the lime.

4 In the Swatches palette, click a swatch to select another color. (We chose the Yellow & Orange radial gradient.)

5 Choose Window > Transparency to display the Transparency palette. Reduce the Opacity to **60**%.

Select artwork.

Select new color and adjust transparency.

Result

You're ready to redefine the edited artwork as a symbol and update the business card.

6 Using the selection tool, drag a selection marquee or Shift-click to select the logo's edited artwork.

7 In the Symbols palette, make sure that the symbol you created earlier is selected.

8 Then choose Redefine Symbol from the Symbols palette menu. All of the logos are updated with the new definition of the symbol.

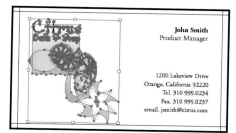

Select artwork.

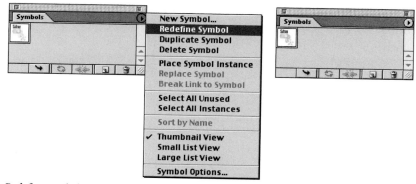

Redefine symbol with selection and create new symbol.

It's easy to update artwork that uses symbols. By breaking the link to a symbol, you can continue to edit instances of the symbol.

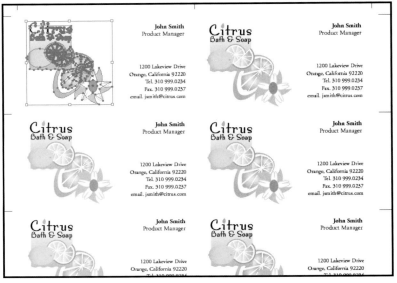

Art updated with new symbol

9 Choose File > Save. Choose File > Close to close the file.

You've completed the lesson on transforming objects.

For more practice with transforming objects, see Lesson 12, "Drawing Cylinders and Boxes."

Exploring on your own

Using variables, you can update text, graph data, linked files, or graphics dynamically and change them in your artwork. For example, you can create a series of business cards in which individual names and titles change, but all other information remains constant.

The Variables feature lets designers create highly formatted graphics as templates (called data-driven graphics), and then collaborate with developers to control the links between a template and its content. For more complex applications, you could, for example, produce 500 different Web banners based on the same template. In the past, you had to manually fill in the template with data (images, text, and so on). With data-driven graphics, you can use a script referencing a database to generate the Web banners for you.

In Illustrator, you can turn any piece of artwork into a template for data-driven graphics. All you need to do is define which objects on the artboard are dynamic (changeable) using variables. In addition, you can create different sets of variable data in order to easily view what your template will look like when it is rendered.

Making text dynamic

To get an idea of the power and usefulness of the Variables feature, you can try out this procedure using the business card artwork in the lesson.

1 Choose File > Open, and open the L6start3.ai file in the Lesson06 folder, located inside the Lessons folder within the AICIB folder on your hard drive.

2 Choose File > Save As, name the file **Buscard2.ai**, and select the Lesson06 folder. Leave the Format option set to Adobe Illustrator® Document, and click Save. In the Illustrator Native Format Options dialog box, select Illustrator 10 Compatibility and click OK.

3 Using the zoom tool, zoom in on the business card artwork in the upper left corner.

4 Choose Window > Variables to display the Variables palette.

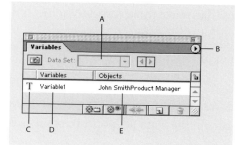

A. Data set *B.* Palette menu *C.* Variable type
D. Variable name *E.* Name of bound object

You'll create some text variables so that you can change the name and title on the business cards. This technique lets you create a series of business cards with a name and title that you can easily modify for other employees. You could also create variables for the address, for example, so that you could change the address for different branch offices.

5 Using the selection tool, in the artwork select the name and title, "John Smith, Product Manager."

6 At the bottom of the Variables palette, click the Make Text Dynamic button. A new variable named Variable1 appears in the palette.

The (**T**) icon appears to the right of the variable, indicating that it's a text string. Objects lists the object to which the variable is bounded—the text you selected in step 5.

7 Double-click the variable, and in the Variables Options dialog box name it **name_title**. The type already is set to Text String. Click OK.

Make Text Dynamic button   *Variable Options dialog box*

You can create four types of variables in Illustrator: Graph Data, Linked File, Text String, and Visibility. A variable's type indicates which object attributes are changeable. For example, you can use a Visibility variable to show or hide any object in your template. The Text String, Linked File, and Graph Data variables make those respective objects dynamic. The Visibility variable makes any object's visibility dynamic.

8 In your artwork, make sure that the text "John Smith, Product Manager" is still selected.

9 In the Variables palette, click the Capture Data Set button in the upper left of the palette to capture the information. Data Set 1 appears in the Data Set pop-up menu as your first variable.

Capture Data Set button and Data Set 1 in Variables palette

A data set is a collection of variables and associated data. When you create a data set, you capture a snapshot of the dynamic data that is currently displayed on the artboard. You can switch between data sets to upload different data into your template.

Now you'll revise the text and create another data set.

10 Select the type tool in the toolbox. In the artwork, drag to select the text "John Smith, Product Manager." Then type **Maggie Riley, Marketing Manager** to replace the text.

11 Notice that the Data Set 1 variable now appears in italics in the Variables palette. The italics indicate that the variable has been edited. You can modify a data set after you create it, as you'll do now.

12 In the Variables palette, click the Data Set button in the upper left of the palette to capture the information. Data Set 2 appears in the pop-up menu as the current variable.

Capturing new data set   *Data Set 2*

Creating variables is a two-step process. First you define the variable, and then you bind it to an object attribute to make the object variable. The type of object and type of variable determine what attributes of the object can change. You can bind a Visibility variable to any object to make the object's state of visibility dynamic. If the object is text, a linked image, or a graph, you can also make the object's content dynamic.

13 To create another variable for the address, click in a blank area of the Variables palette to deselect the variable you just created. If you want to create a new variable that matches the type of the selected object, make sure that no variable is selected in the Variables palette.

14 Use the selection tool ( ) to select the address text.

15 Click the Make Text Dynamic button at the bottom of the Variables palette. A text string variable with the first line of the address as the object appears in the palette. You can double-click the variable and rename it. (We renamed it "address.")

16 Using the type tool (T), revise the telephone number and e-mail address. (We used 310 999.5678 and mriley@citrus.com.)

17 Click the Capture Data Set button at the top left of the Variables palette to capture this information. This creates Data Set 3.

Data Set 3

18 To view the variables you just created, click the Next Data Set button (▸)to the right of the Data Set menu to scroll through the variables.

Notice that Data Set 2 lists the wrong telephone number and e-mail address for Maggie Riley. You can easily delete data sets.

19 With Data Set 2 selected in the Variables palette, choose Delete Data Set from the Variables palette menu, and click Yes at the alert message.

You could create a series of data sets for business card information, and then use a batch process to update all or part of the information—such as the names and titles, branch office addresses, or telephone numbers.

20 Choose File > Save.

Making artwork dynamic

You can also use variables to create artwork for clients that contain different iterations of a design. Now you'll change the visibility of some elements in the artwork.

1 Click in a blank area of the Variables palette to deselect the variable you just created.

2 Choose Window > Layers to display the Layers palette. You use the Layers palette to hide or show artwork.

3 Using the selection tool, drag a marquee to select just the logo in the artwork. If you accidentally select the business card border or text, Shift-click to deselect those objects.

You can also use the Layers palette to select all the objects in a layer or group.

4 Choose Object > Group to group the selected artwork so that it's easier to work with.

5 Expand the Layers palette and Layer1 so that you can see its contents. Notice that the <Group> sublayer is selected, as indicated by the selection indicator to the right of the layer name.

You'll create a variable to show or hide the selection. You can use the Visibility variable to hide or show any object, group, or layer in your artwork. You can also create graph data, linked file, and text string variables to make graphs, linked images, or text dynamic.

6 In the Variables palette, click the Make Visibility Dynamic button. A new variable titled Variable1, with its object listed as <Group>, appears in the palette.

7 Double-click Variable1 to display the Variable Options dialog box. Rename the variable **Logo**. Its type already is set to Visibility because you clicked the Make Visibility dynamic button. Click OK to rename Variable1 as Logo in the Variables palette.

Select object.

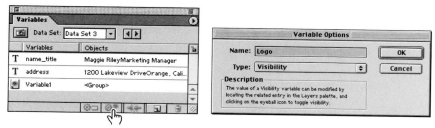

Click Make Visibility Dynamic button.

Name variable.

Now you'll hide the logo artwork.

8 In the Layers palette, click the eye icon to the left of the selected <Group> sublayer to hide the logo and its artwork.

9 In the Variables palette, notice that Data Set 3 now appears in italics, indicating that you have edited the data set.

10 Click the Capture Data Set button in the upper left of the palette to capture the information. Data Set 4 appears in the Data Set pop-up menu.

Lime sublayer selected in
Layers palette

Editing data set

Data Set 3 and logo hidden in artwork

11 To view the variables you just created, click the Next or Previous Data Set button to the right of the Data Set menu to scroll through the variables.

12 Choose File > Save. Then choose File > Close to close the file.

For more information on data-driven graphics and variables, see "Creating Templates for Data-Driven Graphics" in online Help or Chapter 13 in the Adobe Illustrator User Guide.

Review questions

1 How can you select and manipulate individual objects in a group?

2 How do you resize an object? How do you determine the point from which the object resizes? How do you resize a group of objects proportionally?

3 What transformations can you make using the Transform palette?

4 What does the square diagram indicate in the Transform palette, and how will it affect your transformations?

5 What is an easy way to change perspective? List three other types of transformations you can do with the free transform tool.

6 What is a symbol? What is a symbol instance? Why is it useful?

7 How do you create a variable? What are some uses for variables in your artwork?

Review answers

1 You can use the group-selection tool (⬚) to select individual objects or subgroups of objects within a group and change them without affecting the rest of the group.

2 You can resize an object by selecting it and dragging handles on its bounding box or by using the scale tool, the Transform palette, or Object > Transform > Scale to specify exact dimensions. You can also scale by choosing Effect > Distort & Transform > Transform.

To determine the point of origin from which the objects scale, select a reference point in the Transform palette or in the Transform Effect or Transform Each dialog box, or click in the artwork with the scale tool. Holding down Alt (Windows) or Option (Mac OS) and dragging the bounding box or double-clicking the scale tool will resize a selected object from its center point.

Shift-dragging a corner handle on the bounding box scales the objects proportionally, as will specifying a uniform scale value in the Scale dialog box or multiples of the dimensions in the Width and Height text boxes in the Transform palette.

3 You use the Transform palette for making the following transformations:

• Moving or strategically placing objects in your artwork (by specifying the *x* and *y* coordinates and the point of origin).

• Scaling (by specifying the width and height of selected objects).

• Rotating (by specifying the angle of rotation).

- Shearing (by specifying the angle of distortion).

- Reflecting (by flipping selected objects vertically or horizontally).

4 The square diagram in the Transform palette indicates the bounding box of the selected objects. Select a reference point in the square to indicate the point of origin from which the objects will move, scale, rotate, shear, or reflect.

5 An easy way to change the perspective of selected objects is to select the free transform tool (⌖), hold down Shift+Alt+Ctrl (Windows) or Shift+Option+Command (Mac OS), and drag a corner handle on the bounding box.

Other types of transformations you can do with the free transform tool are distorting, scaling, shearing, rotating, and reflecting.

6 A symbol is an art object that you store in the Symbols palette and reuse one or more times in a document. You can create symbols from any Illustrator art object, including paths, compound paths, text, raster images, gradient meshes, and groups of objects. (You can't use nonembedded placed art as a symbol.)

You can then add *instances* of that symbol as many times as you want to your artwork without actually adding the complex art multiple times. Symbols save you time and greatly reduce file size by letting you use the same artwork multiple times (as instances) in a document.

7 To create a variable, you make a selection in your artwork, and then bind a variable to the object. The type of object and type of variable determine what attributes of the object can change. You can bind a Visibility variable to any object to make the object's state of visibility dynamic. If the object is text, a linked image, or a graph, you can also make the object's content dynamic.

Using variables is a quick way to make artwork versions for a client that shows different iterations of the same design. You can also use variables to automate tedious design tasks, such as designing and updating business cards for hundreds of employees. You can use variables to update text, graph data, linked files, or graphics, and change them dynamically in your artwork.

Lesson 7

7 | Working with Type

One of the most powerful features of Adobe Illustrator is the ability to use type as a graphic element. Like other objects, type can be painted, scaled, rotated, and so on. You can also wrap type around objects, make it follow along the shape of a path, create type masks, import text files into containers, and modify the shapes of individual letters in a block of type.

In this lesson, you'll learn how to do the following:

• Create type in containers and along paths.

• Import text files into type containers.

• Apply an envelope effect to type, and edit the effect and the envelope contents.

• Adjust type attributes and formatting, including the font, leading, and paragraph alignment.

• Format text and adjust the text flow.

• Wrap type around a graphic.

• Create stylized letterforms with outlined type.

• Create type masks.

• Save a file in PDF format for online distribution and viewing.

Getting started

In this lesson, you'll create a Tai Chi lecture series poster. Before you begin, you'll need to restore the default preferences for Adobe Illustrator. Then you'll open the finished art file for this lesson to see what you'll create.

1 To ensure that the tools and palettes function exactly as described in this lesson, delete or deactivate (by renaming) the Adobe Illustrator 10.0 preferences file. See "Restoring default preferences" on page 4.

2 Start Adobe Illustrator.

3 Choose File > Open, and open the L7end_win.ai file (Windows) or the L7end_mac.ai file (Mac OS) in the Lesson07 folder, located inside the Lessons folder within the AICIB folder on your hard drive.

4 If you like, choose View > Zoom Out to make the finished artwork smaller and leave it on your screen as you work. (Use the hand tool (🖐) to move artwork where you want it in the window.) If you don't want to leave the image open, choose File > Close.

 For an illustration of the finished artwork in this lesson, see the color section.

Now open the start file to begin the lesson.

5 Choose File > Open, and open the L7start.ai file in the Lesson07 folder, located inside the Lessons folder within the AICIB folder on your hard drive.

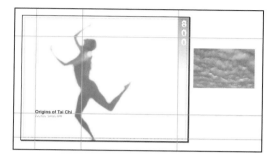

6 Choose File > Save As, name the file **TaiChi.ai**, and select the Lesson07 folder. Leave the Format option set to Adobe Illustrator® Document, and click Save. In the Illustrator Native Format Options dialog box, select Illustrator 10 Compatibility and click OK.

For now you'll hide the palettes that you don't need yet.

7 Click the close boxes or choose Window > Appearance, Window > Color, and Window > Styles to clear their check marks and close these palettes.

8 Bring the Links palette forward by clicking the Links tab behind the Actions palette.

Notice that the Links palette displays two links: the image of the dancing figure, which is linked to the original image file; and the image of the sky to the right of the artboard, which is an embedded image (it was pasted into the document).

9 Click the close box or choose Window > Links to close the Links palette.

For information on using the Links palette, see "Managing linked and embedded images" in online Help or Chapter 2 in the Adobe Illustrator User Guide.

Adding type to a document

Adobe Illustrator lets you add type to a document several different ways. You can type directly in the artwork, copy and paste type from other documents, and import entire text files.

To begin adding type to your artwork, you'll type the Tai Chi title on the poster.

1 Select the type tool (**T**) in the toolbox. Position the pointer so that the I-beam cross hair is in the top left corner of the artwork, using the guides that already exist in the document.

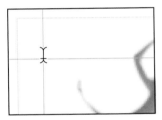

*Position type tool at intersection
of guides.*

The small horizontal line near the bottom of the I-beam—its cross hair—marks the position of the type *baseline*. The baseline is the line on which the type rests.

2 Click to set the type baseline where the guides intersect, and type **Tai Chi**.

By default, the type you create is 12-point Myriad Roman, filled with black, and stroked with None. The Fill and Stroke boxes in the toolbox display the type's current paint attributes.

Sampling type

Now you'll use the eyedropper tool to pick up, or sample, the attributes of other type in the artwork and apply it to the Tai Chi title.

1 Click the selection tool (▶) in the toolbox to select the words *Tai Chi*.

Clicking the selection tool immediately after typing with the type tool automatically selects the words you typed.

2 Click the eyedropper tool (✐) in the toolbox, and click anywhere in the line "Lecture Series 800" to sample the type's attributes (18-pt Adobe Garamond Semibold Italic).

Sampling type attributes

Sampled attributes are applied to any selected text, and the type colors appear in the Fill and Stroke boxes in the toolbox. In this case, 18-point Adobe Garamond Semibold Italic is applied to the *Tai Chi* text.

Changing the character size

Now you'll use the Character palette to make the title bigger.

1 With the Tai Chi type still selected, choose Window > Type > Character to display the Character palette.

By default, the Character palette displays the selected font and its style, size, kerning, leading, and tracking values. If the type selection contains two or more attributes, the corresponding text boxes are blank. (*Leading* is the amount of space between lines or paragraphs. *Kerning* is the space between two characters. *Tracking* is the spacing between a string of characters.)

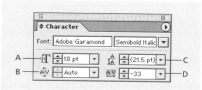

A. Font size B. Kerning C. Leading
D. Tracking

2 Type **125** in the Font Size text box, and press Enter or Return to increase the font size to 125 points.

You can use the Character palette to select or view a font and its attributes.

3 In the Character palette, hold down the mouse button on the Font Menu buttons (in Windows, in the top left and right corners of the palette) or Font Menu button (in Mac OS, in the top right corner of the palette). Notice that the selected font is the one that you sampled in the "Lecture Series 800" (Adobe Garamond Semibold Italic.) Release the mouse button.

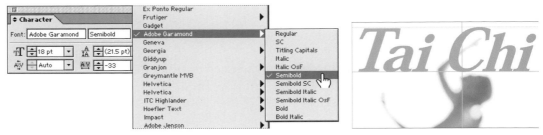

Choosing font from Character palette menu

You can also select a font and size using the Font and Size submenus in the Type menu.

Reshaping text with an envelope

You'll add a simple envelope effect to the *Tai Chi* title to distort the text in the shape of the envelope and make the text follow the curve of the body. Envelopes are objects that distort or reshape selected objects.

1 Click the selection tool ( ) in the toolbox.

2 With the Tai Chi title still selected, choose Object > Envelope Distort > Make With Warp.

3 In the Warp Options dialog box, select Preview to see how the effect will appear.

You'll select a preset warp shape for your envelope. You can also make an envelope using the topmost selected object in your artwork, or a mesh object or objects on your artboard—including text objects, paths, compound paths, meshes, blends, and raster images. You can use envelopes on all artwork except linked objects (with the exception of TIFF, GIF, and JPEG) or artwork to which a third-party plug-in is applied.

4 For Style, choose Flag. Select Horizontal for Bend, and enter an amount using the sliders or entering values in the text box. Then set the Horizontal and Vertical distortions. (We used a Horizontal Bend value of 62%, a Horizontal Distortion of −42%, and a Vertical Distortion of 10%.)

If you like, you can preview other styles and distortion values.

5 Click OK. Illustrator groups the envelope and the original artwork.

Select object to warp.

Set envelope's Warp options.

Result

Now you'll adjust the envelope slightly.

After you apply an envelope, you can continue to edit the original objects. You can edit either the envelope or the artwork, but not both at the same time. At any time you can also edit, delete, or expand an envelope.

6 Select the mesh tool (⬚) in the toolbox.

7 Click the title text three-quarters of the way from the top baseline, and again one-quarter from the bottom baseline to create a series of two horizontal mesh lines with intersecting vertical mesh.

You'll use the direct-selection tool to adjust the mesh.

8 Select the direct-selection tool ( ) in the toolbox. Drag the nodes slightly to distort the text. You can also drag the direction lines to adjust the curve of the warp.

Click with mesh tool to add mesh lines.

Adjust the mesh nodes and lines with the direct-selection tool.

💡 *You can also select the envelope in the artwork, and choose Object > Envelope Distort > Reset With Mesh or Reset With Warp. Then select the desired options.*

You can also edit the contents of an envelope. Now you'll change the font size.

9 Click the selection tool ( ) in the toolbox to select the title text.

10 Choose Object > Envelope Distort > Edit Contents.

11 In the Character palette, decrease the font size to 100 and press Enter or Return.

The Layers palette indicates that you are editing an envelope.

12 Choose Window > Layers to display the Layers palette. In the Layers palette, click the triangle to the left of Layer 1 to expand it. Notice the <Envelope> sublayer; the selection indicator to its right indicates that you are editing the envelope's contents.

13 If you want to edit the text of an envelope, select the type tool (**T**) in the toolbox. Then triple-click the text to select it, and type a new word.

Selection indicator shows
<Envelope> contents
being edited.

Edit envelope contents.

14 Choose Edit > Undo. For this lesson, you'll use the original text.

15 In your artwork, use the selection tool to reposition the title text so that the base of the *T* touches the left guide, and the top of the text touches the dotted line of the printing guide. Press the arrow keys to nudge the text into place.

Repositioning text in an envelope

16 Choose Select > Deselect to deselect your work. Choose File > Save.

Creating columns of type

Another way to add type to your document is to import a text file.

You'll create a container that overlaps the bottom leg of the figure so that later you can wrap the text around the leg. Then you'll divide the type container to hold three columns of type for this layout.

1 If necessary, double-click the hand tool ( ) to fit all of the artwork in the window.

2 Select the type tool (**T**) in the toolbox. Using the vertical guides at the bottom right page for alignment, drag to draw a text container that spans from the intersecting guides beneath the woman's left knee to the lower page boundary and to the right guide.

3 Choose File > Place. Select the text file, Text.rtf, located in the Lesson07 folder, and click Place. The placed text appears within the text container. The plus sign in the lower right corner indicates that not all of the text is displayed.

Placed text fills container drawn within guides.

Illustrator supports more than a dozen text formats for Windows and Mac OS, including Microsoft Word®, Rich Text Format, and WordPerfect®. You can also bring text into Illustrator by copying and pasting text from the Clipboard. However, the copied text may lose its type attributes (such as its font and styles) when pasted into the document.

4 Choose View > Guides > Hide Guides.

You'll divide the type and its container into three type containers, each for a column of type, using the Rows & Columns command.

5 Click the selection tool to select the text block automatically.

6 Choose Type > Rows & Columns.

The Rows & Columns dialog box is useful for changing the height, width, and gutter size between rows and columns. The Text Flow option lets you control the direction in which text flows (from left to right or up and down). The totals in the Rows and Columns section indicate the size of the text block (in this case, the size of the text container you created earlier—approximately 120 pts for Rows and 456 pts for Columns).

You'll divide the text container into columns and gutters.

7 In the Columns area, type **3** in the Number text box for three columns, and click OK.

The three type containers are linked so that text flows between containers in the order that the containers are created and grouped—selecting one container selects all three containers. Each container can be moved and resized individually using the direct-selection tool.

8 Before continuing, choose View > Zoom In to magnify your view of the type containers.

9 Click outside of the artwork to deselect the type columns, and choose File > Save.

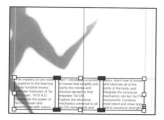

Text container divided into three columns

Changing character attributes of placed text

Next you'll format the type that you just imported. You'll change the character font of the placed text to match the rest of the poster, and reformat the first two paragraphs, which are a quote and a byline.

1 Select the type tool (**T**), click anywhere in one of the three text columns, and then choose Select > All to select all of the imported text automatically after it is placed.

2 In the Character palette, use the Font Menu (at the top of the palette) to choose a font (we chose Adobe Garamond Regular). Enter sizes for the type and the leading in the Font Size and Leading text boxes. (We specified 8.5 in the Font Size text box and 11 in the Leading text box.) Press Enter or Return to apply the attributes.

Choose font from the Character palette menu.

Next you'll select the first two paragraphs and format them as a quote and a byline.

3 First, choose Type > Show Hidden Characters to display all of the hidden characters in the text, such as spaces and paragraph breaks.

4 Using the type tool (**T**), triple-click inside the first paragraph to select only that paragraph. (You can also select it by dragging.)

5 In the Character palette, choose a font from the pop-up menu (we selected Adobe Garamond Italic), and enter sizes for the font and leading (we specified 11 points in the Font Size text box and 16 points in the Leading text box). Press Enter or Return to apply the changes.

6 Using the type tool again, triple-click inside the second paragraph to select it, and experiment with different fonts and sizes for the byline. (We used Adobe Garamond Italic, 11 points for font size, and 16 points for leading.)

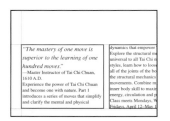

Select and reformat first two paragraphs.

7 Choose Type > Show Hidden Characters to turn off the display of hidden text characters.

8 Choose File > Save.

Changing paragraph attributes

You can set paragraph attributes (such as alignment or indenting) before you enter new type, or reset them to change the appearance of existing, selected type. If you select several type paths and type containers, you can set attributes for all of them at the same time.

Now you'll add more space leading before all of the paragraphs in the column text.

1 Hold down Ctrl (Windows) or Command (Mac OS) to temporarily convert the type tool to the selection tool, and click the edge of one of the type containers to select it. (Clicking one of the type containers selects all three containers.)

2 Click the Paragraph tab behind the Character palette to display the Paragraph palette.

3 In the Paragraph palette, type **6** in the Space Before Paragraph text box (in the bottom right corner), and press Enter or Return to separate all of the paragraphs by 6 points of spacing.

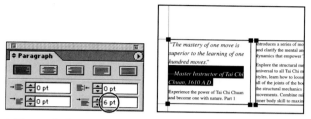

Add space before paragraphs.

4 Choose File > Save.

For information on other features you can use when working with type, such as kerning, tracking, tabs, and searching, see "Using Type" in online Help or Chapter 12 in the Adobe Illustrator User Guide.

Adjusting the text flow

You'll shorten the first text column to fit the quote and byline and force the rest of the type to begin in the second column. Because the type containers are linked, adjusting any of the columns affects all of them and the type within them.

1 Choose Select > Deselect to deselect the artwork.

2 Select the direct-selection tool ( ) in the toolbox. The direct-selection tool lets you resize one type container without resizing the others.

3 Select the bottom of the left column (don't release the mouse button), and then hold down Shift and drag the bottom of the column up to just below the byline (the second paragraph).

You can easily locate the edges of type containers in two ways. Choose View > Smart Guides to turn on the Smart Guides and display the outlines, center points, and points of hidden objects whenever the pointer is over them. Or choose View > Outline to see the outlines of all the objects in the artwork without the fills or strokes hiding them.

Shift-dragging constrains the movement to a straight line. (Shift-clicking the bottom edge of the container with the direct-selection tool alternates between selecting and deselecting the container.)

Shift-drag type container to resize.

Notice how the type flows into the second column as you adjust it. Type flows from one object to another based on the type containers' stacking order. In this case, the stacking order is from left to right, in the order in which the columns were created.

4 Click away from the artwork to deselect it, and then choose File > Save.

Wrapping type around a graphic

You can make type wrap around any graphic object in Illustrator. To complete the column layout, you'll wrap the left column of type around the bottom leg of the figure.

In this example, we've added an unpainted object around the leg in the bitmap image so that you can control the way the type will wrap around the figure.

1 Press Ctrl+Y (Windows) or Command+Y (Mac OS) to switch to Outline view.

2 Click the selection tool ( ) in the toolbox, and choose Object > Unlock All to unlock and select the object that overlaps the left side of the type containers. (The object was locked so that it wouldn't interfere with drawing the containers.)

Objects around which you will wrap type must be in front of the type container.

3 Choose Object > Arrange > Bring to Front, and then Shift-click the border of the left column to select the type containers too.

Because the containers are linked, Shift-clicking one type container selects all three.

4 Choose Type > Wrap > Make to wrap the type around the object, and then choose View > Preview.

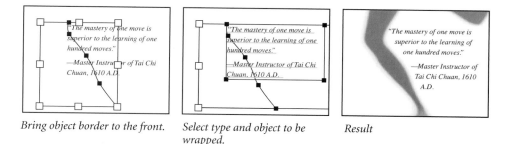

Bring object border to the front.   Select type and object to be wrapped.   Result

The type is wrapped around the object, and the type containers are now grouped with it. You can use the direct-selection tool to select parts of the group and make changes.

5 Press Ctrl+Y (Windows) or Command+Y (Mac OS) to toggle between Preview view and Outline view as you work. Outline view lets you see the unpainted object over the leg.

6 Click away from the artwork to deselect it, and then select the direct-selection tool ( ) in the toolbox.

7 Select the curved path outlining the leg, and drag segments of the path outward, or select an anchor point and drag the direction lines to change the shape of the object and, consequently, the shape of the wrapped type.

8 If necessary, use the direct-selection tool to select the bottom of the left column (don't release the mouse button), and drag it down to adjust the last line of the byline.

You can use the type tool to click anywhere in the columns of placed text and make changes as you wish, such as typing some new words or correcting the spelling.

9 When you are satisfied with how the type wraps, choose Select > Deselect to deselect the artwork.

10 Choose File > Save.

Typing along a path

Another way to create type in Illustrator is to enter type along a path. Now you'll add a credit line to the image of the dancing figure.

1 If necessary, press Ctrl+Y (Windows) or Command+Y (Mac OS) to switch to Preview view.

The current fill and stroke settings were both set to None when you selected the path along the bottom leg. You'll change the paint settings so you can see a path as you draw it along the upper leg in Preview view.

2 With the artwork deselected, set the paint attributes in the toolbox to a fill of none and a black stroke (by clicking the Default Fill and Stroke box in the toolbox, and then with the Fill Box selected, clicking the None button).

3 If desired, press Ctrl+spacebar (Windows) or Command+spacebar (Mac OS), and click the raised leg once or twice to zoom in on it.

4 Select the pencil tool (✐) in the toolbox, and drag it to draw a line along the back of the figure's raised leg. The line remains selected after you draw it.

5 Select the path type tool (✎) from the same group as the type tool in the toolbox, and click at the beginning of the line.

Clicking a line with the path type tool converts the line to an invisible path (without any fill or stroke color), and a blinking insertion point appears.

6 Click the Character tab behind the Paragraph palette to display the Character palette, choose a font from the pop-up menu (we selected Adobe Garamond Regular), type **6** points in the Font Size text box, and press Enter or Return to set the new attributes.

7 Type the credit for the figure: **Photo from Adobe Image Library**.

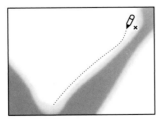
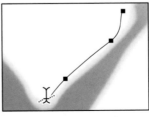

Draw a line.　　　*Convert line to type path.*　　　*Type words along path.*

Turning a path or object into a type path removes any stroke or fill from the path, even if it was originally stroked or filled. When you select a type path, changing the paint settings affects only the type, not the path.

8 To move the type path, use the selection tool ( ).

9 Choose View > Hide Bounding Box so that it doesn't distract you.

10 To adjust the starting position of the type along the path, grab the I-beam using the selection pointer and then drag to move the type along the path. (Dragging across the path flips the type.)

Adjusting type along path

11 If you zoomed in on the artwork, double-click the hand tool ( ) in the toolbox to fit the artwork in the window.

12 Choose Select > Deselect, and then choose File > Save.

Creating type outlines

You can modify the shapes of individual letters in a block of type by converting the block to type outlines or *letterforms*. When you create type outlines, each character becomes a separate object with compound paths outlining the character.

Now you'll convert the number *800* into outlines and change the shape of the letterforms to create a special effect.

1 Choose View > Outline, and then choose Window > Navigator to display a thumbprint of the artboard in the Navigator palette. Click in the top right corner of the thumbprint image to move the red box over the number *800*.

2 Use the selection tool ( ) to select the type *800* in the top right corner of the artwork, and then choose Type > Create Outlines.

The type is converted to a set of compound paths around each number that can be edited and manipulated like any other object.

3 Click away from the artwork to deselect the numbers, and then select the group-selection tool (✛) from the same group as the direct-selection tool in the toolbox.

The group-selection tool lets you select individual outlines in a compound path.

4 Shift-click to select the outer paths of all three numbers, and press the Up Arrow key a few times to move the paths up, leaving the inner paths of all three in their original position.

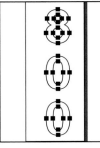 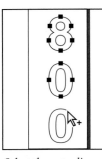 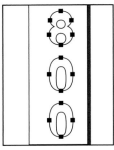

Create outlines.   *Select the outer lines.*   *Press the Up Arrow key.*

You can also change the shape of letterforms by using the direct-selection tool to select path segments or anchor points in the outlines and dragging the direction lines in new directions.

5 Click away from the artwork to deselect it, and press Ctrl+Y (Windows) or Command+Y (Mac OS) to switch back to Preview view.

Creating type masks

Masks crop part of an image so that only a portion of it is revealed through the shape or shapes that you create. You can use type as a mask without having to convert the type to outlines first. After creating a mask using type, you can still edit it—for example, by adjusting the font or size and even by typing in new text.

In this example, you'll create a mask using type and an embedded bitmap image. An image of a cloudy sky was pasted into the document to use as the background of the mask.

[?] For more on embedding and linking image files in your artwork, see "Setting Up Artwork in Illustrator" in online Help or Chapter 2 in the Adobe Illustrator User Guide.

Now you'll add the heading "ASIAN STUDIES PROGRAM" in the top right corner of the poster and convert it to a type mask over the cloudy sky image.

1 Click the selection tool ( ) in the toolbox, and move the image of the sky from the area outside of the artboard to the top right corner of the artwork next to the 800 rectangle.

2 Select the type tool (T) from the same group as the path type tool ( ) in the toolbox, and click in the sky next to the number 8.

Move the sky image.   *Select the type tool and click.*

3 In the Character palette, choose a font from the pop-up menu (we chose Myriad Bold), enter sizes for the font and the leading (we specified 28 points in the Font Size text box and 28 points in the Leading text box), and press Enter or Return to apply the settings.

4 Click the Paragraph tab to display the Paragraph palette. Click the Align Right button.

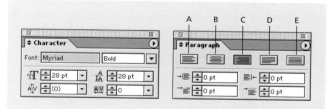

A. *Align left* B. *Align center*
C. *Align right* D. *Justify full lines*
E. *Justify all lines*

5 Press the Caps Lock key to type in all uppercase letters. Type **ASIAN**, and then press Enter or Return to move the insertion point to the next line. Type **STUDIES**, press Enter or Return, and then type **PROGRAM**.

6 Click the selection tool to select the text block. Shift-click to select the image behind it.

The object that will be the mask can be a single shape, multiple shapes, or type. The masking object (in this case, the type) must be on top of the artwork you want to mask.

7 Choose Object > Clipping Mask > Make to convert the front object into a mask and see through to the image.

Select type and sky image.   *Apply clipping mask.*

The type mask loses its paint attributes and is assigned a fill and stroke of None. Thus, if you moved the type away from the background image, you would no longer see the type mask in Preview view unless you select it or assign it new paint attributes.

Once you have created a mask, you can still adjust the artwork and the type (the mask) independently. For example, you can resize either the artwork (here an embedded photo) or the type, as well as rotate, skew, and reflect them.

8 Double-click the hand tool (🖑) in the toolbox to fit the artwork in the window.

9 Choose File > Save.

You've completed the artwork for the Tai Chi poster using various ways to work with type.

Saving your file for electronic distribution

Now you'll save a copy of the poster in Portable Document Format (PDF) so you can distribute it electronically, or link it to your Web site. When you save your artwork in PDF format, Illustrator creates an exact snapshot of the page that lets you view it online without the fonts, linked images, or software used to create it.

1 Choose File > Save a Copy. In the dialog box, choose Adobe PDF (PDF) from the Save as Type (Windows) or Format (Mac OS) pop-up menu, name the file **TaiChi.pdf**, navigate to the Lesson07 folder, and click Save.

2 In the Adobe PDF Format Options dialog box, choose Screen Optimized from the Options Set pop-up menu to display a set of Web options. (Adobe Acrobat® 5.0 automatically converts the document's color mode to RGB for optimal screen viewing.)

```
                    Adobe PDF Format Options
Options Set: [ Screen Optimized    ↕ ]
[ General        ↕ ]                    [    OK     ]
┌─ File Compatibility ──────────┐       [  Cancel   ]
│ ● Acrobat 5.0                  │
│ ○ Acrobat 4.0                  │
│ ☐ Preserve Illustrator Editing Capabilities │
└────────────────────────────────┘
┌─ Options ─────────────────────┐
│ ☑ Embed All Fonts             │
│ ☑ Subset fonts when less than: [ 100% ] │
│   of the characters are used  │
│ ☐ Embed ICC Profile:          │
│ ☐ Generate Thumbnails         │
└────────────────────────────────┘
⚠ The document's color mode will be changed to RGB.
```

3 Leave the other settings as they are, and click OK. In the warning dialog box, click OK to save the file.

Note: In the warning dialog box, select the Preserve Illustrator Editing Capabilities when exporting a file only if you want to be able to reopen and edit the file in Adobe Illustrator. If you are posting the file on a Web site, you probably don't want it to be editable.

Illustrator saves the copy of the poster as a Web-ready PDF file that can be viewed electronically in Adobe Acrobat Reader® and linked to your Web pages to be viewed in a browser. Acrobat Reader—electronic publishing software for Windows, DOS, UNIX®, and Macintosh®—is provided on the Adobe Illustrator CD and is available on the Adobe Web site (http://www.adobe.com) for free distribution.

4 To view the PDF file if you have Acrobat 5.0 installed, launch Acrobat. Then choose File > Open, and open the TaiChi.pdf file you just saved in the Lesson07 folder.

For information on saving Illustrator files in different formats, see "Saving and Exporting Artwork" in online Help or Chapter 14 in the Adobe Illustrator User Guide.

For information on converting artwork to GIF and JPEG images for your Web pages, see Lesson 15, "Creating a Web Publication."

To learn about printing your poster, see Lesson 13, "Printing Artwork and Producing Color Separations."

Review questions

1 Describe three ways to enter text into the artwork.

2 How do you change the leading between lines in a paragraph? How do you change the leading between paragraphs?

3 Describe two ways to change the font and size of type.

4 How can you divide a type container into smaller containers?

5 How do you create type that follows the shape of a path or an object?

6 What is a reason for converting type to outlines?

7 How do you create a type mask?

8 How do you create an envelope effect? How do you edit the effect?

9 How do you create a PDF version of an Illustrator document for online viewing?

Review answers

1 To enter text in the artwork, do any of the following:

• Select the type tool (**T**) and start typing.

• Import text from another file by choosing File > Place.

• Select the path type tool, click on any path, and start typing.

• Click inside any shape, or click and drag a marquee with the type tool. Then start typing or place a text file.

2 To change the leading between lines in a paragraph, select the paragraph and then enter a new leading value in the Character palette. (Choose Type > Character to display the Character palette.) To change the leading (or space) between paragraphs, select the block of type and then enter a new leading value in the Space Before Paragraph text box in the Paragraph palette. (Choose Type > Paragraph to display the Paragraph palette.)

3 To change the font and size of type, you can use the controls in the Character palette, or choose commands from the Font and Size submenus in the Type menu.

4 To divide a type container into smaller containers, select the container and choose Type > Rows & Columns. In the Rows & Columns dialog box, enter the number of horizontal or vertical containers, or both, into which you'll divide the container, their size, and the space between each container.

5 You can use the path type tool (⤴) to type words along an existing path. You can also wrap a block of type around an object by selecting the type and the object and choosing Type > Wrap > Make. (The object must be in front of the type.)

6 To create a PDF version of an Illustrator file for online viewing, you choose File > Save a Copy; then for format or type, you select Adobe PDF.

7 Convert type to outlines when you want to transform (scale, reshape, and so on) letters individually in the word or block of type. Outlines are also useful for filling type with a gradient fill.

8 One way to create a type mask is to select the type that you want to be the mask, and select the object, bitmap image, or type that you want to show through the mask. (The masking type must be in front of any other objects.) Then choose Object > Clipping Mask > Make to create the type mask.

9 You create an envelope by selecting an object and then applying a preset warp shape or mesh using the Object > Envelope Distort > Make With Warp or Make With Mesh command. You can also select a top object that will act as the envelope, select another object to which you apply the envelope, and then choose Object > Envelope Distort > Make With Top Object.

You can edit either an envelope or its contents, but not both at the same time. To edit an envelope, you select the envelope and then choose Object > Envelope Distort > Reset With Warp or Reset With Mesh. You can also use the selection tool or mesh tool to edit the envelope. To edit an envelope's contents, you select the envelope and then choose Object > Envelope Distort > Edit Contents.

Lesson 8

8 | Blending Shapes and Colors

Gradient fills are graduated blends of two or more colors. You use the Gradient palette to create or modify a gradient fill. The blend tool blends the shapes and colors of objects together into a new blended object or a series of intermediate shapes.

In this lesson, you'll learn how to do the following:

• Create and save gradients.

• Add colors to a gradient.

• Adjust the direction of a gradient blend.

• Create smooth-color blends between objects.

• Blend the shapes of objects in intermediate steps.

• Modify a blend, including adjusting its path and changing the shape or color of the original objects.

Getting started

You'll explore various ways to create your own color gradients and blend colors and shapes together using the Gradient palette and the blend tool.

Before you begin, you'll restore the default preferences for Adobe Illustrator. Then you'll open the finished art file for this lesson to see what you'll create.

1 To ensure that the tools and palettes function exactly as described in this lesson, delete or deactivate (by renaming) the Adobe Illustrator 10.0 preferences file. See "Restoring default preferences" on page 4.

2 Start Adobe Illustrator.

3 Choose File > Open, and open the L8end.ai file in the Lesson08 folder, located inside the Lessons folder within the AICIB folder on your hard drive.

The chile peppers, CHILES type, and wavy lines are all filled with gradients. The objects that make up the inside of the bowl, the objects on the outside of the bowl, and the top and bottom wavy lines on the blanket have all been blended to create new objects.

4 If you like, choose View > Zoom Out to make the finished artwork smaller, adjust the window size, and leave it on your screen as you work. (Use the hand tool (✋) to move the artwork where you want it in the window.) If you don't want to leave the image open, choose File > Close.

⬤ For an illustration of the finished artwork in this lesson, see the color section.

To begin working, you'll open an existing art file.

5 Choose File > Open, and open the L8start.ai file in the Lesson08 folder, located inside the Lessons folder within the AICIB folder on your hard drive.

6 Choose File > Save As, name the file **Chiles.ai**, and select the Lesson08 folder. Leave the Format option set to Adobe Illustrator® Document, and click Save. In the Illustrator Native Format Options dialog box, select Illustrator 10 Compatibility and click OK.

7 Click the close box in the Layers palette or choose Window > Layers to close the Layers palette group. You won't need these palettes for this lesson.

Creating a gradient fill

Gradients can be used very much like colors to fill objects that you create. A *gradient fill* is a graduated blend between two or more colors. You can easily create your own gradients, or you can use the gradients provided with Adobe Illustrator and edit them for the desired effect.

To begin the lesson, you'll create a gradient fill for one of the chile peppers.

1 Using the selection tool ( ), click to select the chile pepper in the back.

The pepper is painted with a solid color fill and no stroke, as indicated in the Fill and Stroke boxes in the toolbox. The Gradient button below the Fill and Stroke boxes indicates the current gradient fill (which is by default a black-and-white gradient until you select a gradient-filled object or a gradient swatch in the Swatches palette).

2 Click the Gradient button in the toolbox.

The default, black-and-white gradient appears in the Fill box in the toolbox and is applied to the selected chile pepper.

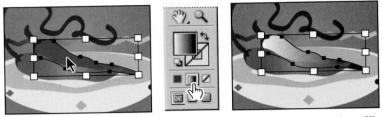

Click Gradient button to paint selected object with default or current gradient fill.

When you click the Gradient button in the toolbox, the Gradient palette appears from behind the Stroke palette. You use the Gradient palette to create your own gradients and to modify the colors of existing gradients.

3 In the Gradient palette, position the pointer on the triangle in the upper right corner of the palette, press the mouse button, and choose Show Options from the palette's menu. (Use the same technique for choosing options from other palette menus.)

4 Now click the Gradient tab on the palette and drag it to move the palette to another area on your screen. This action separates, or undocks, the Gradient palette from the Stroke palette.

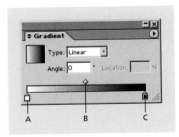

A. *Starting gradient stop*
B. *Midpoint between blended colors*
C. *Ending gradient stop*

In the Gradient palette, the left gradient square, or stop, under the gradient bar marks the gradient's starting color; the right gradient stop marks the ending color. A *gradient stop* is the point at which a gradient changes from one color to the next. A diamond above the bar marks the midpoint where two colors blend equally.

5 Click the left gradient stop to select the starting color of the gradient. The tip of the gradient stop appears darker to indicate that it's selected.

In the Color palette, a gradient stop appears beneath the Fill box, indicating which color in the gradient is currently selected. Now you'll paint the selected color in the gradient with a new color.

6 In the Color palette, position the pointer on the triangle in the upper right corner of the palette, press the mouse button, and choose CMYK to switch from the Grayscale palette to the CMYK palette.

7 With the gradient stop selected, position the eyedropper pointer in the color bar at the bottom of the Color palette, and drag or click to select a new color. Notice the change to the gradient fill in the selected chile pepper.

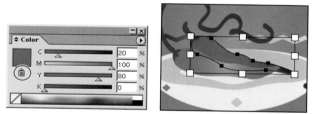

Gradient stop color selected   *Result*

You can also drag the Color palette sliders or enter values in the percent text boxes to select a color. The selected gradient stop changes to reflect your choice.

8 With the left gradient stop still selected, enter these CMYK values in the Color palette: C=**20**, M=**100**, Y=**80**, and K=**0**. (To move between text boxes, press Tab.) Press Enter or Return to apply the last value typed.

9 In the Gradient palette, select the ending gradient stop on the right.

10 In the Color palette, choose CMYK from the palette menu to switch to the CMYK palette from the Grayscale palette.

11 Change the ending color by entering these values in the Color palette: C=**100**, M=**30**, Y=**100**, and K=**0**. (Press Tab to select each text box.) Press Enter or Return to apply the last value typed.

Now you'll save the new gradient in the Swatches palette.

12 Click the Swatches tab to bring the palette to the front of its group. (If the Swatches palette isn't visible on-screen, choose Window > Swatches to display it.)

13 To save the gradient, drag it from the Fill box in the toolbox or the Gradient palette and drop it on the Swatches palette; or select it in the Fill box in the toolbox or in the Gradient palette, and click the New Swatch button at the bottom of the Swatches palette.

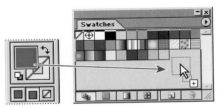

Drag gradient swatch from Fill box to Swatches palette.

14 In the Swatches palette, double-click the new gradient swatch to open the Swatch Options dialog box. Type **Pepper2** in the Swatch Name text box, and click OK.

15 To display only gradient swatches in the Swatches palette, click the Show Gradient Swatches button at the bottom of the Swatches palette.

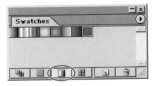

Display only gradient swatches.

16 Try out some of the different gradients in the selected chile pepper.

Notice that some of the gradients have several colors. You'll learn how to make a gradient with multiple colors later in this lesson.

17 Deselect the artwork by choosing Select > Deselect, and then choose File > Save.

Adjusting the direction of the gradient blend

Once you have painted an object with a gradient fill, you can adjust the direction that the gradient colors blend in the object. Now you'll adjust the gradient fill in the other chile pepper.

1 Use the selection tool ( ) to select the chile pepper in front. Notice that it's painted with a radial-type gradient (as indicated in the Gradient palette).

You can create linear or radial gradients. Both types of gradient have a starting and an ending color of the fill. With a radial gradient, the starting color of the gradient defines the center point of the fill, which radiates outward to the ending color.

2 Select the gradient tool ( ) in the toolbox.

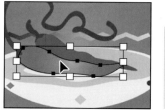
Select gradient-filled object.

Select gradient tool to adjust gradient.

The gradient tool works only on selected objects that are filled with a gradient.

3 Click or drag the gradient tool across the selected chile pepper to change the position and direction of the gradient's starting and ending colors.

Drag gradient tool at an angle.

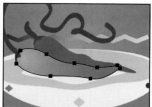
Result

For example, drag within the pepper to create a short gradient with distinct color blends; drag a longer distance outside the pepper to create a longer gradient with more subtle color blends. You can also drag from the ending color to the starting color and vice versa to transpose the colors and reverse the direction of the blend.

4 Deselect the artwork by choosing Select > Deselect, and then choose File > Save.

Adding colors to a gradient

Every gradient in Adobe Illustrator has at least two gradient stops. By editing the color mix of each stop and by adding gradient stops in the Gradient palette, you can create your own custom gradients.

Now you'll paint some type that has been converted to path outlines with a linear gradient fill, and edit the colors in it.

1 Select the magic wand tool ( ), and click to select the letters in the type *CHILES*.

The *CHILES* type has already been converted to path outlines so you can fill it with a gradient. (To convert type to path outlines, select it and choose Type > Create Outlines. See Lesson 7, "Working with Type," for more information.)

2 Choose Object > Group to group the letters.

Select letter outlines and group type.

By grouping the letters, you'll fill each individual letter with the same gradient at once. Grouping them also makes it easier to edit the gradient fill globally.

3 In the toolbox, click the Gradient button (below the Fill and Stroke boxes) to paint the type outlines with the current gradient fill—in this case, with the radial gradient that was last selected in the chile pepper.

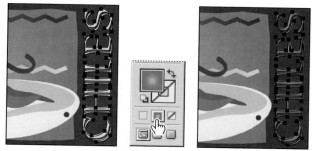

Paint selected type with last-selected gradient fill.

To edit the colors in a gradient, you click their gradient stops below the gradient bar.

4 In the Gradient palette, for Type choose Linear to change the fill to a linear gradient, and then click the left gradient stop to select it so that you can adjust the starting color of the gradient.

The Color palette displays the color of the currently selected gradient stop in the Fill box.

Now you'll change the display of the Swatches palette so that you can choose any color from it.

5 At the bottom of the Swatches palette, click the Show All Swatches button to display all of the color, gradient, and pattern swatches in the Swatches palette.

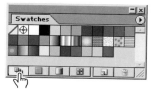

Display all swatches.

6 With the left gradient stop selected in the Gradient palette, hold down Alt (Windows) or Option (Mac OS) and click a color swatch in the Swatches palette to assign the color to the gradient. (We selected the Lime color swatch.)

Holding down Alt/Option as you click a color swatch applies the color to the selected gradient stop in the gradient rather than to the selected objects in the artwork.

Colors in gradients can be assigned as CMYK process colors, RGB process colors, Web Safe RGB colors, or spot colors. When a gradient is printed or separated, mixed-mode gradient colors are all converted to CMYK process color.

Now you'll add intermediate colors to the gradient to create a fill with multiple blends between colors.

7 In the Gradient palette, click anywhere below the gradient bar to add a stop between the other gradient stops.

You add a color to a gradient by adding a gradient stop. When you add a new gradient stop, a diamond appears above the gradient bar to mark the colors' new midpoint.

8 With the new gradient stop selected, hold down Alt (Windows) or Option (Mac OS) and click a color swatch in the Swatches palette to assign it to the gradient. (We selected the Yellow color swatch.)

Observe how the new color looks in the *CHILES* type.

Select gradient stop and change   Result
middle color of gradient.

9 To adjust the midpoint between two colors, drag the diamond above the gradient bar to the right or left.

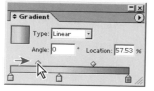

Drag diamond to adjust color midpoint.

Note: *You can delete a color in a gradient by dragging its gradient stop downward and out of the Gradient palette.*

Another way to apply a color to the gradient is to sample the color from the artwork using the eyedropper tool.

10 Select the right gradient stop in the Gradient palette. Select the eyedropper tool (✐) in the toolbox. Then hold down Shift and click a color in the artwork. (We sampled the light red color in the front chile pepper.)

Holding down Shift as you click with the eyedropper tool applies the color sample to the selected gradient stop in the gradient rather than replacing the entire gradient with the color in the selected *CHILES* type.

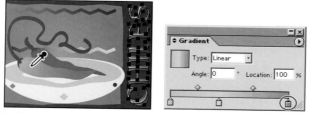

Shift-click to apply sample to selected stop in gradient.

Now you'll save the new gradient.

11 In the Swatches palette, choose New Swatch from the palette menu, type a name for the gradient in the Swatch Name text box (we named it "Chiles type"), and click OK to save the new gradient.

12 Deselect the artwork by choosing Select > Deselect, and then choose File > Save.

Creating smooth-color blends

You can choose several options for blending the shapes and colors of objects to create a new object. When you choose the smooth-color blend option, Illustrator combines the shapes and colors of the objects into many intermediate steps, creating a smooth graduated blend between the original objects.

For an example of smooth-color blends, see figure 8-1 in the color section.

Now you'll combine the two inner shapes of the bowl into a smooth-color blend.

1 Select the selection tool ( ), click the smallest shape inside the bowl to select it, and then Shift-click to select the second shape inside the bowl.

Both objects are filled with a solid color and have no stroke. Objects that have strokes blend differently than those that have no stroke.

2 Choose Object > Blend > Blend Options.

3 In the Blend Options dialog box, for Spacing choose Smooth Color (selected by default), and click OK.

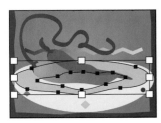

Select two inner shapes.　　　Set blend options.

This action sets up the blend options, which remain set until you change them. Now you'll apply the blend.

4 Choose Object > Blend > Make.

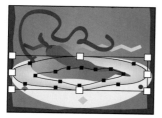

Result

When you make a smooth-color blend between objects, Illustrator automatically calculates the number of intermediate steps necessary to create a smooth transition between the objects.

Note: *To release a blend and revert to the original objects, select the blend and choose Object > Blend > Release.*

Blending intermediate steps

Now you'll create a series of blended shapes between three different-colored shapes on the outside of the bowl by specifying the number of steps in the blend and using the blend tool to create the blend.

1 Click away from the artwork to deselect it, and then double-click the blend tool (🖐) to open the Blend Options dialog box.

2 For Spacing, choose Specified Steps, type **6** for the number of steps, and click OK.

Blend Options
Spacing: Specified Steps   6   OK
Orientation: Cancel
Preview

3 Using the blend tool, click the red diamond with the tool's upper hollow square, and then click the green diamond to make a blend between them.

A new object is created that blends the shapes of the diamonds and their colors together in six steps.

4 Now click the blue circle to complete the blended path.

Click objects with blend tool to   Result
create a blend.

Note: *To end the current path and continue blending other objects on a separate path, click the blend tool in the toolbox first and then click the other objects.*

Modifying the blend

Now you'll modify the shape of the path or *spine* of the blend using the convert-anchor-point tool.

1 Select the convert-anchor-point tool (⌐) from the same group as the pen tool (✒) in the toolbox.

2 Select the endpoint of the spine at the center of the blue circle (don't release the mouse button). Drag slowly down until you see two direction lines, and continue dragging down and a little to the left until the path runs parallel to the bottom edge of the bowl.

3 Repeat step 2 with the endpoint of the spine at the center of the red diamond, but drag up instead of down.

Now you'll adjust the spacing between the center shapes on the blend.

4 Using the convert-anchor-point tool, select the middle anchor point of the spine (at the center of the green diamond)—don't release the mouse button—and drag to the left to lengthen the direction line and stretch out the spacing between the blend steps.

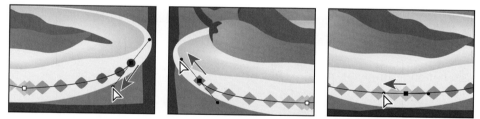

Select end and middle anchor points and drag direction handles to reshape blend path.

💡 *A quick way to reshape the blend's path is to wrap it around another path or object. Select the blend, select the other object or path, and then choose Object > Blend > Replace Spine.*

You can modify the blend instantly by changing the shape or color of the original objects. Now you'll delete an anchor point on an object and reshape the object to modify the blend.

5 Zoom in closer on the red diamond by using the zoom tool (🔍) or the Navigator palette.

6 Hold down Ctrl (Windows) or Command (Mac OS), and click the red diamond to select it.

7 Select the delete-anchor-point tool (✒) from the same group as the convert-direction-point tool in the toolbox and click a corner point on the red diamond to delete it.

Notice how changing the shape of the diamond affects the shape of the intermediate steps in the blend.

8 Select the direct-selection tool (↖) in the toolbox and drag another anchor point on the diamond out to extend the shape of the corner.

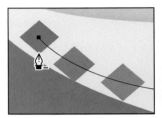  

Delete anchor point on
original object.

Drag anchor point to
reshape object.

Result

💡 *You can switch the starting and ending objects in the blend without affecting the shape of the spine by selecting the blend and choosing Object > Blend > Reverse Spine.*

9 Choose File > Save.

🌑 For an example of modified blends, see figure 8-2 in the color section.

Combining blends with gradients

You can blend objects that are filled with gradients to create different effects of color blending. The two zigzag lines in the artwork are filled with gradients. (See "Exploring on your own" on page 258 to learn how to create them.)

Now you'll blend the gradient-filled lines to create a multicolored blend in the artwork.

1 Double-click the hand tool (✋) in the toolbox to fit the artwork in the window.

2 Select the blend tool (▦) in the toolbox and click the top zigzag line to select the first object for the blend. Then click the corresponding point on the bottom zigzag line to create the blend. (If you don't click the corresponding point, you'll get a distorted result.)

The current blend settings for six specified steps are applied to the blend. You can change these settings for an existing blend.

  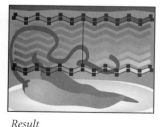

Click top line to select first object for blend. | *Click corresponding point on bottom line.* | *Result*

3 Click the selection tool ( ) to select the bounding box of the new blend, and choose Object > Blend > Blend Options.

4 In the Blend Options dialog box, select Preview, type a number in the text box (we specified 4 steps), and press Tab to see the effect in the artwork. Click OK.

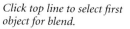 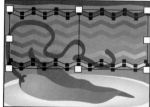

Change number of steps in the blend. *Result*

5 Click away from the artwork to deselect it.

Now you'll adjust the blend by changing a gradient color in one of the original objects.

6 Select the direct-selection tool ( ), and select one of the original zigzag lines. (We selected the bottom zigzag line.)

Select original object.

7 In the Gradient palette, click a gradient stop to select a color in the gradient fill. (We selected the right gradient stop to select the ending color of the gradient.)

8 Hold down Alt (Windows) or Option (Mac OS), and click a color in the Swatches palette to apply it to the selected gradient stop. (We selected the Teal color swatch.)

Holding down Alt/Option as you click applies the color swatch to the selected gradient stop rather than to the selected zigzag line.

 You can paint the individual steps in the blend with separate gradients or colors by expanding the blend. Select the blend and choose Object > Blend > Expand.

9 To view your final artwork, press Tab to hide the toolbox and all of the open palettes.

Pressing Tab toggles between hiding and showing the toolbox and palettes. Pressing Shift+Tab toggles between hiding and showing just the palettes (and not the toolbox).

10 Deselect the artwork.

11 Choose File > Save. Choose File > Close to close the file.

This completes the lesson. To learn how to use the gradient mesh tool to make colors in an object blend in multiple directions, see Lesson 11, "Creating Airbrush Effects." To learn how to use the color modes or transparency to blend colors together, see Lesson 9, "Using Appearance Attributes, Styles, and Effects."

Exploring on your own

The two wavy lines in the artwork were created by applying the Zig Zag distort filter to two straight lines, and then they were converted to path outlines so that they could be filled with gradients.

To create a gradient-filled zigzag line like those in the artwork, do the following:

1 Draw a straight line using the pen tool.

2 Select the line, remove the fill, paint the stroke with a color, and increase the stroke weight to **10** points.

3 With the line selected, choose Filter > Distort > Zig Zag. (Choose the top filter command in the menu.)

4 In the Zig Zag dialog box, enter **0.15 in** in the Size text box and **11** in the Ridges per segment text box. Click OK.

For more on the Zig Zag filter, see "Converting straight lines to zigzags" on page 184.

5 Choose Object > Path > Outline Stroke.

Notice that the stroke color has switched with the fill of None, so now you can fill the object with a gradient.

Review questions

1 What is a gradient fill?

2 Name two ways to fill a selected object with a gradient.

3 What is the difference between a gradient fill and a blend?

4 How do you adjust the blend between colors in a gradient?

5 How do you add colors to a gradient?

6 How do you adjust the direction of a gradient?

7 Describe two ways to blend the shapes and colors of objects together.

8 What is the difference between selecting a smooth-color blend and specifying the number of steps in a blend?

9 How do you adjust the shapes or colors in the blend? How do you adjust the path of the blend?

Review answers

1 A gradient fill is a graduated blend between two or more colors or tints of the same color.

2 Select an object and do one of the following:

• Click the Gradient button in the toolbox to fill an object with the default white-to-black gradient or with the last selected gradient.

• Click a gradient swatch in the Swatches palette.

• Make a new gradient by clicking a gradient swatch in the Swatches palette and mixing your own in the Gradient palette.

• Use the eyedropper tool to sample a gradient from an object in your artwork, and then apply it to the selected object.

3 The difference between a gradient fill and a blend is the way that colors combine together—colors blend together within a gradient fill and between objects in a blend.

4 You drag one of the gradient's stops in the Gradient palette.

5 In the Gradient palette, click beneath the gradient bar to add a gradient stop to the gradient. Then use the Color palette to mix a new color, or in the Swatches palette, Alt-click (Windows) or Option-click (Mac OS) a color swatch.

6 You click or drag with the gradient tool to adjust the direction of a gradient. Dragging a long distance changes colors gradually; dragging a short distance makes the color change more abrupt.

7 You can blend the shapes and colors of objects together by doing one of the following:

• Clicking each object with the blend tool to create a blend of intermediate steps between the objects according to preset blend options.

• Selecting the objects and choosing Object > Blend > Blend Options to set up the number of intermediate steps, and then choosing Object > Blend > Make to create the blend.

Objects that have painted strokes blend differently than those with no strokes.

8 When you select the Smooth Color blend option, Illustrator automatically calculates the number of intermediate steps necessary to create a seamlessly smooth blend between the selected objects. Specifying the number of steps lets you determine how many intermediate steps are visible in the blend. You can also specify the distance between intermediate steps in the blend.

9 You use the direct-selection tool ( ) to select and adjust the shape of an original object, thus changing the shape of the blend. You can change the colors of the original objects to adjust the intermediate colors in the blend. You use the convert-anchor-point tool ( ) to change the shape of the path, or spine, of the blend by dragging anchor points or direction handles on the spine.

Lesson 9

9 Using Appearance Attributes, Styles, and Effects

You can alter the look of an object without changing its structure using appearance attributes—fills, strokes, effects, transparency, blending modes, or any combination of these object properties. You can edit or remove appearance attributes at any time. You can also save them as styles and apply them to other objects. You can edit an object that has a style applied to it at any time, plus edit the style—an enormous time-saver.

In this lesson, you'll learn how to do the following:

- Create an appearance attribute.
- Reorder appearance attributes and apply them to layers.
- Copy and remove appearance attributes.
- Add an effect to an appearance and edit an effect.
- Save an appearance as a style.
- Apply a style to a layer.
- Select appropriate resolution settings for printing or exporting files with transparency.

Getting started

In this lesson, you'll enhance the basic design for a Web page by applying appearance attributes and styles to the page's type, background, and three buttons. Before you begin, you'll restore the default preferences for Adobe Illustrator. Then you will open the finished art file for this lesson to see what you'll create.

1 To ensure that the tools and palettes function exactly as described in this lesson, delete or deactivate (by renaming) the Adobe Illustrator 10.0 preferences file. See "Restoring default preferences" on page 4.

2 Start Adobe Illustrator.

3 Choose File > Open, and open the L9end.ai file located in the Lesson09 folder inside the Lessons folder within the AICIB folder on your hard drive.

The artwork in this file is a design mock-up of a Web home page. The design for the completed page includes several styles and effects, including overlapping gradients, transparent type, drop shadows, and texturized and shaded graphics.

4 If you like, choose View > Zoom Out to make the design mock-up smaller, adjust the window size, and leave it on-screen as you work. (Use the hand tool (🖐) to move the artwork where you want it in the window.) If you don't want to leave the artwork open, choose File > Close.

For an illustration of the finished artwork in this lesson, see the color section.

Using appearance attributes

You can apply appearance attributes to any object, group, or layer by using effects and the Appearance and Styles palettes. An appearance attribute is a property—such as a fill, stroke, transparency, or effect—that affects the look of an object, but does not affect its basic structure. An appearance attribute can be changed or removed at any time without changing the underlying object or any other attributes applied to the object.

The advantage to using the Appearance palette to add effects or other attributes is that they can be selected and edited at any time.

For example, if you apply a drop shadow effect to an object, at any time you can change the drop shadow distance, blur, or color. You can also copy that effect and apply it to other shapes, groups, or layers. You can even save it as a style and use it for other objects or other files. In contrast, if you apply the Drop Shadow filter to an object, you cannot edit the filter results, copy the filter effect, or apply it to other objects globally.

The Appearance palette contains the following types of editable attributes:

• Fill lists all fill attributes (fill type, color, transparency, and effects).

• Stroke lists some stroke attributes (stroke type, brush, color transparency, and effects). All other stroke attributes are displayed in the Stroke palette.

• Transparency lists opacity and blending mode.

• Effects lists commands in the Effect menu.

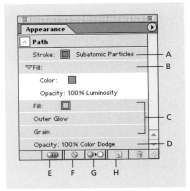

A. Stroke color and paintbrush name
B. Fill color and opacity
C. Second fill color and effects
D. Fill opacity and blending mode
E. New Art Maintains Appearance
F. Clear Appearance
G. Reduce to Basic Appearance
H. Duplicate Selected Item

Adding an appearance attribute

You'll start by selecting the star shape and adding to its basic appearance using the Appearance palette.

1 Choose File > Open, and open the L9start.ai file, located in the Lesson09 folder inside the Lessons folder within the AICIB folder on your hard drive.

2 Choose File > Save As, name the file **StarArt.ai**, and select the Lesson09 folder. Leave the Format option set to Adobe Illustrator® Document, and click Save. In the Illustrator Native Format Options dialog box, select Illustrator 10 Compatibility and click OK.

3 Using the selection tool ( ), select the star shape.

4 In the Layers palette, expand the Star Button layer so that you can see its contents. Notice that the star shape is selected, as indicated by the square to the right of the layer name, and its path is targeted, as indicated by the double-circle (target) icon to the right of the path name.

5 Notice the stroke and fill attributes of the star shape listed in the Appearance palette. (If the palette isn't visible on-screen, choose Window > Appearance to display it; a check mark indicates that the palette is open on-screen.)

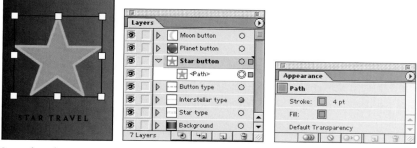

Star selected   *Expanded Star button layer*   *Stroke and fill attributes*

6 In the Appearance palette, click the Stroke attribute to select it.

Selecting the Stroke attribute lets you change just the stroke in the artwork.

7 In the Transparency palette, choose Multiply from the blending modes pop-up menu.

You can expand and collapse attributes in the Appearance palette by clicking the triangle (▷) to the left of the attribute in the palette list.

8 Using the keyboard shortcut, press Ctrl+spacebar (Windows) or Command+spacebar and click the star shape to zoom in on it to about 200% without deselecting the star shape or selection tool. Inspect the stroke around the star to see how it has changed. The effect of the Multiply blending mode is similar to drawing on a page with transparent marker pens.

Strokes are centered on a path outline—half of the stroke color overlaps the filled star shape and half of the stroke color overlaps the background gradient.

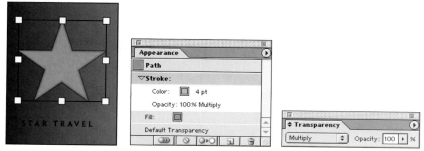

Star shape with Multiply blending mode applied

For a color illustration of the Multiply blending mode, see figure 9-1 in the color section.

Reordering appearance attributes

Now you'll change the appearance of the Multiply blending mode by rearranging the attributes in the Appearance palette.

1 Resize the Appearance palette so that you can view all of its contents. Click the Fill attribute and drag it above the Stroke attribute. (This technique is similar to dragging layers in the Layers palettes to adjust their stacking order.)

Drag Fill attribute above Stroke attribute.   *Result*

Moving the Fill attribute above the Stroke attribute changes the look of the Multiply blending modes on the stroke. Half of the stroke has been covered up. Blending modes work only on objects that are beneath them in the stacking order.

You'll add another stroke to the object using the Appearance palette.

2 With the star shape still selected, choose Add New Stroke from the Appearance palette menu. A stroke is added to the top of the appearance list. It has the same color and stroke weight as the first stroke.

3 Select the new stroke in the Appearance palette.

4 In the Color palette, choose RGB from the palette menu, and then use the sliders or text boxes to change the color to a dark orange. (We used a color mix of R=255, G=73, and B=0.)

5 Click the Stroke palette tab to bring it to the front of its group. Then change the Stroke weight to **2** points. Press Enter or Return.

You'll rearrange the order of the appearance attributes to prepare for adding live effects in the next part of the lesson.

6 In the Appearance palette, click the triangle to the left of the 4-point Stroke attribute to collapse the attribute. Then drag it to the very top of the Appearance attributes list. (It should be directly above the 2-point stroke.)

Add new stroke.   Change stroke color.   Rearrange stroke order.

7 Choose File > Save to save the artwork.

Using live effects

The Effect menu commands alter the appearance of an object without changing the underlying object. Many Effect commands also appear in the Filter menu, but only the Effect commands are fully editable. Applying an effect to an object automatically adds the effect to the object's appearance attribute. You can select and edit the effect at any time using the Appearance palette.

You can apply more than one effect to an object. In this part of the lesson, you'll apply two effects to the star shape—an outer glow to make the star appear to glow and a texture using a Photoshop effect called Grain.

1 With the star shape still selected, choose Effect > Stylize > Outer Glow.

Note: *Choose the top Stylize command in the Effect menu.*

2 Click the Preview option and try different Opacity and Blur amounts until you are satisfied with the result. Leave the blend mode set to Screen. (We used 86% opacity and a 19-point blur.) Don't click OK yet.

3 Click the color square next to the Mode menu to change the glow color. (We used a color mix of R=255, G=255, and B=51 to get a richer, brighter yellow.) Click OK to exit the Color Picker, and click OK again to apply the effect.

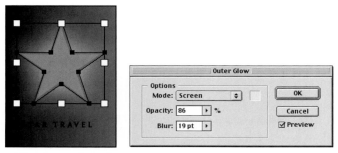

Adding Outer Glow effect

Now you'll add a second effect to the star shape.

4 Choose Effect > Texture > Grain.

5 Adjust the settings until you are satisfied with the preview in the Grain dialog box. (We used an Intensity of 30, Contrast of 100, and Regular type.)

6 Click OK to see the result. Notice that Grain has been added to the list of attributes in the Appearance palette.

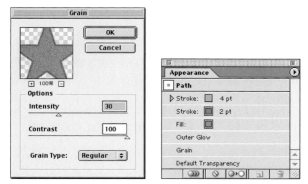

Adding Grain effect

7 Choose File > Save to save your changes.

Editing an effect

Effects can be edited at any time. To edit an effect, you simply double-click its name in the Appearance palette to display that effect's dialog box. Changes you make update the artwork.

You'll change the texture you applied to the star in the last section.

1 Make sure that the star is still selected.

2 If necessary, resize the Appearance palette to view all of its contents. Then double-click the Grain attribute.

3 In the Grain dialog box, change the Type to Soft and click OK.

Now you'll adjust the blending mode of the star's fill to make it glow more.

4 With the star shape still selected, click the Fill attribute in the Appearance palette.

5 In the Transparency palette, choose Luminosity from the blending mode menu.

6 Choose File > Save to save the artwork.

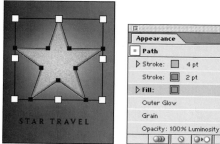

Luminous fill added to effect

Now you're ready to save the star's appearance as a style.

Using styles

A style is a named set of appearance attributes. By applying different styles, you can quickly and globally change the entire appearance of an object.

For example, you may have a symbol on a map that represents a city, with a style applied that paints the symbol green with a drop shadow. You can use that style to paint all of the cities' symbols on the map. If you change your mind, you can change the fill color of the style to blue. All the symbols painted with that style will be updated automatically.

The Styles palette lets you create, name, save, and apply styles to objects, layers, or groups. Just like attributes and effects, styles are completely reversible. For example, you could apply a style to a circle that contains the Zig Zag effect, turning the circle into a starburst. You can revert the object to its original appearance with the Appearance palette or you can break the link with that style and edit one of its attributes without affecting other objects that are painted with the same style.

Creating and saving a style

Now you'll save and name a new style using the appearance attributes you just created for the star button.

1 Click the Styles tab to bring the palette to the front of its group. (If the Styles palette isn't visible on-screen, choose Window > Styles; a check mark indicates that the palette is open on-screen.)

2 Position the Styles palette and the Appearance palette so that you can see both of them at the same time.

3 Make sure that the star shape is still selected so that its appearance attributes are displayed in the Appearance palette.

The appearance attributes are stored in the appearance thumbnail, named Path in the Appearance palette.

4 In the Appearance palette, drag the appearance thumbnail onto the Styles palette.

5 Release the mouse button when a thick black border appears on the inside of the palette. The border indicates that you are adding a new style to the palette.

The path thumbnail in the Appearance palette changes to Path: Graphic Style.

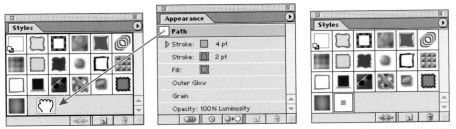

Drag object's appearance thumbnail onto Styles palette to save appearance attributes as new style.

6 In the Styles palette, choose Style Options from the palette menu. Name the new style **Grainy Glow.** Click OK.

7 Choose Select > Deselect to deselect the star shape, and then choose File > Save.

Applying a style to a layer

Once a style is applied to a layer, everything added to that layer also will have that style applied to it. Now you'll create a new style and apply it to a layer. Then you'll create a few new shapes on that layer to see the effect of the style.

1 In the Appearance palette, click the Clear Appearance button at the bottom of the palette. Then select the appearance name or thumbnail.

The Clear Appearance option removes all appearance attributes applied to an object, including any stroke or fill.

2 Choose Effect > Stylize > Drop Shadow.

3 Use the default settings. If desired, click the color swatch in the Drop Shadow dialog box to change the shadow color. (We picked a red color of R=215, G=65, and B=4.) Click OK to exit the Color Picker, and click OK again to apply the effect.

Note: *Because the Drop Shadow appearance has no stroke or fill, its thumbnail will be blank. But once applied to a shape, the drop shadow will appear.*

Clear appearances.   *Choose Drop Shadow effect.*   *Result*

When creating a new style, the Style palette automatically uses the current appearance attributes displayed in the Appearance palette.

4 In the Styles palette, Alt-click (Windows) or Option-click (Mac OS) the New Style button at the bottom of the palette, and type **Drop Shadow** as the name of the new style. Click OK.

Now you'll target the Planet Button layer, to apply a drop shadow to all the shapes on that layer.

5 In the Layers palette, click the triangle to the left of the Planet Button layer to expand the layer. Then click the target indicator (○) to the right of the Planet Button layer. (Be careful not to target the mesh-filled path (the Planet Button sublayer). If you target the path, only the planet shape will have a drop shadow.

6 In the Styles palette, click the Drop Shadow style to apply the style to the layer.

7 Choose Select > Deselect to deselect the planet shape.

Now you'll test the layer effect by adding some shapes to the Planet Button layer.

8 Select the star tool (☆) in the same group as the rectangle tool (▭) in the toolbox.

9 Click the Color tab to bring the palette to the front of its group or choose Window > Color to display it. In the Color palette, choose a fill color (we used R=129, G=23, B=136 for a purple color) and a stroke of None.

10 With the Planet Button layer still selected, in the artwork draw several small stars around the planet shape.

Because the Drop Shadow style contains only an effect and no stroke or fill, the objects retain their original stroke and fill attributes.

Layer targeted   *Style applied to layer*   *Stylized artwork added to layer*

11 Notice the following icons on the right side of a layer in the Layers palette, indicating whether any appearance attributes are applied to the layer or whether it is targeted:

• (◎) indicates that the layer, group, or object is targeted but has no appearance attributes applied to it.

- (o) indicates that the layer, group, or object is not targeted and has no appearance attributes applied to it.

- (●) indicates that the layer, group, or object is not targeted but has appearance attributes applied to it.

- (◉) indicates that the group is targeted and has appearance attributes applied to it. This icon also designates any targeted object that has appearance attributes more complex than a single fill and stroke applied to it.

12 Choose File > Save to save the artwork.

Applying existing styles

Adobe Illustrator comes with a palette of premade styles that you can apply to your artwork. Now you'll finish the button designs by adding an existing style to the Moon Button layer.

It's a good habit to use the Layers palette to select objects or layers to which you'll apply styles. An effect or style varies, depending on whether you're targeting a layer, or an object or group within a layer. Now you'll select the Moon button shape, not the layer.

1 In the Layers palette, click the triangle (▹) to expand the Moon Button layer.

2 Select the <Path> sublayer to select it. Then click the target indicator (o) to the right of the <Path> sublayer to target it. Targeting the sublayer selects the path in the artwork.

Note: If you target a layer or sublayer by mistake, Ctrl/Command-click the target indicator to remove it.

3 Click the Swatches tab to bring the palette to the front of its group. In the Swatches palette, select the Moon gradient to fill the selected path.

Select path in Layers palette.   *Target path in Layers palette*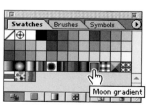

Change fill color to Moon gradient.

Now you'll apply a style to the Moon Button layer. The style contains a color, which you'll apply to the layer in place of the moon's existing color.

4 In the Layers palette, click the target indicator (○) for the Moon Button layer.

5 Click the Styles tab to bring the palette to the front of its group. In the Styles palette, click the Green relief style (fourth row, leftmost swatch) to apply it to the layer.

6 Choose File > Save to save the artwork.

Layer selected *Style applied to layer* *Result*

Applying an appearance to a layer

You can also apply simple appearance attributes to layers. For example, to make everything on a layer 50% opaque, simply target that layer and change the opacity in the Transparency palette.

Next you'll target a layer and change its blending mode to soften the effect of the type.

1 In the Layers palette, click the downward triangle next to the Moon Button layer to collapse the layer.

2 If necessary, scroll to the Star Type layer. Then click the target indicator (○) for the Star Type layer. This action selects everything on the layer and targets all of its objects.

3 In the Transparency palette, choose Soft Light from the blending mode menu.

4 Choose File > Save to save the artwork.

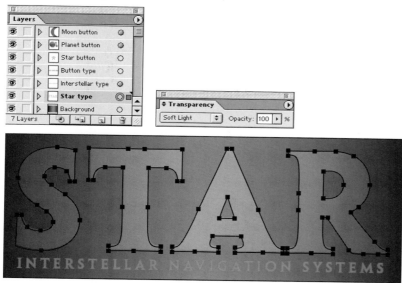

Star Type layer targeted; Soft Light mode applied; result

Copying, applying, and removing styles and appearances

Once you've created several styles and appearances, you may want to use them on other objects in your artwork. You can use the Styles palette, the Appearance palette, the eyedropper tool, or the paintbucket tool to apply and copy appearance attributes.

Next you'll apply a style to one of the objects using the Appearance palette.

1 Choose Select > Deselect.

2 Select the selection tool ( ) in the toolbox, and click the star shape to select it.

3 In the Appearance palette, drag the appearance thumbnail (labeled "Path: Grainy Glow") onto the moon shape to apply those attributes to it.

You can apply styles or attributes by dragging them from the Styles palette or the Appearance palette onto any object. The object doesn't have to be selected.

Star shape attributes   *Drag thumbnail onto new object to apply the same attributes.*

4 Ctrl-click (Windows) or Command-click (Mac OS) away from the artwork to deselect it.

Next you'll apply a style by dragging it directly from the Styles palette onto an object.

5 In the Styles palette, drag the Green relief style thumbnail onto the moon shape in the artwork.

6 Release the mouse button to apply the style to the shape.

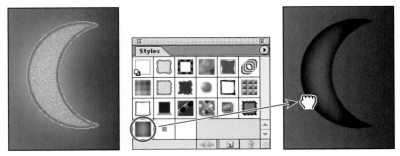

Drag style thumbnail onto object (selected or not) to apply the style.

Now you'll use the Layers palette to copy an attribute from one layer to another.

7 Expand the Layers palette to see all the layers. Then in the Layers palette, Alt-drag (Windows) or Option-drag (Mac OS) the appearance indicator from the Planet Button layer onto the appearance indicator of the Button Type layer.

Using Alt or Option copies one layer effect onto another, as indicated by the hand pointer with the plus sign. To simply move an appearance or style from one layer or object to another, just drag the appearance indicator.

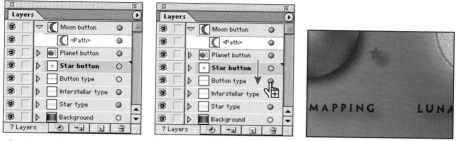

Alt/Option drag appearance attribute to copy it from one layer to another.

Now you'll remove an appearance from a layer using the Layers palette.

8 In the Layers palette, click the target indicator to the right of the Button Type layer.

9 Drag the appearance indicator to the Trash button at the bottom of the Layers palette to remove the appearance.

Another way to remove attributes of a selected object or layer is by using the Appearance palette. You select the object and then click the Reduce to Basic Appearance button at the bottom of the palette to return the object to its original state (including any stroke or fill) before the appearance attribute or style was applied.

Drag appearance indicator to Trash button to remove attributes.

10 Choose File > Save.

Printing and saving files with transparency effects

Once you've created a document with transparency, blending modes, feathering, or other effects that produce artwork with transparency effects, you must set up the document for printing or exporting. The best way to preserve transparency effects is to export the document to the Photoshop (PSD) file format. Exporting to the Photoshop file format retains the transparency masks and links created in the Transparency palette and the layers as they were created in Illustrator. However, only top-level layers are preserved; any nested layers in Illustrator are flattened into the top-level layer.

Illustrator flattens artwork containing transparency before printing or saving the artwork. During flattening, Illustrator looks for areas where transparent objects overlap other objects and isolates these areas by dividing the artwork into components. Illustrator then analyzes each component to determine if the artwork can be represented using vector data or if the artwork must be rasterized.

In most cases, the flattening process produces excellent results. However, if your artwork contains complex, overlapping areas and you require high-resolution output, you can control the degree to which artwork is rasterized. To preserve as much of the vector art in your document as possible, use the Raster/Vector Balance slider in the Document Setup dialog box. Illustrator uses these settings to determine the quality, printing speed, or both, for your artwork.

Specifying rasterization settings

Even though the image created in this lesson is meant for a Web page, not for print, you can still experiment with the settings to use for exporting or printing the file.

Now you will specify the degree of rasterization of flattened artwork using the Raster/Vector Balance slider in the Document Setup dialog box. You will also set the resolution for objects that will be rasterized (drop shadows and gradient mesh objects).

1 Choose File > Document Setup.

2 Choose Transparency from the pop-up menu in the Document Setup dialog box.

3 Drag the Raster/Vector Balance slider to determine the percentage of rasterization. The settings vary from 0 on the left for the greatest rasterization, to 100 on the right for the least rasterization on artwork. Select the highest setting to represent as much artwork as possible using vector data; select the lowest setting to rasterize all the artwork.

Each setting has trade-offs. Rasterizing everything in a file degrades some of vector graphics' crisp edges. But maintaining too much of the vector artwork may make a file difficult to print due to your printer's memory limitations.

You can also specify an output resolution for rasterized artwork (except for gradient mesh objects).

Using the Raster/Vector slider to specify rasterization at setting 50

4 In this case, leave the Rasterization Resolution at 300. In most cases, 300 is sufficient.

If you know that all or part of your file will be rasterized, you must determine the resolution for the rasterization, based on your desired end result. If your file ultimately will be separated and printed on a high-quality, four-color press, you'll want to choose a higher resolution than if it will appear in a black-and-white, laser-printed newsletter.

5 Leave the Convert All Text to Outlines and Convert All Strokes to Outlines options deselected. These options ensure that the width of text and strokes, respectively, stay consistent during flattening.

6 Leave the Clip Complex Regions option deselected. When selected, this option ensures that the boundaries between vector artwork and rasterized artwork fall along object paths, but may result in paths that are too complex for the printer to handle.

7 Select Preserve Overprints When Possible if you are printing separations and the document contains overprinted objects.

8 Do not click OK yet. You'll look at the resolution setting for rasterizing gradient meshes.

9 Choose Printing & Export from the pop-up menu in the upper left corner.

10 Note the default values for the rasterization resolution of gradient mesh objects. The Gradient Mesh Resolution option sets an output resolution for gradient mesh objects.

11 Click OK.

12 Choose File > Save.

Specifying the resolution of filters and live effects

Some filter effects and live effects, such as drop shadows and bevels, use settings in the Rasterize Effects Settings dialog box. Now you'll change the resolution in the Rasterize Effects Settings dialog box and see the effect on your artwork.

1 Select the zoom tool ( ) in the toolbox. Position the zoom tool over the star shape in the artwork and click. Continue clicking the center of the star until you have zoomed in to 200%. You should be able to see the pixelated texture of the star button.

Notice the edges of the star shape, with stair-stepping on the angled edges. This is due to the resolution setting for the raster effects. The default setting is 72 ppi.

You will change that setting to improve the edge quality of the star shape.

2 Choose Effect > Document Raster Effects Settings.

3 Change the Resolution setting to Medium (150 ppi).

4 Leave the other settings as they are, and click OK.

5 Notice that the grain texture has become finer and the edge quality smoother.

Now you'll see how the star looks at a higher resolution.

6 To see detail more easily, use the zoom tool to zoom in closer on the artwork.

7 Choose Effect > Document Raster Effects Settings.

8 Change the Resolution setting to High (300 ppi), and click OK.

9 If you prefer the texture that the medium resolution gives, choose Edit > Undo.

You can switch between Edit > Undo and Edit > Redo to compare the resolution settings.

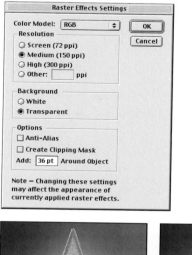

Raster Effects resolution: 72 ppi   150 ppi   300 ppi

10 Choose File > Save to save the artwork. Choose File > Close to close the file.

This completes the lesson. Now you're ready to create your own styles and effect combinations.

🔲 To learn more about styles, effects, and appearance attributes, see "Using Appearance Attributes, Styles, and Effects" in online Help or Chapter 10 of the Adobe Illustrator User Guide.

Exploring on your own

Now that you've learned the basic steps about creating and using effects and styles, experiment with different combinations of appearance attributes to create interesting special effects. Try combining different styles to create new ones.

For example, here's how to merge two existing styles to create a brand new style.

1 Choose File > New to open a new file.

2 If the Styles palette isn't visible on-screen, choose Window > Styles to display it.

3 In the Styles palette, select the Rustic Pen style (second row, rightmost style).

4 Add the Phantasmagoric style to the selection by Ctrl-clicking (Windows) or Command-clicking (Mac OS) the style to the left of the Rustic Pen style (second row, second style from the right) in the Styles palette.

5 Choose Merge Styles from the Styles palette menu.

6 Name the Style in the Style options dialog box, and click OK.

7 In the artwork, draw a shape and apply the new style.

Merged styles   *Result*

If you want to edit the style and save it again, do the following:

8 Deselect the artwork.

9 In the Appearance palette, drag the 6-point stroke to the top, above the three fills.

10 Create a new shape or drag the appearance thumbnail onto the existing shape to view the results.

If you like the new effect, you can replace the first merged style with it.

11 To replace a style, Alt-drag (Windows) or Option-drag (Mac OS) the appearance thumbnail onto the style you are replacing in the Styles palette. The style being replaced displays a thick black border when you position the pointer over it.

12 Release the mouse button, and save the file.

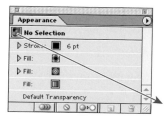
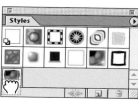

Select appearance thumbnail.   *Alt/Option-drag onto style*   *Result*
                                      in Styles palette.

Review questions

1 Name two types of Appearance attributes.

2 How do you add a second stroke to an object?

3 What's the difference between a filter and an effect?

4 How do you edit an effect that's part of an object's appearance attributes?

5 What's the difference between applying a style to a layer versus an object?

6 How do you remove an appearance using the Layers palette?

7 How do you set the resolution for a file that contains filter effects?

8 How do you preserve transparency effects when printing or exporting?

Review answers

1 The Appearance palette contains the following types of editable attributes:

• Fill attributes (fill type, color, transparency, and effects).

• Stroke attributes (stroke type, brush, color transparency, and effects).

• Transparency attributes (opacity and blending mode).

• Effects commands from the Effect menu.

2 From the Appearance palette menu choose Add New Stroke. A stroke is added to the top of the appearance list. It has the same color and stroke weight as the first stroke.

3 Many commands in the Effect menu also appear in the Filter menu, but only the Effect menu commands are fully editable.

4 To edit an effect you simply double-click its name in the Appearance palette to display that effect's dialog box. You can then make changes and click OK to update them in the artwork.

5 Once a style is applied to a layer, everything you add to that layer will have that style applied to it. For example, if you create a circle on Layer 1 and then move it to Layer 2, which has a Drop Shadow effect applied, the circle would adopt that effect. When a style is applied to an object, nothing else on that object's layer is affected by the object's style. For example, if a triangle has a Roughen effect applied to its path, and you move it to another layer, it will still retain the Roughen effect.

6 In the Layers palette, click the target indicator of a layer. Drag the appearance indicator down to the Trash icon in the Layers palette to remove the appearance. You can also remove the appearance of a selected object or layer by using the Appearance palette. Select the object and click the Reduce to Basic Appearance button to return the object to its original state before the appearance attribute or style was applied.

7 You change the resolution in the Rasterize Effects Settings dialog box. Choose Effect > Document Raster Effects Setting. Change the Resolution setting to Low (72 ppi), Medium (150 ppi), High (300 ppi), or Other. Click OK.

8 To best preserve transparency effects, make sure that any transparency resides on the top layers (including any nested layers). Illustrator flattens artwork containing transparency before printing or saving artwork; flattening preserves only top-level layers, including nested layers. You can control the degree to which Illustrator maintains vector data or rasterizes the artwork to preserve transparency when flattening by using the Raster/Vector Balance slider in the Document Setup dialog box.

In addition, export the document to the Photoshop (PSD) file format. Exporting to the Photoshop file format retains the transparency masks and links created in the Transparency palette, and (top-level) layers as they were created in Illustrator.

Lesson 10

10 | Working with Layers

Layers let you organize your work into distinct levels that can be edited and viewed as individual units. Every Adobe Illustrator document contains at least one layer. Creating multiple layers in your artwork lets you easily control how artwork is printed, displayed, and edited.

In this lesson, you'll learn how to do the following:

- Work with the Layers palette.
- Create, rearrange, and lock layers, nested layers, and groups.
- Move objects between layers.
- Paste layers of objects from one file to another.
- Merge layers into a single layer.
- Apply a drop shadow to a layer.
- Make a layer clipping mask.
- Apply an appearance attribute to objects and layers.

Getting started

In this lesson, you'll finish the artwork of a wall clock as you explore the various ways to use the Layers palette. Before you begin, you must restore the default preferences for Adobe Illustrator and then you will open the finished art file for this lesson to see what you'll create.

1 To ensure that the tools and palettes function exactly as described in this lesson, delete or deactivate (by renaming) the Adobe Illustrator 10.0 preferences file. See "Restoring default preferences" on page 4.

2 Start Adobe Illustrator.

3 Choose File > Open, and open the L10end.ai file in the Lesson10 folder, located inside the Lessons folder within the AICIB folder on your hard drive.

Separate layers are used for the objects that make up the clock's frame, striped clock face, hands, and numbers—as indicated by their layer names in the Layers palette.

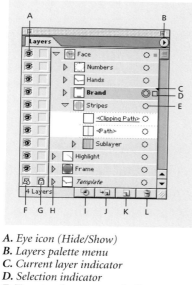

A. Eye icon (Hide/Show)
B. Layers palette menu
C. Current layer indicator
D. Selection indicator
E. Target and appearance indicator
F. Template layer icon
G. Edit column (Lock/Unlock)
H. Expand/Collapse triangle
I. Make/Release Clipping Mask
J. Create New Sublayer button
K. Create New Layer button
L. Delete button

4 If you like, choose View > Zoom Out to make the finished artwork smaller, adjust the window size, and leave it on your screen as you work. (Use the hand tool (🖑) to move the artwork where you want it in the window.) If you don't want to leave the image open, choose File > Close.

For an illustration of the finished artwork in this lesson, see the color section.

To begin working, you'll open an existing art file.

5 Choose File > Open, and open the L10start.ai file in the Lesson10 folder, located inside the Lessons folder within the AICIB folder on your hard drive.

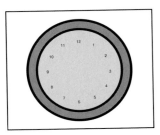

The artwork contains some of the basic objects for the clock illustration.

6 Choose File > Save As, name the file **Clock.ai**, and select the Lesson10 folder. Leave the Format option set to Adobe Illustrator® Document, and click Save. In the Illustrator Native Format Options dialog box, select Illustrator 10 Compatibility and click OK.

Using layers

Using the Layers palette, you can create multiple levels of artwork that reside on separate, overlapping layers, sublayers, and groups in the same file. Layers act like individual, clear sheets containing one or more objects. Where no filled (or nontransparent) objects overlap, you can see through any layer to the layer below.

You can create and edit objects on any layer without affecting the artwork on any other layer. You can also display, print, lock, and reorder layers as distinct units.

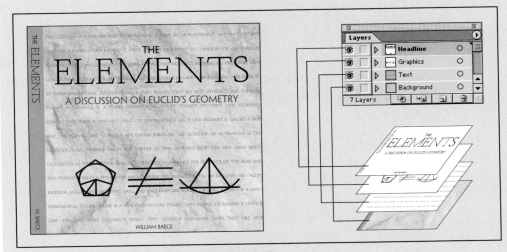

Example of composite art and how layers break out individually

Creating layers

Every document in Illustrator contains one layer by default. You can rename the layer and add more layers at any time as you create the artwork. Placing objects on separate layers lets you easily select and edit them by their organization. For example, by placing type on a separate layer, you can change the type all at once without affecting the rest of the artwork.

You'll change the layer name to "Clock," and then you'll create another layer.

1 If the Layers palette isn't visible on-screen, choose Window > Layers to display it.

Layer 1 (the default name for the first layer) is highlighted, indicating that it is selected. The layer also has a triangle (▾), indicating that it's active and that objects on the layer can be edited when you use the tools.

2 In the Layers palette, double-click the layer name to open the Layer Options dialog box. Type **Clock** in the Name text box, and then click OK.

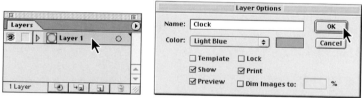

Double-click layer name.   Change layer name to Clock.

Now you'll create a sublayer for the clock numbers.

3 Alt-click (Windows) or Option-click (Mac OS) the Create New Sublayer button at the bottom of the Layers palette to create a new sublayer and display the Layer Options dialog box.

(If you simply want to create a new sublayer without setting any options or naming the layer, you can click the Create New Sublayer button. New sublayers created this way are numbered in sequence, for example, Layer 2.)

4 In the Layer Options dialog box, type **Numbers** in the Name text box, and click OK. The new sublayer appears directly beneath its main layer name (Clock) and is selected.

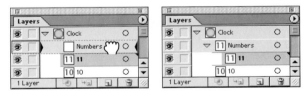

Create sublayer named Numbers.

Moving objects and layers

By rearranging the layers in the Layers palette, you can reorder layered objects in your artwork. You can also move selected objects from one layer or sublayer to another.

First you'll move the clock numbers onto their own sublayer.

1 In the Layers palette, grab the thumbnail for the 11 layer and drag it onto the thumbnail for the Numbers layer. Release the mouse button when you see the large black triangles at either end of the Numbers layer in the palette. (The large triangles indicate that you are adding something to that layer.)

Grab thumbnail and move it onto sublayer thumbnail.

2 Repeat step 1 for each of the twelve numbers in the Layers palette.

To select multiple layers or sublayers quickly, select a layer and then Shift-click additional layers.

3 Choose Select > Deselect. Then choose File > Save.

4 To simplify your work, click the triangle to the left of the Numbers layer to collapse the layer view.

Now you'll move the face of the clock to a new layer to use later when you add the stripes, hands, and brand name of the clock, and you'll rename the Clock layer to reflect the new organization of the artwork.

5 In the artwork, click behind the numbers to select the clock face. In the Layers palette, the layer named <Path> becomes active (as indicated by the small square selection indicator (■) in the far right column.

6 Alt-click (Windows) or Option-click (Mac OS) the Create New Layer button at the bottom of the Layers palette, or choose New Layer from the Layers palette menu.

7 In the Layer Options dialog box, enter **Face** in the Name text box, choose a different layer color from the pop-up menu (such as Orange), and click OK.

The new Face layer is added above the Clock layer and becomes active.

8 In the Layers palette, select the small square selection indicator on the <Path> layer, and drag it directly up to the right of the target indicator (○) on the new Face layer.

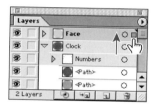

Drag selection indicator up to move object to another layer.

This action moves the selected object to the new layer. The color of the selection lines in the artwork changes to the color of the new Face layer (such as Orange).

Now that the Face layer is on top of the Clock layer and the Numbers layer, the clock numbers are covered up. You'll move the Numbers sublayer onto a different layer and rename the Clock layer to reflect the new organization of the artwork.

9 In the Layers palette, drag the Numbers sublayer thumbnail onto the Face layer thumbnail. Release the mouse button when you see the indicator bar with large black triangles at either end of the Face layer in the palette.

Now you can see the numbers again.

10 Double-click the Clock layer to display the Layer Options dialog box, and change the layer name to **Frame**. Then click OK.

Drag sublayer thumbnail to move it to another layer.   *Change layer name.*

11 Choose Select > Deselect, and then choose File > Save.

Locking layers

As you edit objects on a layer, you can use the Layers palette to lock other layers and prevent selecting or changing the rest of the artwork.

Now you'll lock all the layers except the Numbers sublayer so that you can easily edit the clock numbers without affecting objects on other layers. Locked layers cannot be selected or edited in any way.

1 To simplify your work, click the triangle to the left of the Frame layer to collapse the layer view.

2 Click the edit column to the right of the eye icon on the Frame layer to lock the layer. The padlock icon (🔒) indicates that a layer is locked.

3 Click the edit column to the right of the eye icon on the <Path> layer below the Numbers layer.

4 Click the Numbers sublayer in the Layers palette to select the layer.

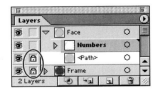

Click the edit column to lock layer.

You can unlock individual layers by clicking the padlock icon to make it disappear from the edit column. Clicking again in the edit column locks the layer. Holding down Alt (Windows) or Option (Mac OS) as you click in the edit column alternately locks and unlocks all other layers.

Now you'll change the type size and font of the numbers.

5 In the Layers palette to the right of the Numbers layer, click the selection column to select all objects on that layer.

A quick way to select all of the type or objects on a layer is to click the selection column—the blank area to the right of the target indicators—in the Layers palette.

The Numbers layer now has a large red square, indicating that everything on the layer is selected.

6 Choose Window > Type > Character to display the Character palette.

7 In the Character palette, select another font or size for the group of numbers. (We used Myriad Bold, size 28 points.)

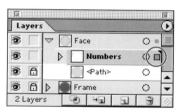 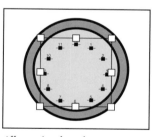 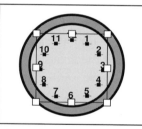

Click the selection column.   *All type is selected.*   *Change font and size globally*

8 If you wish, use the Color palette or Swatches palette to change the color of the selected numbers.

9 In the Layers palette, click the padlock icons next to the <Path> and the Frame layers to unlock them.

Viewing layers

The Layers palette lets you hide layers, sublayers, or individual objects from view. When a layer is hidden, objects on the layer are also locked and cannot be selected or printed. You can also use the Layers palette to display layers or objects in either Preview or Outline view independently from other layers in the artwork.

Now you'll edit the frame on the clock, using a painting technique to create a three-dimensional effect on the frame.

1 In the Layers palette, click the Frame layer to select it, and then Alt-click (Windows) or Option-click (Mac OS) the eye icon next to the Frame layer name to hide the other layers.

Alt/Option-clicking the layer eye icon alternately hides and shows a layer. Hiding layers also locks them and prevents them from being changed.

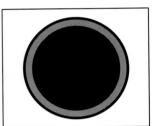

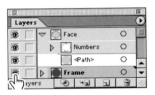

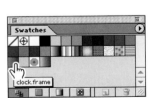

Alt/Option-click eye icon.   Only objects on Frame layer   Only Frame layer is showing
                               appear.   and unlocked.

2 Using the selection tool (➤), click the inside circle of the frame to select it. Then Shift-click to select the next largest circle.

3 With the two inner circles selected, make sure that the Fill box is selected in the toolbox, and then click the Clock.frame swatch in the Swatches palette to paint the circles with a custom gradient.

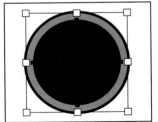

Select two inner circles.   Paint with gradient fill.

4 Shift-click the second largest circle to deselect it and keep the in:

5 Select the gradient tool (▭) in the toolbox. Drag the tool in a vert of the circle straight down to the bottom to change the direction of

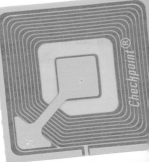

The gradient tool works only on selected objects that are filled with gradients. To learn more about using the gradient tool, see Lesson 8, "Blending Shapes and Colors."

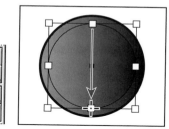

*Select
gradient
tool.*   *Drag over selected object.*

6 Choose Select > Deselect to deselect the artwork, and then choose File > Save.

7 In the Layers palette, choose Show All Layers from the palette menu.

As you edit objects in layered artwork, you can display individual layers in Outline view, keeping the other layers in Preview view.

8 Ctrl-click (Windows) or Command-click (Mac OS) the eye icon next to the Face layer to switch to Outline view for that layer.

This action lets you see the gradient-filled circle behind the clock face. Displaying a layer in Outline view also is useful for viewing the anchor points or center points on objects without selecting them.

*White fill in eye icon
indicates Outline view.*   *Preview view of other layers shows
through Face layer in Outline view.*

9 Ctrl/Command-click the eye icon next to the Face layer to return to Preview view for that layer.

Pasting layers

To complete the clock, you'll copy and paste the finishing parts of artwork from another file. You can paste layered files into another file and keep all the layers intact.

1 Choose File > Open, and open the Details.ai file, located in the Lesson10 folder, inside the Lessons folder within the AICIB folder on your hard drive.

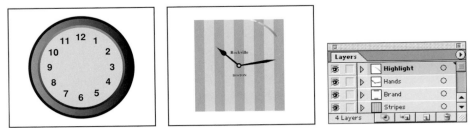

Clock.ai file   Details.ai file   Layers palette for Details.ai file

2 If you want to see how the objects are organized on the layers, Alt/Option-click the eye icons in the Layers palette to alternately display each layer and hide the others. You can also click the triangles (▷) to the left of the layer names to expand and collapse the layers for further inspection. When you've finished, make sure that all the layers are showing and that they are fully collapsed.

If a layer is hidden, its objects are locked and cannot be selected or copied.

3 Choose Select > All and then Edit > Copy to select and copy the clock details to the Clipboard.

4 Choose File > Close and click No (Windows) or Don't Save (Mac OS) to close the Details.ai file without saving any changes.

5 In the Clock.ai file, choose Paste Remembers Layers from the Layers palette menu to select the option. (A check mark next to the option indicates that it's selected.)

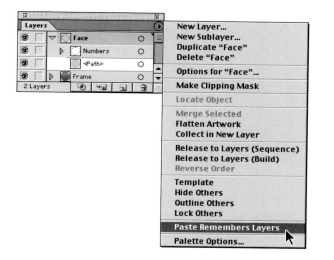

Selecting the Paste Remembers Layers option indicates that when layers from another file are pasted into the artwork, they're added separately to the Layers palette. If the option is not selected, all objects are pasted into the active layer.

6 Choose Edit > Paste In Front to paste the details into the clock.

The Paste In Front command pastes the objects from the Clipboard to a position relative to the original position in the Details.ai file. The Paste Remembers Layers option causes the Details.ai layers to be pasted as four separate layers (Highlight, Hands, Brand, Stripes) at the bottom of the Layers palette.

7 Drag the Layers palette by its lower right corner to resize it and display all of the layers in the palette. As you can see, some of the layers need to be repositioned.

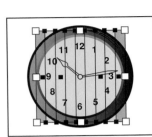

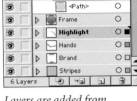

Paste artwork from Details.ai file.

Layers are added from Details.ai file.

Now you'll move the brand and hands into the Face layer and the highlight in front of the Frame layer.

8 Select the selection tool ( ), and click away from the artwork to deselect it.

9 In the Layers palette, select the Highlight layer, and drag it up between the <Path> sublayer and Frame layer. Release the mouse button when the indicator bar with large black triangles extends the full column width above the Frame layer. (You want to create a separate layer, not a sublayer.)

Move Highlight layer up above Frame layer.

10 Shift-click the Hands and Brand layers in the Layers palette.

11 Drag the selected layers up between the Numbers and <Path> sublayers; when the insertion bar appears between those sublayers, release the mouse button to make the Hands and Brand layers sublayers of the Face layer.

Drag Hands and Brand layers up into Face layer.

12 Choose File > Save to save the changes.

Creating clipping masks

The Layers palette lets you create clipping masks to control how artwork on a layer (or in a group) is hidden or revealed. A *clipping mask* is an object or group of objects whose shape masks artwork below it so that only artwork within the shape is visible.

Now you'll create a clipping mask with the circle shape in the Face layer. You'll group it with the Stripes sublayer so that only the stripes show through the circle shape.

1 In the Layers palette, drag the Stripes layer up until the insertion bar's double lines are highlighted above the <Path> layer within the Face layer. Release the mouse button when the indicator bar appears.

Drag Stripes layer up above <Path> sublayer within Face layer.

For the clipping mask to mask only the stripes, you must move it into the Stripes sublayer. You'll move the <Path> into the Stripes sublayer and then create the clipping mask.

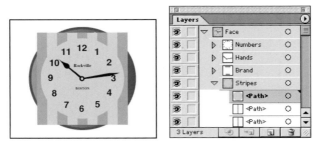

Drag circle named <Path> into Stripes layer.

2 Drag the <Path> layer with the circle color fill onto the Stripes thumbnail to add it to that layer as the top sublayer.

3 In the Layers palette, click the triangle (▶) to the left of the Stripes layer to expand the layer view.

4 Make sure that the <Path> with the circle color fill is the topmost sublayer in the Stripes layer, moving it if necessary. (Clipping masks are always the first object in a layer or group.)

5 Select the Stripes layer. Then click the selection area to the right of the Stripes layer to select the stripes and the colored circle path.

6 Click the Make/Release Clipping Mask button at the bottom of the Layers palette. Notice that all the layer's dividing lines are now dotted and the first path's name has changed to <Clipping Path>. The clipping path name is also underlined to indicate that it is the masking shape.

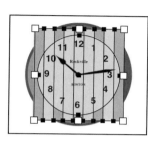
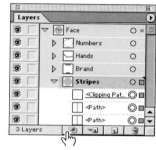

Select Stripes layer.   *Click Make/Release Clipping Mask button.*   *Result*

7 Click the triangle next to the Stripes layer name to collapse the layers in the Layers palette.

8 Choose Select > Deselect. Then choose File > Save.

Merging layers

To streamline your artwork, you can *merge* layers. Merging layers combines the contents of all selected layers onto one layer.

As a final step, you'll combine some of the artwork from the Details.ai file with your other layers.

1 In the Layers palette, click the Numbers layer to select it, and then Shift-click to select the Hands layer.

Notice the current layer indicator (◥) shows the last selected layer as the active layer. The last layer you select will determine the name and color for the merged layer.

2 Choose Merge Selected from the Layers palette menu to merge both layers into one layer called Hands.

The objects on the merged layers retain their original stacking order.

3 Now click the Highlight layer to select it, and then Shift-click to select the Frame layer.

4 Choose Merge Selected from the Layers palette menu to merge the two layers into one layer called Frame.

5 Choose File > Save.

Applying appearance attributes to layers

You can apply appearance attributes such as styles, effects, and transparency to layers, groups, and objects with the Layers palette. When an appearance attribute is applied to a layer, any object on that layer will take on that attribute. If an appearance attribute is applied only to an object on a layer, it affects only that object, not the entire layer.

You will apply an effect to an object on one layer. Then you'll copy that effect to a layer to change all objects on that layer.

1 In the Layers palette, collapse the Face layer and expand the Frame layer to reveal all of its objects.

2 Select the bottom path in the Frame layer.

3 To the right of the bottom path's layer name, click the target indicator (o) to target the bottommost object. Clicking the target indicator indicates that you want to apply an effect, style, or transparency change.

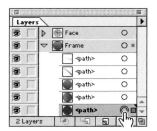

Click the target indicator to target the bottom path

4 Choose Effect > Stylize > Drop Shadow. Leave the settings at their default values and click OK. A drop shadow appears on the outer edge of the clock.

Note: *Select the top Effect > Stylize command.*

5 Notice that the target indicator is now shaded, indicating that the object has appearance attributes applied to it.

6 Click the Appearance tab to bring the palette to the front of its group. (If the Appearance palette isn't visible on-screen, choose Window > Appearance.) Notice that Drop Shadow has been added to the list of appearance attributes for the selected shape.

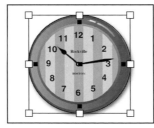
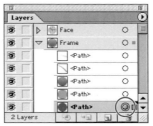
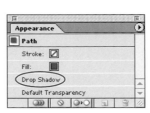

Apply drop shadow effect to clock edge.   *Shaded target indicator indicates appearance attributes.*   *Appearance palette lists selection's attributes.*

You will now use the Layers palette to copy an appearance attribute onto a layer and then edit it.

7 Expand the Face layer to reveal its contents. Drag the bottom right corner of the Layers palette to display the entire list.

8 Hold down Alt (Windows) or Option (Mac OS) and drag the shaded target indicator of the <Path> sublayer to the target indicator of the Hands layer, without releasing the mouse button. The hand pointer with a plus sign indicates that the appearance is being copied.

9 When the target indicator of the Hands layer turns light gray, release the mouse button. The drop shadow is now applied to the entire Hands layer, as indicated by the shaded target indicator.

Drag target indicator to copy effect.   *Result*

Now you'll edit the drop shadow attribute for the type and clock hands, to tone down the effect.

10 In the Layers palette, click the target indicator for the Hands layer. This automatically selects the objects on the Hands layer and deselects the object on the Frame layer.

11 In the Appearance palette, double-click the Drop Shadow attribute. In the Drop Shadow dialog box, enter 3 points for the X and Y offsets and the Blur amount. Click OK.

Target Hands layer. *Edit Drop Shadow effect.* *Result*

For more information on appearance attributes, see Lesson 9, "Using Appearance Attributes, Styles, and Effects."

12 Choose Select > Deselect.

13 Choose File > Save. Choose File > Close to close the file.

You have completed building a layered file.

In some cases after the artwork is complete, you may want to place all the layers of art onto a single layer and delete the empty layers. This is called *flattening* artwork. Delivering finished artwork in a single layer file can prevent accidents from happening, such as hiding layers and not printing parts of the artwork.

To flatten specific layers without deleting hidden layers, select the layers you want to flatten, and then choose Merge Layers from the Layers palette menu.

Merging and flattening artwork

Merging and flattening are similar in that they let you consolidate paths, groups, and sublayers. With merging, you can select which items you want to consolidate; with flattening, all visible items in the artwork are consolidated in a single, parent layer. With either option, the stacking order of the artwork remains the same.

To merge artwork into a single layer or group:

1. Select the items that you want to merge in the Layers palette.

2. Choose Merge Selected from the Layers palette menu. Items will be merged into the layer or group that you selected last. In flattened artwork, all visible layers are merged into the selected layer, and hidden layers are deleted. If you flatten a hidden layer that contains artwork, you can choose to delete the artwork along with the hidden layer, or make all artwork visible and flatten it into one layer. In most cases, you won't want to flatten a file until you finish editing individual layers.

To flatten artwork:

1. Make sure that all the layers you want to flatten are visible.

2. Select the layer into which you will flatten the artwork. You cannot flatten artwork into hidden, locked, or template layers. Doing this results in the topmost layer that is not hidden, locked, or a template being chosen instead. Regardless of the layer you select, the options for the layer and the stacking order of the artwork don't change.

3. Choose Flatten Artwork from the Layers palette menu.

If artwork is present on a hidden layer, a dialog box prompts you to choose whether to make all artwork visible and flatten it into one layer, or delete the artwork along with the layer.

–From online Help and the Adobe Illustrator User Guide, Chapter 9

For information on opening layered Photoshop files in Illustrator and working with layered Illustrator files in Photoshop, see Lesson 14, Combining Illustrator Graphics and Photoshop Images.

For a complete list of shortcuts that you can use with the Layers palette, see "Quick reference" in online Help or the printed *Quick Reference Card*.

Exploring on your own

When you print a layered file, only the visible layers print in the same order in which they appear in the Layers palette—with the exception of *template layers*, which do not print even if they're visible. Template layers are locked, dimmed, and previewed. Objects on template layers neither print nor export.

Now that you've learned how to work with layers, try creating layered artwork by tracing an image on a template layer. We've provided a bitmap photo image of a goldfish that you can use to practice with or use your own artwork or photo images.

1 Choose File > New to create a new file for your artwork.

2 Choose File > Place. In the dialog box, select the Goldfish.eps file, located in the Lesson10 folder, inside the Lessons folder within the AICIB folder on your hard drive; or locate your file containing the artwork or image you want to use as a template and click Place to add the placed file to Layer 1.

For information on importing files, see "About imported artwork" and "Opening and placing artwork" in online Help or in Chapter 2 of the Adobe Illustrator User Guide.

3 Create the template layer by choosing Template from the Layers palette menu or choosing Options for Layer1 and selecting Template in the Layer Options dialog box.

4 Click the New Layer button to create a new layer on which to draw.

5 With Layer 2 active, use any drawing tool to trace over the template, creating new artwork.

6 Create additional layers to separate and edit various components of the new artwork.

7 If you wish, delete the template when you've finished to reduce the size of the file.

You can create custom views of your artwork with some layers hidden and other layers showing, and display each view in a separate window. To create a custom view, choose View > New View. To display each view in a separate window, choose Window > New Window.

For information on custom views, see "Viewing artwork" in online Help or in Chapter 1 in the Adobe Illustrator User Guide.

Review questions

1 Name two benefits of using layers when creating artwork.

2 How do you hide layers? Display individual layers?

3 Describe how to reorder layers in a file.

4 How can you lock layers?

5 What is the purpose of changing the selection color on a layer?

6 What happens if you paste a layered file into another file? Why is the Paste Remembers Layers option useful?

7 How do you move objects from one layer to another?

8 How do you create a layer clipping mask?

9 How do you apply an effect to a layer? How can you edit that effect?

Review answers

1 Benefits of using layers when creating artwork include: You can protect artwork that you don't want to change, you can hide artwork that you aren't working with so that it's not distracting, and you can control what prints.

2 To hide a layer, you click the eye icon to the left of the layer name; you click in the blank, leftmost column to redisplay a layer.

3 You reorder layers by selecting a layer name in the Layers palette and dragging the layer to its new location. The order of layers in the Layers palette controls the document's layer order—topmost in the palette is frontmost in the artwork.

4 You can lock layers several different ways:

• You can click in the column to the left of the layer name; a padlock icon appears, indicating that the layer is locked.

• You can choose Lock Others from the Layers palette menu to lock all layers but the active layer.

• You can hide a layer to protect it.

5 The selection color controls how selected anchor points and direction lines are displayed on a layer, and helps you identify the different layers in your document.

6 The Paste commands paste layered files or objects copied from different layers onto the active layer by default. The Paste Remembers Layers option keeps the original layers intact when the objects are pasted.

7 Select the objects you want to move and drag the square selection indicator icon (■) (to the right of the target indicator) to another layer in the Layers palette.

8 Create a clipping mask on a layer by selecting the layer and clicking the Make/Release Clipping Mask button. The topmost object in the layer will become the clipping mask.

9 Click the target indicator (○) for the layer to which you want to apply an effect. Then choose an effect from the Effect menu. To edit the effect, make sure that the layer is selected; then double-click the name of the effect in the Appearance palette. The effect's dialog box will open, and then you can change the values.

Lesson 11

11 | Creating Airbrush Effects

Converting shapes into mesh objects lets
you blend colors in multiple directions
within the shapes, for a watercolor or airbrush effect. It's easy to modify mesh
objects. You can add or remove colors
from points on the mesh, to adjust the
direction and amount of color blending.

In this lesson, you'll learn how to do the following:

• Create a mesh object using two methods.

• Apply colors to a mesh.

• Edit a mesh for a variety of effects.

• Apply warp effects.

• Select objects in different groups and layers.

• Use Smart Guides to display information about mesh objects.

Getting started

In this lesson, you'll convert the shapes of two butterflies into meshes, paint them, and manipulate the color blending. Before you begin, you must restore the default preferences for Adobe Illustrator and then you will open the finished art file for the lesson to see what you'll create.

1 To ensure that the tools and palettes function exactly as described in this lesson, delete or deactivate (by renaming) the Adobe Illustrator 10.0 preferences file. See "Restoring default preferences" on page 4.

2 Start Adobe Illustrator.

3 Choose File > Open, and open the L11end.ai file in the Lesson11 folder, located inside the Lessons folder within the AICIB folder on your hard drive.

4 If you like, choose View > Zoom Out to make the finished artwork smaller, adjust the window size, and leave it on your screen as you work. (Use the hand tool (🖐) to move the artwork where you want it in the window.) If you don't want to leave the image open, choose File > Close.

For an illustration of the finished artwork in this lesson, see the color section.

To begin working, you'll open an existing art file.

5 Choose File > Open, and open the L11start.ai file in the Lesson11 folder, located inside the Lessons folder within the AICIB folder on your hard drive.

6 Choose File > Save As, name the file **Buttrfly.ai**, and select the Lesson11 folder. Leave the Format option set to Adobe Illustrator® Document, and click Save. In the Illustrator Native Format Options dialog box, select Illustrator 10 Compatibility and click OK.

Setting Smart Guides preferences

Smart Guides are useful for working with mesh objects because they display information about the mesh without the need to select the object first. You'll set preferences for hiding the construction guides (which are useful for drawing and aligning objects) and text labels (which you won't need for this lesson), and you'll change the snapping tolerance (the distance that the pointer must be from an object before Smart Guides take effect).

1 Choose Edit > Preferences > Smart Guides & Slices (Windows and Mac OS 9) or Illustrator > Preferences > Smart Guides & Slices (Mac OS X).

2 In the Preferences dialog box, deselect the display options for Text Label Hints and Construction Guides, and make sure that Transform Tools and Object Highlighting are selected. Enter **1 pt** in the Snapping Tolerance text box. Click OK to set the preferences.

The Transform Tools option is useful for scaling, rotating, reflecting, and shearing objects. The Object Highlighting option displays mesh lines and anchor points when the mouse is positioned over the object.

3 Choose View > Smart Guides to activate them. (A check mark in the menu indicates that they're turned on.)

Painting with the mesh tool

You can convert any object into a mesh object by using the mesh tool and creating one mesh point at a time. Each time you click an object using the mesh tool, a new color is added to the object.

First you'll paint a color on one of the tail wings on a butterfly, and then you'll paint the other tail wing with the same color.

1 Select the zoom tool ( ) in the toolbox and click the butterfly at the top of the artwork a few times to zoom in to 300% (as indicated in the lower left corner of the window). Then select the hand tool ( ), and use it to move the butterfly to the center of the window.

2 Click a color in the Color palette or Swatches palette to specify the current fill. (We selected the Color 2 swatch.) To display the Swatches palette, click its tab to bring it to the front of its palette group.

3 Select the mesh tool ( ) in the toolbox, and click in the center of the upper left tail wing to apply a mesh point with the currently selected color.

The tail wing is automatically converted to a mesh object. The first time you click an object with the mesh tool, the object is converted to a mesh object with one mesh point and two intersecting mesh lines.

4 Now click in the center of the right tail wing to apply a mesh point with the same color and convert it to a mesh object.

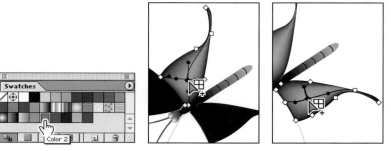

Select color.   Click with mesh tool to apply selected color.

5 Hold down Ctrl (Windows) or Command (Mac OS), and click away from the tail wing to deselect it, and then select another color from the Color or Swatches palette. (We selected the Color 3 swatch.)

6 Click in the left tail wing to add a mesh point with the new color, and then click in the right tail wing to add one with the same color.

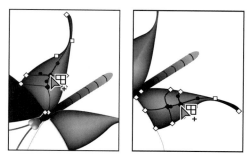

Add mesh points to mesh object with another color.

7 Ctrl-click (Windows) or Command-click (Mac OS) away from the object to deselect it, and then continue adding a few more colors and mesh points.

8 When you have finished, choose File > Save.

Specifying the number of mesh lines

When you use the mesh tool to create a mesh object, two intersecting mesh lines are created for every mesh point you create. Before converting an object to a mesh object, you'll specify its number of mesh lines using the Create Gradient Mesh command.

1 Select the selection tool ( ) in the toolbox, and click the black forewing on the butterfly to select it.

2 Choose Object > Create Gradient Mesh.

3 In the Create Gradient Mesh dialog box, select the Preview option to see the changes to the selected object without closing the dialog box. Type **3** in the Rows text box; press Leave the Columns set to **4** (the default) and leave the Appearance as Flat (the default). Click OK.

The black forewing is converted to a mesh object with three rows separated by two horizontal mesh lines and four columns separated by three vertical mesh lines.

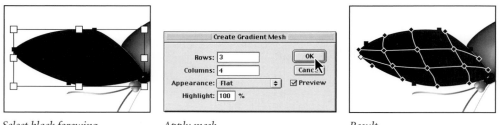

Select black forewing.   Apply mesh.   Result

The mesh object is automatically selected when you create it.

4 Notice that the points in the selected object are all a solid color, indicating that they're selected. Also, the object has a mesh point at the intersection of every mesh line, anchor points at the ends of the mesh lines, and some anchor points on the segments of the outlining edge that are from the original object.

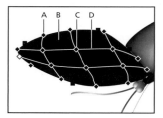

A. Anchor point **B.** Mesh patch
C. Mesh point **D.** Mesh line

For a color illustration of selected mesh objects, see figure 11-1 and figure 11-2 in the color section.

Applying colors to the mesh

You can select points on a mesh object using either the direct-selection tool or the mesh tool and paint them with different colors. Now you'll practice selecting mesh points using the direct-selection tool and apply three colors to the butterfly's forewing.

1 Select the direct-selection tool (▶), and click away from the object to deselect it. Then move the pointer over the top left side of the forewing. (Smart Guides display the mesh as you move the pointer over it.)

2 Click in the center of a mesh patch to select the four mesh points where the lines intersect. (We clicked in the patch above the top horizontal line and to the right of the left vertical line.)

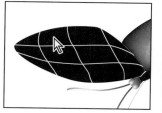 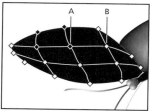

Position pointer over mesh patch. **A.** *Selected mesh point* **B.** *Deselected mesh point*

Clicking with the direct-selection tool in a mesh patch is an easy way to select all of the mesh points and direction handles on the lines surrounding the patch. All the other points become white diamonds, indicating they're not selected.

3 Click a color in the Color palette or Swatches palette (we selected the Color 2 swatch) to apply it to the four selected points.

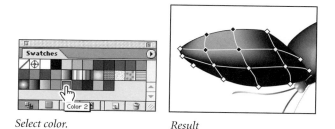

Select color.   *Result*

4 Select the direct-select lasso tool (🔗) in the toolbox.

5 With the forewing still selected, draw a selection marquee around the two left mesh points on the bottom horizontal line.

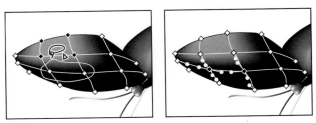

Draw selection marquee around mesh points to select them.

If you inadvertently select the wrong mesh points, draw the selection marquee again. You can also Ctrl-click (Windows) or Command-click (Mac OS) away from the artwork to deselect it, Ctrl/Command-click the artwork to reselect it, and then redraw the selection marquee.

6 Paint the two selected mesh points with a color from the Color palette or Swatches palette (we selected the Color 3 swatch).

7 Use the direct-select lasso tool to select the two middle mesh points on the right vertical mesh line. Select a third color in the Color palette or Swatches palette (we selected the Color 4 swatch) to paint the selected mesh points.

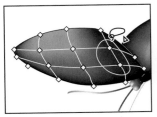
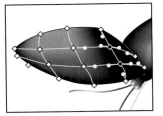

Select two right mesh points.   *Select color.*   *Result*

8 Choose File > Save.

Highlighting a mesh object

To give an object a three-dimensional appearance, you can create a mesh that highlights the center or the edge of an object. Now you'll create a mesh with highlighting.

1 Use the hand tool (🖐) to move the second butterfly at the bottom of the artwork to the center of the window.

2 Select the selection tool (➤), and click the top forewing on the pink butterfly to select it.

3 Choose Object > Create Gradient Mesh.

4 In the Create Gradient Mesh dialog box, leave **3** entered in the Rows text box. Type **3** in the Columns text box, and make sure that the Preview option is selected.

5 For Appearance, choose To Edge in the dialog box; notice the change to the highlighting in the selected object. Then choose To Center from the pop-up menu.

To Edge creates a highlight on the edges of the object. To Center creates a highlight in the center of the object.

For a color illustration of highlighted mesh objects, see figure 11-1 in the color section.

6 Type a value between 0% and 100% in the Highlight text box (we entered 60%), and press Tab to see the change to the artwork without closing the dialog box.

A value of 100% applies a maximum white highlight to the object. A value of 0% applies no white highlight to the object.

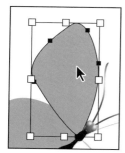

Create Gradient Mesh	
Rows: 3	OK
Columns: 3	Cancel
Appearance: To Center ↕	☑ Preview
Highlight: 60 %	

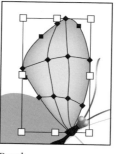

Select top forewing. *Apply highlight and preview.* *Result*

7 Click OK to close the dialog box and create the highlighted mesh object.

8 Select the direct-select lasso tool ( ), and drag to draw a marquee over the tip of the forewing to select the four upper left anchor points on the mesh.

9 With the anchor points selected, click a color in the Color palette or Swatches palette to apply it to the points. (We selected the Color 4 swatch.)

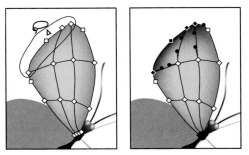

Drag direct-select lasso to select mesh points.

Editing mesh points

You can use the mesh tool to select, add, and delete mesh points to change the way colors blend in a mesh object. Every mesh point has a set of direction handles that let you adjust the distance and direction that a color blends with neighboring colors in the mesh object.

First, you'll use the mesh tool to select a mesh point and add a color to the butterfly's forewing.

1 Select the mesh tool ( ) in the toolbox and position the pointer over a mesh point. The plus sign on the pointer disappears when it's over a mesh point. Click to select the mesh point. (We selected the lower right mesh point where the right vertical line intersects with the bottom horizontal line.) Choose Edit > Undo if you add a mesh point by mistake.

2 Click a color in the Color palette or Swatches palette to apply it to the selected mesh point. (We selected the Color 5 swatch.)

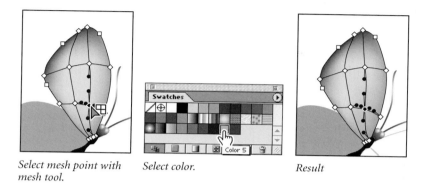

Select mesh point with mesh tool.   Select color.   Result

Now you'll use the mesh tool to delete a mesh point on the forewing and see how the colors and highlighting readjust.

3 Using the mesh tool, hold the pointer over the top left mesh point where the top horizontal line and left vertical line intersect. Hold down Alt (Windows) or Option (Mac OS) to display a minus sign on the pointer, and click the mesh point to delete it.

Deleting a mesh point also deletes the two intersecting mesh lines.

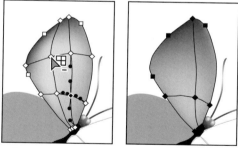

Delete mesh point.   Result

Notice that the highlighting from the center of the object is diminished as the remaining colors on the anchor points now blend with the original base color.

4 If you want to take a look at that change again, press Ctrl+Z (Windows) or Command+Z (Mac OS) to undo the deletion, and then press Shift+Ctrl+Z (Windows) or Shift+Command+Z (Mac OS) to redo it.

Now you'll use the mesh tool to add a mesh point to the tail wing on the butterfly and then change the direction in which the color of the mesh point blends from the center.

5 With the mesh tool selected, hold the pointer over the bottom tail wing, and click anywhere inside it to add a mesh point.

6 Click a color in the Color palette or Swatches palette to apply it to the new mesh point. (We selected the Color 5 swatch.)

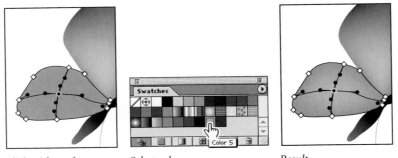

Click with mesh   Select color.   Result
tool to add mesh point.

7 Select the direct-selection tool ( ) in the toolbox. Drag a marquee over the bottom tip of the tail wing to select the anchor points along the edge, and click a color in the Color palette or Swatches palette to apply it to the selected points. (We selected the Color 4 swatch.)

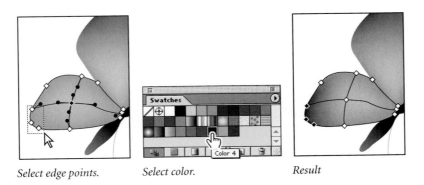

Select edge points.   Select color.   Result

8 Select the mesh tool ( ) in the toolbox, and click the mesh point you created in the center of the tail wing to select it. (The plus sign on the pointer disappears when it's over a mesh point.)

The selected mesh point displays four direction points (or handles) that lie along the mesh lines until you move them. Now you'll use the handles to adjust the direction and distance of the mesh point's color.

9 Using the mesh tool, select the left direction handle (don't release the mouse button) and drag it to the left about midway to the edge of the object; then release the mouse button. Notice how the mesh point's color extends further out before it starts to blend with the other colors.

10 Select another direction handle and drag it in an arc to swirl the direction of the blending colors.

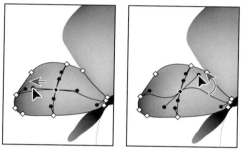

Drag direction handles to lengthen or swirl color blending.

11 Ctrl-click (Windows) or Command-click (Mac OS) away from the object to deselect it.

12 Choose File > Save.

Reflecting mesh objects

You can use the reflect tool and other tools in the toolbox on a mesh object just like any other type of object. Now you'll reflect a copy of the two wing parts to complete the butterfly.

1 Select the selection tool ( ) in the toolbox, and Shift-click to select both the tail wing and the forewing on the bottom butterfly.

2 Select the reflect tool ( ) from the same group as the rotate tool ( ) in the toolbox, hold down Alt (Windows) or Option (Mac OS), and click in the center of the butterfly's body, midway between the selected wing parts and the wing guides on the right.

Clicking the body of the butterfly designates the point of origin from which the object will reflect. Holding down Alt/Option as you click displays the Reflect dialog box.

3 In the Reflect dialog box, select the Angle option and type **46** in the degree text box. Click Copy. (Don't click OK.)

Depending on where you clicked to set the reflecting reference point in step 2, you may need to slightly adjust the position of the reflected copy using the arrow keys—or choose Edit > Undo and repeat steps 2 and 3.

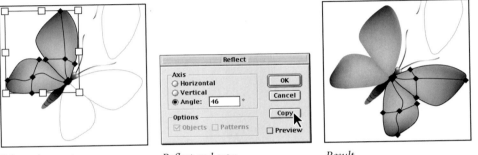

Select wing parts. *Reflect and copy.* *Result*

4 Ctrl-click (Windows) or Command-click (Mac OS) away from the object to deselect it.

5 Choose File > Save to save the artwork.

Modifying mesh lines

You'll use the mesh tool to reshape mesh lines by moving mesh points on them, add mesh lines with an unpainted mesh point to the mesh, and delete a single mesh line in the forewing of the first butterfly.

1 Select the hand tool ( ), and move the butterfly at the top of the artwork down to the center of your window.

2 Select the mesh tool ( ), and position it over the left forewing. Select the left mesh point on the top horizontal line (don't release the mouse button); then hold down Shift, and drag the mesh point to the left.

As you drag to the left, the intersecting vertical mesh line is reshaped. Holding down Shift as you drag constrains the movement horizontally, leaving the horizontal mesh line unaffected.

3 Select the bottom mesh point on the right vertical line (don't release the mouse button), and Shift-drag to move it down without affecting the vertical mesh line.

Notice how the color blending readjusts to the new position of the mesh point.

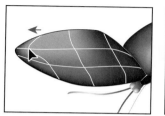

Shift-drag left to move mesh point along horizontal line.

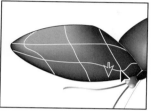

Shift-drag down to move mesh point along vertical line.

For a color illustration of the edited mesh point, see figure 11-2 in the color section.

You can add a mesh point to a mesh object without applying the current fill color to it or changing the existing colors in the object.

4 Ctrl-click (Windows) or Command-click (Mac OS) away from the object to deselect it.

5 Select a new color fill by clicking a color in the Color palette or the Swatches palette. (We selected the Color 6 swatch.)

6 Using the mesh tool, position the pointer in the center of a patch. (We chose the middle right patch; see the following illustration.) Shift-click to add a new mesh point with two intersecting mesh lines—without changing the color in the object. Notice that the Fill box in the toolbox changes to the existing color of the object where you clicked.

7 If you want to change the color of the new mesh point, click a new color in the Color palette or Swatches palette. (We selected the Color 6 swatch again.)

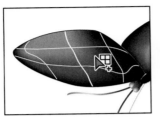

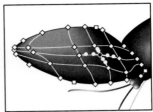

Shift-click to add unpainted mesh point.

New mesh point picks up underlying mesh colors.

Note: *You can add anchor points to an existing mesh line by selecting the object and using the add-anchor-point tool (✑).*

Now you'll delete a mesh line.

8 Using the mesh tool, position the pointer over a mesh line and hold down Alt (Windows) or Option (Mac OS) to display a minus sign on the pointer. Alt/Option-click a segment (between two mesh points) on the mesh line to delete the line.

Notice how the color on the new mesh point spreads into the area where the line was.

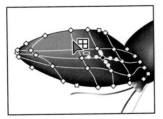

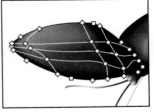

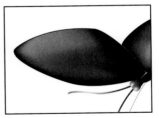

Position pointer over line to left of new mesh point.

Alt/Option-click segment to delete mesh line.

Result

You'll complete the butterfly body by reflecting a copy of the forewing.

9 Select the selection tool ( ) in the toolbox to select the bounding box of the mesh object.

10 Select the reflect tool ( ) in the toolbox, and Alt-click (Windows) or Option-click (Mac OS) in the body of the butterfly, about midway between the existing wing and the wing guide.

11 In the Reflect dialog box, make sure that the Angle option is selected, type **36** in the degree text box, and click Copy. (Don't click OK.)

Depending on where you clicked in the body, you may have to adjust the position of the reflected copy by using the arrow keys.

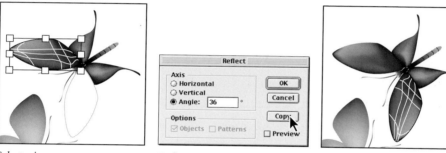

Select wing.   Reflect copy.   Result

12 Choose Select > Deselect.

13 Choose File > Save to save your work.

Warping a mesh

Now you'll experiment with changing the shape of the butterfly wing and its meshes using the warp tool. The warp tool, along with the other liquify tools, changes an object's shape.

1 Double-click the warp tool ( ) in the toolbox to select the tool and display its Options dialog box.

The warp tool molds objects in the same way as if they were modeling clay. Dragging or pulling parts of an object with the warp tool causes the pulled areas to thin out. First you'll set the tool's options.

2 In the Warp Tool Options dialog box, enter **10 pt** for both the Global Brush Dimensions Width and Height to set the size of the tool cursor.

3 Set the Intensity to **25%**. The lower the intensity, the slower the rate of change when dragging the warp tool.

4 Leave the remaining Warp options as is.

Detail specifies the spacing between points introduced into the object's outline; the higher the value, the more closely spaced are the points. Simplify is related to Detail and reduces superfluous points that do not noticeably affect the shape's overall appearance.

5 Click OK.

6 In the artwork, position the warp tool over the right butterfly wing, and drag to warp the meshes. Continue to drag the tool and try out its effect.

Drag warp tool to warp mesh.

You can apply preset warp effects to paths, text, blends, and raster images. In addition, you can apply a warp effect as a live effect that can be removed at any time using the Effect menu. Once you apply the Warp effect, the warp appears in the Appearance palette, where you can save it as part of a style, select it for editing, expand it, or delete it. The effect also appears in the Layers palette, which displays the object as having an appearance applied.

If you don't like the effect, you can remove it before continuing with the lesson by choosing the File > Revert command.

7 Choose Select > Deselect. Choose File > Save to save your work.

Modifying shapes with liquify tools

Illustrator provides a variety of liquify tools for changing an object's shape. Using these tools alters the original object's shape. To distort objects with liquify tools, simply draw over the object with the tool—the tool adds anchor points and adjust paths as you draw.

Note: *you cannot use liquify tools on objects that contain text, graphs, or symbols.*

Use any of the following tools to distort an object:

Warp tool ( ) *Molds objects in the same way as if they were modeling clay. When you drag or pull portions of an object using this tool, the pulled areas attenuate.*

Twirl tool ( ) *Creates swirling distortions of an object.*

Pucker tool ( ) *Deflates an object by moving control points toward the cursor.*

Bloat tool ( ) *Inflates an object by moving control points away from the cursor.*

Scallop tool ( ) *Adds scallop-like details to the outline of an object.*

Crystallize tool ( ) *Adds crystal-like details to the outline of an object.*

Wrinkle tool ( ) *Adds wrinkle-like details to the outline of an object.*

–From online Help and the Adobe Illustrator User Guide, Chapter 5

Applying transparency to a mesh

Mesh objects can be transparent or opaque, just like nonmesh objects. Now you'll scroll down to the dragonfly in your lesson art. You'll create an iridescent mesh in the dragonfly's wing and then you'll adjust its transparency to make it appear translucent.

1 In the Layers palette, click to the left of both the Dragonfly and Leaves layers to display the artwork on those layers. If necessary, resize the Layers palette to view all the contents.

2 Press the spacebar to get the hand tool (🖐), and drag the image up until the dragonfly is visible in the center of the window.

3 Select the direct-selection tool (▵) in the toolbox, and click in the center of the lower left wing of the dragonfly.

4 Apply a mesh to the dragonfly wing:

• Choose Object > Create Gradient Mesh.

• In the Create Gradient Mesh dialog box, enter **3** in the Rows text box, press Tab and enter **2** in the Columns text box, and make sure that the Preview option is selected.

• For Appearance, choose To Center to highlight the center of the object. Enter a highlight of **80%**. Click OK.

Select lower wing.   *Create gradient mesh with highlight.*   *Result*

5 In the Layers palette, click the triangle (▸) to the left of the Dragonfly layer to view its contents.

6 Now click the triangle to the left of the Lower Wings sublayer to expand its view. This sublayer has two paths, named <Path> and <Mesh>. The solid square selection indicator (■) and the shaded target indicator (◎) show that the <Mesh> path is selected.

7 Click the selection indicator area for the <Path> sublayer to select the lower right wing.

Using the selection indicators in the Layers palette is a quick and easy way to select objects that are in different groups or on different layers.

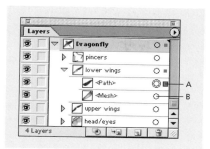

A. Selection indicator   *B. Target indicator*

8 Repeat step 4 for the lower right wing. Notice that the sublayer's name changes to <Mesh> from <Path>.

9 In the Layers palette, click the triangle to the left of the Lower Wings sublayer to collapse it.

Now you'll repeat these steps to apply a mesh to the upper wings.

10 Click the triangle to the left of the Upper Wings sublayer to expand its view. This sublayer also has two paths.

11 Now apply a mesh to each of the upper right wings:

• To select the upper right wing, click the selection indicator area for the first <Path> sublayer. Repeat step 4.

• To select the upper left wing, click the target indicator for the second <Path> sublayer. Repeat step 4.

Now you'll select the wings using the Layers palette and adjust their transparency.

12 In the Layers palette, click the selection indicator area to the far right of the Upper Wings sublayer. Shift-click the selection indicator for the Lower Wings sublayer to add the wings to the selection. All four dragonfly wings are now selected.

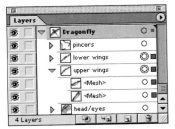

Shift-click target indicators to select multiple sublayers.

13 Choose Window > Transparency or click the Transparency palette tab to display the Transparency palette.

14 Use the Opacity slider to decrease the opacity of the dragonfly wings. (We used 29%.)

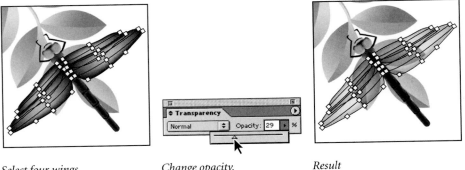

Select four wings.   *Change opacity.*   *Result*

For a color illustration of the opacity change, see figure 11-3 in the color section.

Now you're ready to view the finished artwork. You'll clear the guides and selection lines.

15 Double-click the zoom tool (🔍) to zoom out to 100%.

16 Choose View > Smart Guides, and then choose Select > Deselect.

17 Choose File > Save to save the artwork. Choose File > Close to close your file.

This completes the lesson. You're ready to create your own watercolor or airbrush effects. To learn other ways to blend colors in objects, see Lesson 8, "Blending Shapes and Colors."

Tips for creating mesh objects

You can create a mesh object from any path object or any bitmap image (such as a photographic image imported from Adobe Photoshop). Keep these important guidelines in mind when creating mesh objects:

- *You cannot create gradient mesh objects from compound paths, text objects, or placed EPS files.*

- *Once a mesh object has been created, it cannot be converted back to a path object.*

- *When converting complex objects, use the Create Gradient Mesh command for the best results.*

- *When converting simple objects, use either the mesh tool or the Create Gradient Mesh command. However, if you want to add a highlight to a particular spot, use the mesh tool and click at the point you want the highlight to appear.*

- *To create a mesh object with a regular pattern of mesh points and mesh lines, use the Create Gradient Mesh command.*

- *When converting complex objects, Illustrator can add hidden anchor points to maintain the shape of a line. If you want to edit, add, or remove one or more of these anchor points, use the add-anchor-point tool or the delete-anchor-point tool.*

- *To improve performance and speed of redrawing, keep the size of mesh objects to a minimum. Complex mesh objects can greatly reduce performance. Thus, it is better to create a few small, simple mesh objects than to create a single, complex mesh object.*

–From online Help and the Adobe Illustrator User Guide, Chapter 8

Review questions

1 Describe two methods for creating a mesh.

2 How do you change a color on the mesh?

3 How do you add a mesh point to a mesh object? How do you add the mesh point without adding a color?

4 How do you delete a mesh line?

5 Describe how to move a mesh point without affecting the intersecting line.

6 How do you make a mesh transparent?

7 How do you add a warp effect?

Review answers

1 To create a mesh, you select the mesh tool and click an object; or you can select the object first, choose Object > Create Gradient Mesh, and specify the number of mesh lines and highlighting in the Create Gradient Mesh dialog box. Another way to create a mesh is to select a gradient-filled object, choose Object > Expand, and select the Mesh option in the Expand dialog box to expand the gradient.

2 To change a color on the mesh, use the direct-selection tool or the mesh tool to select the mesh point for the color, and then select a different color.

3 To add a mesh point to a mesh object, click in a mesh patch or on a mesh line segment with the mesh tool. (You can also add anchor points to mesh lines using the add-anchor-point tool.) To add the mesh point without adding a color, hold down Shift as you click.

4 To delete a mesh line, select the mesh tool, and Alt/Option-click a segment on the line.

5 To move a mesh point without affecting the intersecting line, use the mesh tool to select the point, and without releasing the mouse button, Shift-drag the mesh point.

6 To make a mesh transparent, select the mesh object and change its opacity in the Transparency palette.

7 To add a warp effect, select the warp tool in the liquify tool set in the toolbox. Then simply drag over the artwork you want to warp. To set tool options, double-click the warp tool in the toolbox. You can also apply warp effects as live effects that can be removed at any time, using the Effect > Warp menu.

Lesson 12

12 | Drawing Cylinders and Boxes

It's easy to transform two-dimensional designs into three-dimensional shapes. Use Smart Guides and the free transform tool to shape objects precisely. Envelope distortions let you warp objects and type to create the illusion of depth. You can also use gradients to give the illusion of depth.

In this lesson, you'll learn how to do the following:

- Use the Envelope Distort feature to create a banner logotype.
- Precisely align points using Smart Guides as you draw objects.
- Use the Pathfinder palette to create shapes.
- Use gradients to provide the illusion of depth.
- Use brushes and custom brushes to paint the package.
- Construct and rotate objects using the free transform tool.

Getting started

In this lesson, you'll use a round and a rectangular box top as the basis for creating cylindrical and rectangular boxes. Before you begin, you'll need to restore the default preferences for Adobe Illustrator. Then you'll open a file containing the finished artwork to see what you'll create.

1 To ensure that the tools and palettes function exactly as described in this lesson, delete or deactivate (by renaming) the Adobe Illustrator 10.0 preferences file. See "Restoring default preferences" on page 4.

2 Start Adobe Illustrator.

3 Choose File > Open, and open the L12end_win.ai file (Windows) or the L12end_mac.ai file (Mac OS) in the Lesson12 folder, located inside the Lessons folder within the AICIB folder on your hard drive.

This file displays both the cylindrical and rectangular completed boxes. You'll create the boxes from two separate start files.

4 Choose View > Zoom Out to make the finished artwork smaller, adjust the window size, and leave it on your screen as you work. (Use the hand tool (✋) to move the artwork where you want it in the window.) If you don't want to leave the image open, choose File > Close.

For an illustration of the finished artwork in this lesson, see the color section.

To begin working, you'll open an existing art file set up for the cylindrical box.

5 Choose File > Open, and open the L12strt1_win.ai file (Windows) or the L12strt1_mac.ai file (Mac OS) in the Lesson12 folder, located inside the Lessons folder within the AICIB folder on your hard drive.

6 Choose File > Save As, name the file **Lemon.ai**, and select the Lesson12 folder. Leave the Format option set to Adobe Illustrator® Document, and click Save. In the Illustrator Native Format Options dialog box, select Illustrator 10.0 Compatibility and click OK.

Creating a banner logo with an envelope

You can use envelopes to create a warped shape or other distortions to selected objects. Once you apply an envelope, you can edit the original objects at any time. At any time you can also edit, delete, or expand an envelope.

In this part of this lesson, you'll create a logotype with a preset warp shape and use the warp shape as a ribbon on top of which to place the logotype. Then you'll add some transparency and drop shadow effects to the logotype.

Creating the logotype

You can make an envelope out of objects in your artwork, or you can use a preset warp shape or a mesh object as an envelope.

1 Select the selection tool ( ) in the toolbox. Then click to select the *Lots O' Lemon* type with the selection tool.

You can use envelopes with text objects, paths, compound paths, meshes, blends, and raster images.

2 Choose Object > Envelope Distort > Make with Warp.

3 In the Warp Options dialog box, select Preview to preview the effect of changes.

4 Drag the Warp Options dialog box by its title bar so that you can see the dialog box and the selected type in the artwork.

5 Choose Rise from the Style pop-up menu, and set the Bend amount to **93**% to create a ribbon effect. Click OK.

6 Choose File > Save to save your work.

Creating the banner shape

Now you'll create the banner envelope shape by copying the logotype, releasing its type from the envelope shape, and then deleting the type copy.

1 With the logotype still selected, use the selection tool and Alt-drag (Windows) or Option-drag (Mac OS) the logotype to a blank area of the artwork. Release the mouse button and then release the Alt/Option key to copy the logotype and leave the original behind.

Next, you'll release the type from the envelope shape.

2 With the copy still selected, choose Object > Envelope Distort > Release. Releasing the type separates the original text from the warp shape and leaves both selected.

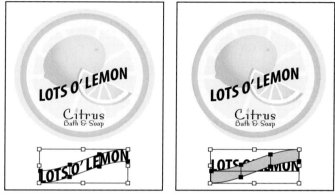

Selected copy of envelope type   Envelope type released

You've used the copy of the type as a template for the warp shape. Once the shape is created, you can delete the type copy because you no longer need it.

3 Click in a blank area of the screen to deselect the artwork. Then click the released type to select it.

4 Delete the type by pressing Backspace or Delete.

You'll enlarge the envelope shape and remove its mesh points. Then you'll place it behind the logotype on the package design.

5 Select the zoom tool (⬚) in the toolbox, and drag a zoom marquee around the entire banner shape. Marquee-zooming is a quick way of zooming on a specific area of your artwork and ensuring that the entire shape is contained in the window.

6 Select the selection tool (⬚) in the toolbox, and click the banner shape to select it.

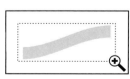 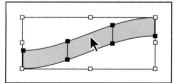

Drag a marquee with   Select the banner shape.
the zoom tool.

7 Choose Object > Path > Offset Path. Leave the Offset amount set to **10 pt**, and click OK.

A larger banner is created outside the boundaries of the gray, original banner.

8 Click the Color palette to make it active, or choose Window > Color to display the palette if it's not visible on-screen.

9 With the larger banner still selected, paint the banner with a stroke of None and a lime green fill of C=**50**, M=**4**, Y=**100** and K=**0**.

Adding the banner to the package design

Now you'll add the green banner behind the logotype on the package design.

1 Using the selection tool (▶), click the smaller gray banner and delete it.

Now that you've created the larger banner, the original warp shape is no longer needed.

2 Press Ctrl+Alt+spacebar (Windows) or Command+Option+spacebar and click the artwork to zoom out to 150%.

3 Click the Layers palette tab to make it active, or choose Window > Layers if the palette is not visible on-screen.

Next you'll move the <Envelope> layer so that the type will remain visible.

4 In the Layers palette, click the triangle to the left of the Banner layer to display its contents. Then drag the <Envelope> layer above the <Path> sublayer.

Move the envelope layer above the banner's <Path> sublayer.

5 In the artwork, use the selection tool to drag the banner until it is centered behind the distorted logotype. Use the arrow keys on the keyboard to nudge the banner into place, as needed.

Stylizing the banner and logotype

To complete the banner and logotype, you'll add some drop shadows and transparency to give the artwork more dimension and sophistication.

1 With the banner still selected, choose Window > Transparency or click the Transparency palette tab to bring it to the front of its group.

2 Set the blending mode to Multiply and the Opacity to **50%**.

Next you'll add a drop shadow to the banner.

3 Choose Effect > Stylize > Drop Shadow.

Note: *Choose the top Effect > Stylize command; the bottom Effect > Stylize command applies effects to bitmap images.*

4 In the Drop Shadow dialog box, use the following settings: Mode=Multiply, Opacity = **50%**, X Offset=**4 pt**, Y Offset=**4 pt**, and Blur = **0pt**. Select Color, and click the color swatch to open the Color Picker.

5 In the Color Picker, set the color for the shadow to a marine blue, using the following values: C=**94**, M=**65**, Y=**4**, and K=**0**. Click OK to exit the Color Picker and click OK to exit the Drop Shadow dialog box.

Set the transparency. *Set the drop shadow options and color.*

Result

Now you'll make a few changes to stylize the logotype and then group it with the banner for final positioning. To be able to edit the type, you need to access it without its envelope. First you'll select the type.

6 Click the type to select it and the envelope.

7 Choose Object > Envelope Distort > Edit Contents. This command lets you access just the type for editing. The type is selected automatically.

8 In the Color palette, select a Fill of white for the type.

9 With the type still selected, choose Effect > Stylize > Drop Shadow.

10 In the Drop Shadow dialog box, use the following settings: Mode=Multiply, Opacity=**15**%, X Offset=**2 pt**, Y Offset=**2 pt**. With the Color option selected, click the color swatch to open the Color Picker. Set the color for the shadow to a gray-blue with the following values: C=**49**, M=**34**, Y=**21**, and K=**7**. Click OK to exit the Color Picker and click OK to exit the Drop Shadow dialog.

11 To return the envelope to its editable state, choose Object > Envelope Distort > Edit Envelope.

12 Select the selection tool ( ), and Shift-click the banner to add it to the selection.

Type selected   *Envelope selected*

13 Choose Object > Group to group the logotype with the banner.

14 Use the selection tool to move the logotype banner up so that it looks more visually centered.

15 Choose Select > Deselect, and choose File > Save to save the file.

Finished logotype banner

Drawing three-dimensional objects

In this part of the lesson, you'll use two-dimensional shapes as the basis for creating more complex, three-dimensional objects.

Illustrator has several tools that are helpful in creating complex shapes, including Smart Guides and the Pathfinder palette. Smart Guides help you select and snap to points to create, edit, move, align, and transform objects by creating temporary guides that indicate paths, anchor and path points, and angles. Pathfinder commands combine, isolate, and subdivide shapes as part of creating complex objects.

Drawing cylinders

You'll use the round box top as a basis for creating the cylindrical box.

1 In Layers palette, click the padlock icon (🔒) to the left of Layer 1 to unlock the layer.

2 Choose Select > All to select all of the artwork.

You'll begin by scaling the box top to create perspective.

3 Select the selection tool ( ) in the toolbox. Then drag the center bottom handle on the bounding box up to scale the artwork vertically.

Select objects.

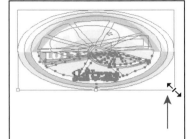

Drag bounding box handle up to scale objects.

4 Click outside the artwork to deselect the box top.

Clicking outside the artwork with the selection tool, the direct-selection tool, or the group-selection tool deselects all selected objects.

5 Choose File > Save to save the artwork.

Creating the cylinder bottom and sides

Now you'll create the cylinder's bottom and sides, using Smart Guides to align the shapes precisely. You can use Smart Guides with the pen tool or the shape tools, the selection tools, and the transformation tools.

You'll use Smart Guides to locate and join anchor points on the top and bottom ellipses.

1 Choose Edit > Preferences > Smart Guides & Slices (Windows and Mac OS 9) or Illustrator > Preferences > Smart Guides & Slices (Mac OS X).

Objects in artwork snap to Smart Guides when they're within the designated tolerance range. The default setting is 4 points. You'll decrease the snapping tolerance to create more precise alignment.

2 Set the Snapping Tolerance to **1 point**. (Leave other Smart Guides options at their default settings.) Click OK.

3 Choose View > Smart Guides to turn on Smart Guides. A check mark next to the command indicates that Smart Guides are turned on.

4 Use the selection tool ( ) to select the outer ellipse in the artwork.

5 Start dragging the ellipse downward; then press Alt+Shift (Windows) or Option+Shift (Mac OS), and drag a copy of the ellipse directly below the original.

Note: *Drag the ellipse by positioning the pointer within its path, not on a segment.*

The copy of the ellipse will become the bottom of the cylinder.

6 Select the pen tool ( ). Roll over the left edge of the upper ellipse until you see the Smart Guides text label for the anchor point on that edge.

Smart Guides text labels appear when you roll over anchor points or path points with the mouse. You'll use the Smart Guides text labels to locate the anchor points on the outer edges of the upper and lower ellipses, and to join the anchor points with the pen tool to create a rectangle that will become part of the cylinder barrel.

7 Click the left anchor point with the pen tool.

8 Roll over the left edge of the lower ellipse until you see the Smart Guides text label for the anchor point on that edge.

9 Shift-click the anchor point with the pen tool to create the left side of a rectangle that will join the two ellipses.

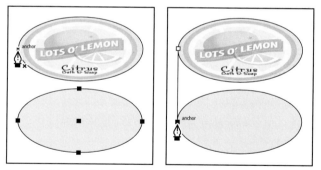

Smart Guides text labels indicate anchor points beneath tool.

10 Roll over the right edge of the lower ellipse until you see the Smart Guides text label for the anchor point on that edge. Then click the anchor point with the pen tool to create the bottom side of the rectangle.

11 As you did in the previous step, use Smart Guides to locate the anchor point on the right edge of the upper ellipse, and click the anchor point with the pen tool to create the right side of the rectangle.

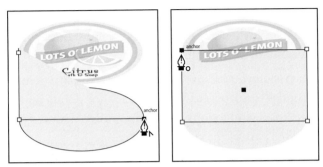

Smart Guides text labels indicate anchor and alignment points.

12 Click the anchor point on the left edge of the upper ellipse again to close the rectangle.

13 Ctrl-click (Windows) or Command-click (Mac OS) away from the artwork to deselect it. Then choose File > Save to save the file.

How Smart Guides work

When Smart Guides are turned on and you move the cursor over your artwork, the cursor looks for objects, page boundaries, and intersections of construction guides to snap to that are within the tolerance range set in Smart Guides Preferences.

You can use Smart Guides in the following ways when you create, move, and transform objects:

• When you create an object with the pen or shape tools, use the Smart Guides to position the new object's anchor points relative to the other object.

• When you move an object, use the Smart Guides to align to the point on the object that you have selected. You can align to the anchor point at the corner of a selected object near the bounding box. To do so, select the object just inside the bounding box handle. If the tolerance is 5 points or greater, you can snap to the corner point from 5 points away.

• When the Transform Tools option is selected in Smart Guides Preferences and you transform an object, Smart Guides appear to assist the transformation.

Note: *When Snap to Grid is turned on, you cannot use Smart Guides (even if the menu command is selected).*

–From online Help and the Adobe Illustrator User Guide, Chapter 4

Completing the cylinder

You'll use Pathfinder commands to complete construction of the cylinder, and add a gradient fill to the cylinder barrel to give the illusion of depth. Then you'll reduce the cylinder depth to complete the project.

1 Click the selection tool ( ). Then Shift-click the rectangle and the bottom ellipse you created to select them.

2 Choose Window > Pathfinder if the Pathfinder palette is not visible.

Pathfinder commands combine, isolate, and subdivide shapes as part of creating complex objects. You can further modify shapes by changing their size, shape, or orientation with the free transform tool or the reflect, rotate, scale, and shear tools.

3 In the Pathfinder palette, click the Add to Shape Area button ( ). The Add to Shape Area command creates a single object from overlapping objects.

If you know you won't want to access the original shapes you are combining you can click the Expand button to make the shape change permanent.

4 Click the Expand button in the Pathfinder palette.

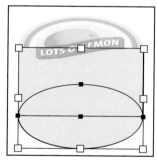 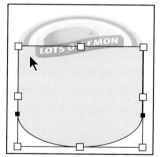

Add to shapes with Pathfinder.   *Click Expand button to expand the shapes.*

5 Display the context-sensitive menu for the consolidated shape:

• (Windows) Press Ctrl and right-click over the shape.

• (Mac OS) Press Control and then click over the shape to view the context-sensitive menu.

Now you will complete the shape of the cylinder by cutting away the curved shape at the top. You'll do this using the Pathfinder commands.

6 From the context-sensitive menu, choose Arrange > Send to Back.

7 Select the top ellipse, and choose Edit > Copy.

8 Select the cylinder barrel shape, and choose Edit > Paste in Front.

9 With the ellipse still selected, Shift-click the cylinder barrel shape to add it to the selection.

10 In the Pathfinder palette, Alt/Option-click the Subtract from Shape Area button ( ).

The Subtract from Shape Area command removes hidden parts of overlapping filled objects. Alt/Option-clicking the button is equivalent to clicking the Expand button to make the command permanent instead of live and editable.

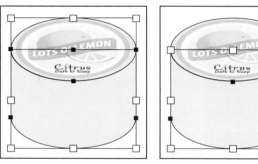

Top ellipse and barrel selected   Alt/Option-click Subtract from Shape Area button.

The Pathfinder palette contains many commands in addition to the Add to Shape Area and Subtract from Shape Area commands, which let you divide and combine shapes to create complex objects. You can also apply Pathfinder commands with the Effect menu. For more information on Pathfinder commands, see "Using the Pathfinder palette" in online Help or Chapter 5 in the Adobe Illustrator User Guide.

For an illustration of effects applied by the Pathfinder commands, see figure 12-1 in the color section.

Now you'll apply color and refine the shape you just created. You'll paint the cylinder barrel with a swatch from the Swatches palette.

11 With the barrel shape still selected, click the Swatches tab to bring the palette to the front of its group.

12 In the Swatches palette, click the Cylinder gradient swatch to fill the cylinder barrel.

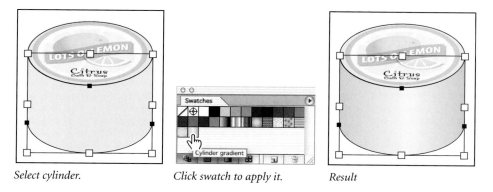

Select cylinder.   *Click swatch to apply it.*   *Result*

13 Click outside the artwork to deselect the cylinder barrel.

14 To reduce the depth of the cylinder, select the direct-selection tool ( ), and Shift-click or drag a marquee to select the left, bottom, and right anchor points on the bottom ellipse. Begin to drag the bottom of the cylinder up; then press Shift, and release when the cylinder height is about half the original size.

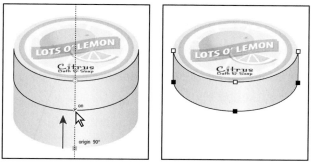

Shift-drag bottom ellipse.   *Result*

15 Click outside the artwork to deselect the object.

16 Choose File > Save to save your work, and choose File > Close to close the file.

Drawing boxes

Now you'll create a rectangular box. You'll use Smart Guides, as you did to create the cylinder, but this time you'll use the Smart Guides angle alignment guides to create precise side panels for the box.

You'll start this part of the lesson by opening a flat view (the box top). You'll use this flat view to create the box sides and then you'll decorate the sides and shear the box panels to construct the box.

1 Choose File > Open, and open the L12strt2.ai file in the Lesson12 folder, located inside the Lessons folder within the AICIB folder on your hard drive.

2 Choose File > Save As, name the file **Lime.ai**, and select the Lesson12 folder. Leave the Format option set to Adobe Illustrator® Document, and click Save. In the Illustrator Native Format Options dialog box, select Illustrator 10 Compatibility and click OK.

Creating box sides

You'll use Smart Guides to create sides for the box based on the dimensions of the box top.

First you'll roll the mouse over anchor points on the left side of the box top and practice using Smart Guides to find intersection points.

1 In the Layers palette, click Layer 1 to select it. Selecting the layer ensures that all the artwork you create will be placed on that layer.

2 Select the pen tool (🖊). Roll the pointer over the anchor points at the two left-side corners on the box top. Then roll the pointer over the artboard to the left of the box top.

Smart Guides alignment guides and text labels appear, indicating angles of alignment for the points you rolled over.

Note: *If the alignment guides and text labels seem too elusive, you can change the snapping tolerance to make them easier to find. Choose Edit > Preferences > Smart Guides (Windows and Mac OS 9) or Illustrator > Preferences > Smart Guides & Slices (Mac OS X). Set the Snapping Tolerance to 2 pt. (Leave other Smart Guides options at their default settings.) Then click OK.*

3 Roll the pointer along the alignment guides until you see the "intersect" text label. This label marks the intersection point of the points you rolled over.

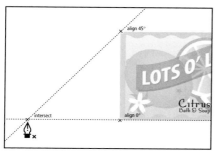

Smart Guides indicate alignment points, angles, and intersection points.

Now that you've practiced, you're ready to use Smart Guides to draw the side panels for the box.

4 Roll the mouse pointer over the bottom left anchor point on the box top. Then click the anchor point with the pen tool to create the first point of the longer side panel for the box.

5 Roll the pointer slowly downward from the anchor point. Use the alignment guide and the "align 90°" text label to align the pointer with the left side of the box top.

By default, Smart Guides show alignment guides and points for 0°, 45°, and 90° angles. You can change Smart Guides to show alignment guides and points for other angles.

See "Using Smart Guides" in online Help or Chapter 4 in the Adobe Illustrator User Guide.

6 Click with the pen tool along the alignment guide to create the bottom left corner point of the longer side panel (so that the side panel is about one-third the height of the box top).

Roll tool pointer to see Smart Guides.   *Click alignment guides to draw points.*

Now you'll create the right edge of the side panel in the same manner and use the alignment guides to create the bottom edge of the side panel precisely.

7 Roll over the bottom right corner point of the box top. Don't click the mouse button; just let it display the position of the corner point.

8 Roll the mouse pointer slowly downward from the anchor point to view the alignment guide and the "align 90°" text label.

9 Continue rolling downward along the alignment guide until a perpendicular alignment guide and the "intersect" text label appear, marking the lower right corner of the side panel.

Roll over anchor points and roll along alignment guide to see intersection point.

10 Click the intersect point to create the lower right anchor point for the side panel.

Now you'll complete the side panel.

11 Roll upward and click the bottom right anchor point of the box top to create the top right anchor point for the side panel.

12 Click the upper left anchor point of the side panel to close the path (point A in the following illustration).

You'll use alignment guides in a similar manner to create the shorter side panel for the box.

13 With the pen tool still selected, Shift-click the same point (A) you just clicked in step 12 to close the path. This creates the upper right anchor point for the shorter side panel.

14 Roll over the upper left anchor point of the box top (point B in the following illustration).

You'll use angle alignment guides and intersection points to create the top edge of the shorter panel.

15 Roll down to the left at a 45° angle to find the intersection between the 45° alignment guide of the box top upper left corner and the 0° alignment guide for the upper right corner of the shorter side panel (point C in the following illustration). Then click the intersection point to create the upper left anchor point for the shorter side panel.

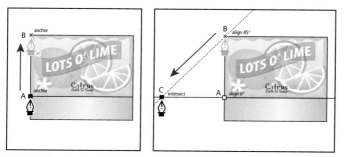

Shift-click point A, roll up to point B and along alignment guide to display intersection point (C).

Now you'll use alignment guides to create the left edge of the shorter panel.

16 Roll over the lower left corner of the longer side panel (point E in the following illustration); then roll slowly to the left to find the intersection point between the 0° alignment guide of the longer side panel and the 90° alignment guide of the upper left corner of the shorter side panel (point D in the following illustration). Then click the intersection point to create the lower left anchor point for the shorter side panel.

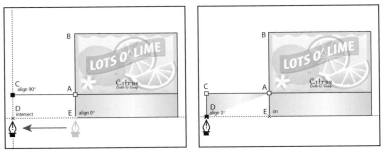

Roll over point E to see intersection point (D).   Click point D to create anchor point.

17 Click the lower left corner of the longer side panel (point E) to create the lower right anchor point for the shorter side panel.

18 Click the upper right corner of the shorter side panel to close the path (point A in the illustration on page 365).

Adding depth with fills

Now you'll paint the panels. By painting with various shades of color, you can create the illusion of shading and depth.

1 Select the selection tool (⬉), and select the shorter side panel.

2 In the Swatches palette, click the Bright Yellow-Green swatch to fill the shorter panel. Choose None for the Stroke.

3 With the selection tool, click the longer side panel to select it.

4 In the Swatches palette, click the Pale Yellow-Green swatch to fill the longer panel. Choose None for the Stroke.

Select longer side panel.   *Select color.*

5 Click outside the artwork to deselect the side panel. Then choose File > Save to save your work.

Using brushes to decorate the panels

Next you'll use the paintbrush tool and custom brushes to add illustrations to the box's side panels.

1 Select the paintbrush tool (✐).

2 In the toolbox, set the Fill to None.

Brushes apply art to the stroke of a path. Use a fill of None when painting with brushes to avoid filling the brushed path with color. For more information on applying brushes to paths, see Lesson 5, "Working with Brushes."

3 Click the Brushes tab to bring the palette to the front of its group. (Choose Window > Brushes to bring the palette to the front.) If necessary, resize the palette to see all of its brushes.

The Brushes palette displays the default brushes provided with the Illustrator program. The Brushes palette also includes a brush created specially for this lesson, the Lime Scatter brush. (You won't see the Lime Scatter brush when you open the Brushes palette in other lessons.)

4 In the Brushes palette, select the Lime Scatter brush.

5 Paint a wavy stroke on the shorter side panel. (Make sure that the brush stroke stays within the panel.)

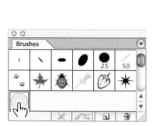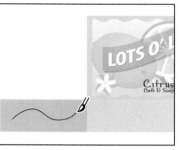

Select brush in Brushes palette.   *Draw with paintbrush tool.*

6 Use the selection tool ( ) to select the flower on the box top.

7 In the Brushes palette, select New Brush from the Brushes palette menu.

8 Select New Scatter Brush, and click OK.

9 In the Scatter Brush Options dialog box, name the brush **Flower**. Then set the following options by entering values in the text boxes or dragging the sliders, pressing Tab to move between text boxes:

• For Size, choose Random. Set the size values to **36%** and **70%**.

• For Spacing, choose Random. Set the spacing values to **65%** and **118%**.

• For Scatter, leave the default setting (Fixed, 0%).

• For Rotation, choose Random. Set the rotation values to **60%** and **–10%**.

Select object to use as new brush.   *Enter settings for new brush.*

10 Click OK.

For more information about making your own brushes, see "Creating brushes" in online Help or Chapter 3 in the Adobe Illustrator User Guide.

11 Click outside the artwork to deselect the flower.

12 In the toolbox, set the Fill to None.

13 In the Brushes palette, select the new Flower Scatter brush. Then use the paintbrush tool to paint a wavy stroke on the longer side panel. (Make sure that the brush stroke stays within the panel.)

14 Select the selection tool. In the artwork, Shift-click the Lime Scatter brush stroke and the Flower Scatter brush stroke.

15 Choose Object > Expand Appearance.

The Expand Appearance command creates closed paths from stroked paths—similar to the Create Outlines command used to create closed paths from type. You must expand brushstrokes to be able to transform the paths, as you'll do in the following sections.

Select brush strokes.   *Expand strokes to create closed paths.*

16 Click away from the artwork to deselect it, and choose File > Save to save your work.

Constructing the box

To join the box elements into a three-dimensional object, you'll use the free transform tool and the rotate tool to shear and rotate the box top and panels.

As you'll see, you can perform the same transformation several ways. When you shear an object, you skew the object along the axis that you designate. Rotating an object turns it around a fixed point that you designate. See Lesson 6, "Transforming Objects," to learn more about the various transformation tools.

The type used in the box top artwork has been converted to outlines using the Type > Create Outlines command. Type must be converted to outlines before you can use the free transform tool to shear, distort, or change perspective in the type

Transforming selected objects

You can transform selected objects—that is, change their size, shape, and orientation by selecting one or more objects and then applying various transformation actions on them. For example, you can change the angle of an object by rotating it, or add perspective to an angle by shearing it.

To transform an object, you can use the free transform tool, individual transformation tools, the Transform palette, or the Transform Effect command:

- *Use the free transform tool to rotate, scale, reflect, shear, and distort objects quickly.*

- *Use the transformation tools to change the size, shape, and orientation of selected objects. The transformation tools are the rotate tool, scale tool, reflect tool, and shear tool. You can also use individual transform dialog boxes to specify numeric values, to preview the transformation before applying it, and to select other transformation options.*

- *Use the Transform palette to modify selected objects by changing information in the palette.*

- *Use the Transform Effect command to transform a selection, group, or layer without altering the original artwork.*

–From online Help and the Adobe Illustrator User Guide, Chapter 5

If you want your type to remain editable while distorting it, select the type and choose Effect > Distort & Transform > Free Distort. For more information on applying editable effects, see Lesson 9, "Using Appearance Attributes, Styles, and Effects."

You'll start by grouping the elements of each box panel so that you can work with each panel as a unit.

1 In the Layers palette, click the padlock icon (🔒) next to the Banner layer to unlock that layer.

2 Select the selection tool ( ), and drag a selection marquee over the box top to select all the objects that are part of the top.

3 Choose Object > Group to group the objects in the box top.

4 Repeat steps 1 and 2 with the two side panels to select and group each panel separately.

Select and group box top.   *Select and group side panels.*

Next you'll shear and rotate the box top to give it perspective.

5 Use the selection tool to select the box top group.

6 Select the free transform tool ( ); then position the pointer on the center point on the right side of the box top.

7 Click, and without releasing the mouse button, press Ctrl (Windows) or Command (Mac OS), and drag the center point down to shear the box top downward.

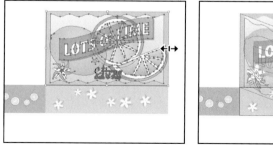

Select object.   *Drag bounding box handle with free transform tool to shear.*

8 Select the rotate tool ( ), and click at the box top's lower left corner to set the point of origin for the rotation.

9 Hold down the Shift key, click near the right edge of the box top, and drag counter-clockwise to rotate the box top 45°. (The pointer can be inside or outside the box top when you drag.) Holding down the Shift key constrains the rotation so that it snaps to a 45° angle.

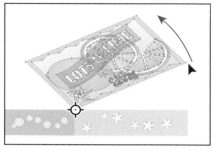

Drag with rotate tool to rotate object around point of origin.

Now you'll fit the longer side panel to the box top and shear the panel to adjust its perspective.

10 Use the selection tool to select the longer side panel.

11 Select the free transform tool.

12 Position the pointer on the center point on the right side of the panel. Click, and without releasing the mouse button, press Ctrl (Windows) or Command (Mac OS), and drag the center point up to shear the panel upward, until the upper right corner of the panel meets the lower right corner of the box top. Then release the mouse button.

To complete the box, you'll fit the shorter side panel to the box top and shear the shorter panel.

13 Press Ctrl (Windows) or Command (Mac OS) to temporarily select the selection tool, and then select the shorter side panel.

Pressing Ctrl/Command temporarily activates the selection tool (or the direct-selection or group-selection tool, whichever was used most recently) when another tool is selected in the toolbox.

14 Repeat step 11, dragging the center point on the left side of the panel upward, until the upper left corner of the panel meets the upper left corner of the box top.

Select object.

Drag with free transform tool to shear.

As a final step, you'll rotate and reposition the artwork.

15 Press Ctrl (Windows) or Command (Mac OS) to temporarily select the selection tool, and drag a marquee over the box top and side panels to select all elements in the artwork.

16 Choose Object > Group.

17 Click the selection tool in the toolbox, and drag the grouped box to the center of the artboard.

18 Move the pointer near any of the four corners of the artwork until you see the rotation pointer, and then drag clockwise to rotate the artwork.

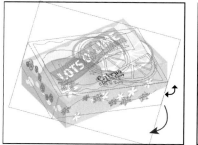

Drag outside bounding box corner to rotate artwork.

Result

19 Click outside the artwork to deselect the box.

20 Choose File > Save to save the file. Choose File > Close to close the file.

This completes the lesson on creating a three-dimensional box.

Review questions

1 How do you quickly scale an object using its bounding box?

2 What features of Smart Guides help you to draw an object that aligns precisely with another object in the artwork?

3 What transformations can you perform with the free transform tool?

4 How do you edit text that is contained in an envelope?

Review answers

1 With the bounding box, you can scale objects easily by dragging the selection or a handle (one of the hollow squares surrounding the selected objects). The bounding box creates a temporary border around the selected object. You see an outline of the selection as you drag it. When you release the mouse button, the object snaps to the current border created by the bounding box, and you see the object's outline move.

2 Smart Guides have the following features to help you align objects precisely as you draw:

• Smart Guides snap objects to guides when the objects fall within a specified tolerance (distance from the guides).

• Text labels identify anchor points, intersection points, and alignment angles when the pointer is positioned over the points in the artwork.

• Alignment guides indicate alignment angles or intersection angles when you roll over one or more anchor points with the mouse, then roll away from the anchor point or points.

3 You can distort, reflect, rotate, scale, and shear objects with the free transform tool.

4 To edit text contained in an envelope, choose Object > Envelope Distort > Edit Contents. Edit the text as desired. Then choose Object > Envelope Distort > Edit Envelope.

1-1: **Toolbox Overview**

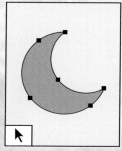

The selection tool (V) selects entire objects.

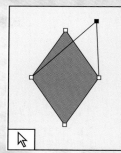

The direct-selection tool (A) selects points or path segments within objects.

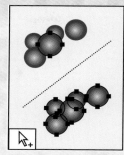

The group-selection tool (Shift+A) selects objects and groups within groups.

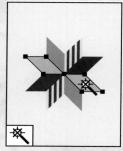

The magic wand tool (Y) selects objects of similar attributes.

The direct-select lasso tool (Q) selects points or path segments within objects.

The lasso tool selects entire objects.

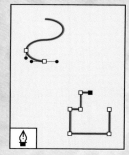

The pen tool (P) draws straight and curved lines to create objects.

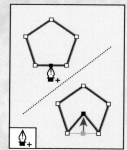

The add-anchor-point tool (+) adds anchor points to paths.

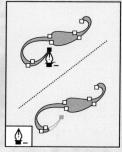

The delete-anchor-point tool (-) deletes anchor points from paths.

The convert-anchor-point tool (Shift+C) changes smooth points to corner points and vice versa.

The type tool (T) creates individual type and type containers and lets you enter and edit type.

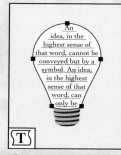

The area type tool changes closed paths to type containers and lets you enter and edit type within them.

The path type tool *changes paths to type paths and lets you enter and edit type on them.*

The vertical type tool *creates vertical type and vertical type containers and lets you enter and edit vertical type.*

The vertical area-type tool *changes closed paths to vertical type containers, and lets you enter and edit type within them.*

The vertical path-type tool *changes closed paths to vertical type paths and lets you enter and edit type on them.*

The line segment tool (\) *draws individual straight line segments.*

The arc tool *draws individual concave or convex curve segments.*

The spiral tool (Shift+L) *draws clockwise and counterclockwise spirals.*

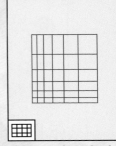

The rectangular grid tool *draws rectangular grids.*

The polar grid tool *draws circular chart grids.*

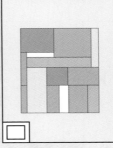

The rectangle tool (M) *draws squares and rectangles.*

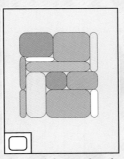

The rounded rectangle tool (Shift+M) *draws squares and rectangles with rounded corners.*

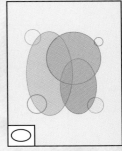

The ellipse tool (L) *draws circles and ovals.*

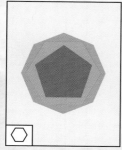

The polygon tool (Shift+L) *draws regular, multisided shapes.*

The star tool (Shift+L) *draws stars.*

The flare tool *creates lens-flare or solar-flare-like effects.*

The paintbrush tool (B) *draws freehand and calligraphic lines, as well as art and patterns on paths.*

The pencil tool (N) *draws and edits freehand lines.*

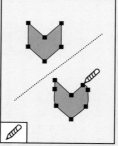

The smooth tool *smooths Bézier paths.*

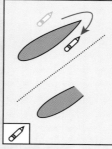

The erase tool *erases paths and anchor points from the artwork.*

The rotate tool (R) *rotates objects around a fixed point.*

The reflect tool (O) *flips objects over a fixed axis.*

The twirl tool (Shift+R) *twirls objects around a fixed point.*

The scale tool (S) *resizes objects around a fixed point.*

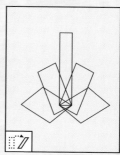

The shear tool (Shift+O) *skews objects around a fixed point.*

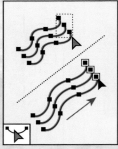

The reshape tool *smooths or changes a path while retaining the path's overall shape.*

The warp tool (Shift+R) *molds objects with the movement of the cursor (like molding clay, for example).*

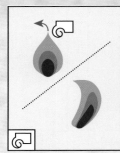

The twirl tool *creates swirling distortions within an object.*

The pucker tool *deflates an object.*

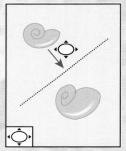

The bloat tool *inflates an object.*

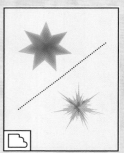

The scallop tool *adds many curved details to the outline of an object.*

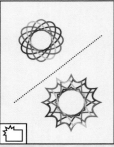

The crystallize tool *adds many spiked details to the outline of an object.*

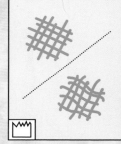

The wrinkle tool *adds wrinkle-like details to the outline of an object.*

The free transform tool (E) *scales, rotates, or skews a selection.*

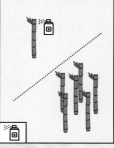

The symbol sprayer tool (Shift+S) *places multiple symbol instances as a set on the artboard.*

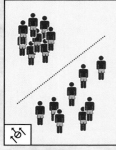

The symbol shifter tool *moves symbol instances away from each other.*

The symbol scruncher tool *moves symbol instances closer to each other.*

The symbol sizer tool *resizes symbol instances.*

The symbol spinner tool *rotates symbol instances.*

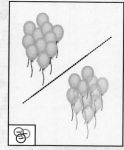

The symbol stainer tool *colorizes symbol instances.*

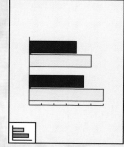

The symbol screener tool *applies opacity to symbol instances.*

The symbol styler tool *applies the selected style to symbol instances.*

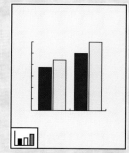

The column graph tool (J) *positions columns vertically.*

The stacked column graph tool *stacks columns on top of one another.*

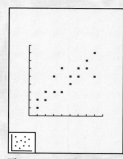

The bar graph tool *positions columns horizontally.*

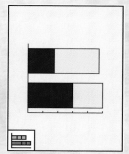

The stacked bar graph tool *stacks columns and positions them horizontally.*

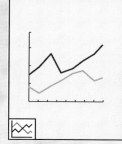

The line graph tool *shows the trend of one or more subjects over time.*

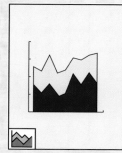

The area graph tool *emphasizes totals as well as changes in values.*

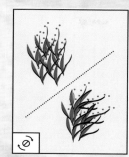

The scatter graph tool *plots data as paired sets of X and Y coordinates.*

1-1: **Toolbox Overview (cont.)**

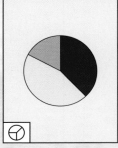

The pie graph tool *creates a circle graph with wedges showing relative percentages of the compared values.*

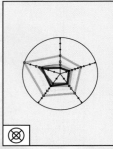

The radar graph tool *uses a circle to compare sets of values at given points in time or in particular categories.*

The mesh tool **(U)** *creates multicolored objects and applies a mesh for adjusting color shading.*

The gradient tool **(G)** *adjusts the beginning and ending points of gradients within objects.*

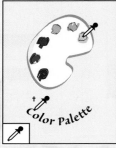

The eyedropper tool **(I)** *samples paint or type attributes from objects.*

The paint bucket tool **(K)** *fills objects with the current paint or type attributes.*

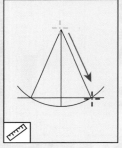

The measure tool *measures the distance between two points.*

The blend tool **(W)** *creates a blend between the color and shape of multiple objects.*

The auto trace tool *traces the outlines of objects.*

The slice tool **(Shift+K)** *creates Web slices.*

The slice select tool *selects Web slices.*

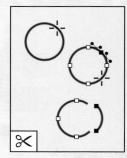

The scissors tool **(C)** *splits paths.*

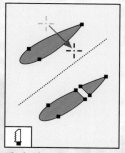

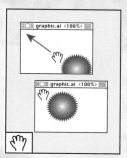

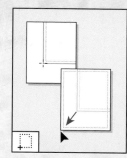

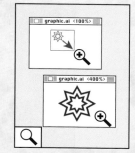

The knife tool *slices objects and paths.*

The hand tool *(H) moves the Illustrator artboard within the illustration window.*

The page tool *(Shift+H) adjusts the page grid to control where artwork appears on the printed page.*

The zoom tool *(Z) increases and decreases the magnification in the illustration window.*

Illustrator Tour

Lesson 1

Lesson 2

Lesson 3

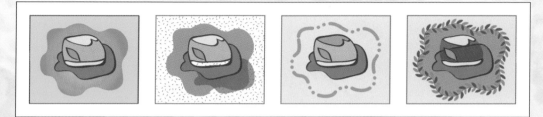

3-1: **Global and nonglobal color**

Global process color

Global colors are created by selecting the Global option in the Swatch Options dialog box and are identified by a white corner icon on the swatch. Tints of global colors are chosen using the Color palette.

When the process mix of a global color is edited in the Swatch Options dialog box, any object in the artwork painted with that color is automatically updated. Individual tints are retained, eliminating the need to select and repaint each object.

Nonglobal process color

CMYK mix for a nonglobal process color swatch is edited using the Swatch Options dialog box. Edits made using the Color palette will not update the saved swatch.

When the color is edited using the Swatch Options dialog box, only the swatch and any currently selected artwork are updated—other artwork painted with that color is unaffected.

Lesson 4

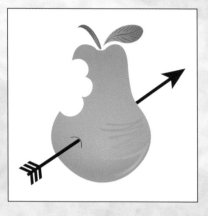

Lesson 5

5-1: **Colorization methods**

None, Tints, Tints and Shades, Hue Shift

When you choose a colorization method for a brush, the current stroke color is applied to the brush. (To apply a different color to the brush after choosing a colorization method, select the brush and select a new stroke color.)

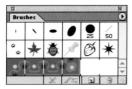 

To apply a colorization method: Select the brush in the Brushes palette, open the Brush Options dialog box, and then select a colorization method from the Method pop-up menu. (The default colorization method varies among different brushes.)

Note: Colorization changes appear when you apply brushes to artwork. Changes do not appear in the Brush Options dialog box or the Brushes palette.

 None leaves the brush color unchanged.

 Tints applies a single hue (the stroke color) to the brush. Black areas in the original brush take on the new hue, and lighter areas take on the new hue with white added.

Tints and Shades applies a single hue (the stroke color) to the brush. Darker areas take on the hue with black added; lighter areas take on the hue with white added.

Hue Shift shifts the selected color to the new hue. All other colors in the brush shift in relation to the selected color.

More about Hue Shift

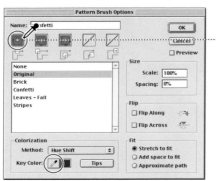

To apply Hue Shift colorization: Choose Hue Shift from the Method pop-up menu. Then click the Key Color eyedropper, and select a key color in the brush example in the dialog box. The key color shifts to the current stroke color, and other colors in the brush shift around the color wheel, according to their relation to the key color.

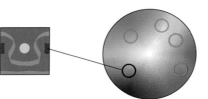

Key color selected in the brush example, and other colors indicated in relation to the key color in the color wheel

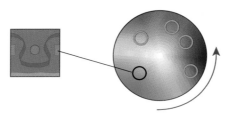

Key color shifted in the brush example, and other colors shifted in relation to the key color in the brush example and the color wheel

Lesson 6

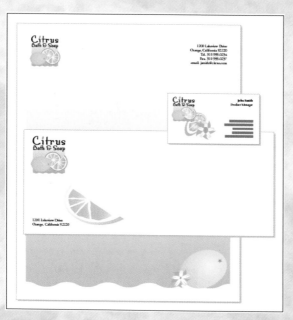

Lesson 7

8-1: **Smooth-color blends**

Starting colors

Blends between subtle changes in color require fewer steps.

Starting colors

Blends between distinct changes in color require more steps.

8-2: **Modifying blends**

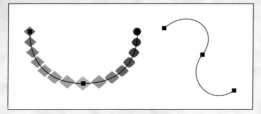

Before applying Replace Spine command

After applying Replace Spine command

After applying Reverse Spine command

Lesson 9

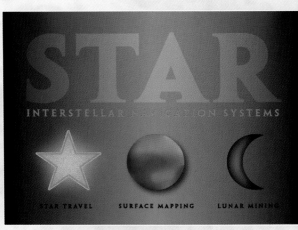

Lesson 10

11-1: **Creating gradient mesh objects**

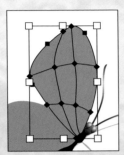 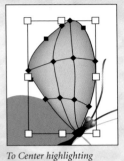 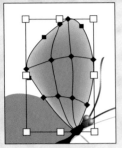

Flat appearance
(no highlighting)

To Center highlighting

To Edge highlighting

11-2: **Modifying a gradient mesh**

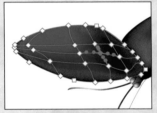  

Gradient mesh applied to object

Mesh points selected before applying
color

Moving a mesh point vertically

 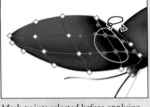 

Mesh point added with new color
applied

Deleting a mesh line

Result of color blending

11-3: **Changing the opacity of a gradient mesh**

Mesh objects selected

Opacity lowered

12-1: **Pathfinder Gallery**

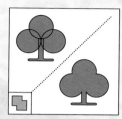

Add to Shape Area *creates one shape from overlapping shapes.*

Subtract from Shape Area *subtracts the front object from the back object.*

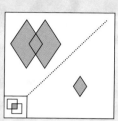

Intersect *creates a new object from shared space.*

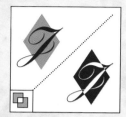

Exclude *removes an overlapping area.*

Divide *creates independent objects from component faces.*

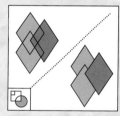

Trim *removes the hidden part of filled paths.*

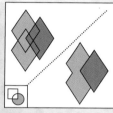

Merge *removes the hidden part of filled paths and merges overlapping objects.*

Crop *divides shapes and crops images.*

Outline *creates independent lines divided at each intersection.*

Minus Back *subtracts back object from front.*

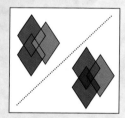

Hard Mix *mixes colors of overlapping areas using the highest value of each color component.*

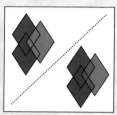

Soft Mix *makes the top color semitransparent and applies the specified transparency to overlapping colors.*

13-1: **Separating colors**

Artwork can consist of spot colors, process colors (global or nonglobal), registration colors, or a combination. When you separate artwork containing spot colors, a separate plate is created for each spot color. The plate contains only objects of that specific color.

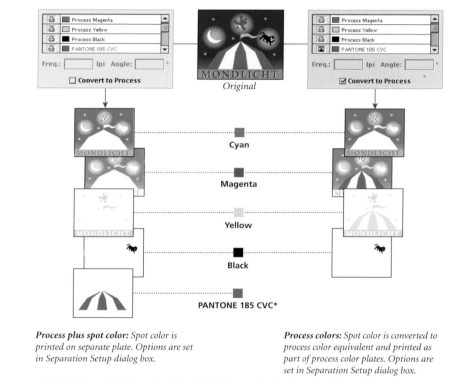

Original

Cyan

Magenta

Yellow

Black

PANTONE 185 CVC*

Process plus spot color: *Spot color is printed on separate plate. Options are set in Separation Setup dialog box.*

Process colors: *Spot color is converted to process color equivalent and printed as part of process color plates. Options are set in Separation Setup dialog box.*

* PANTONE 185 CVC is simulated here. This book was printed using only the four process colors.

13-2: **Overprint option**

Colors knocked out by default

Overprint option selected for shadow

13-3: **RGB and CMYK color models**

Additive colors (RGB)

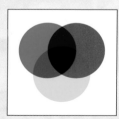

Subtractive colors (CMYK)

Lesson 14

14-1: **Color filters**

Adjust filter on placed photo: Original, and after increasing Magenta and Yellow

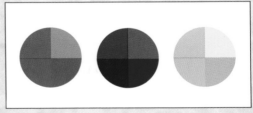

Saturate filter: Original, and after saturating and desaturating

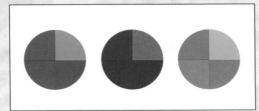

Adjust filter on artwork: Original, and after increasing and decreasing Magenta

Invert filter: Original, and after inverting

Illustrator art

After rasterizing

Dry Brush

Film Grain

Plastic Wrap

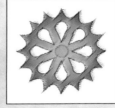

Rough Pastels

Smudge Stick

Sponge

Watercolor

Radial Blur

Accented Edges

Angled Strokes

Crosshatch

Ink Outlines

Sprayed Strokes

Sumi-e

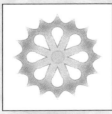

Diffuse Glow

Ocean Ripple

14-2: **Filters Gallery (cont.)**

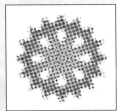

Color Halftone

Crystallize

Mezzotint

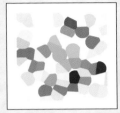

Pointillize

Bas Relief

Chalk & Charcoal

Chrome

Conté Crayon

Graphic Pen

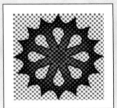

Halftone Pattern

Note Paper

Photocopy

Reticulation

Torn Edges

Water Paper

Glowing Edges

Mosaic Tiles

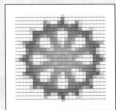

Patchwork

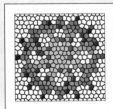

Stained Glass

Texturizer

Lesson 15

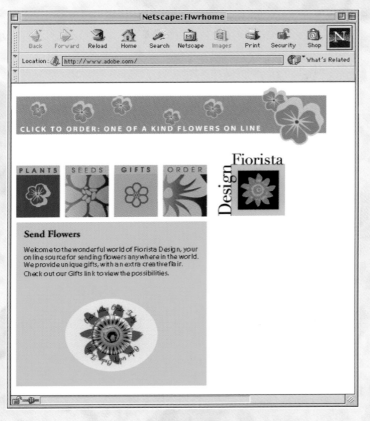

15-1: **Dithering examples**

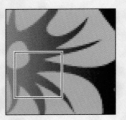

Artwork painted with CMYK colors   *Colors dithered in GIF image*   *No color dithering in GIF image*

Lesson 13

13 Printing Artwork and Producing Color Separations

The quality and color of your final printed output are determined by the process you follow to prepare an image for print. Whether you're printing a draft of your work on a desktop printer or outputting color separations to be printed on a commercial press, learning fundamental printing concepts helps ensure that your printed results meet your expectations.

In this lesson, you'll learn about the following:

- Different types of printing requirements and printing devices.
- Printing concepts and printing terminology.
- Basic color principles.
- How to separate your color artwork into its component colors for output to print.
- How to use spot colors for two-color printing.
- Special considerations when outputting to print.

Printing: An overview

When you print a document from a computer, data is sent from the document to the printing device, either to be printed on paper or to be converted to a positive or negative image on film. For black-and-white, grayscale, or low quantities of color artwork, many people use desktop printers. However, if you require large quantities of printed output, such as a brochure or magazine ad, you'll need to prepare your artwork for output on a commercial printing press. Printing on a commercial press is an art that requires time and experience to perfect. In addition to close communication with a printing professional, learning basic printing concepts and terminology will help you produce printed results that meet your expectations.

Note: This lesson assumes that you have a desktop printer for use with the exercises. If you don't have a desktop printer available, read the sections and skip the step-by-step instructions.

Different printing requirements require different printing processes. To determine your printing requirements, consider the following: What effect do you want the printed piece to have on your audience? Will your artwork be printed in black and white? Color? Does it require special paper? How many printed copies do you need? If you're printing in color, is precise color matching necessary, or will approximate color matching suffice?

Take a minute to consider several types of printing jobs:

- A black-and-white interoffice newsletter, requiring a low quantity of printed copies. For this type of printing job, you can generally use a 300- to 600-dpi desktop laser printer to output the original, and then use a copy machine to reproduce the larger quantity.

• A business card using black and one other color. The term *two-color* printing typically refers to printing with black and one other color, although it may also refer to printing with two colors that are not black. Two-color printing is less expensive than four-color printing and lets you select exact color matches, called *spot* colors, which can be important for logos. For precise color matching, two-color printing is done on a printing press; if only an approximate color match is required, you might use a desktop color printer.

• A party invitation using two colors and tints of those colors. In addition to printing two solid colors, you can print tints of the colors to add depth to your printed artwork. Two-color printing is often done on colored paper that complements the ink colors and might be done on a desktop color printer or on a printing press, depending on the desired quantity and the degree of color matching required.

• A newspaper. Newspapers are typically printed on a printing press because they are time-sensitive publications printed in large quantities. In addition, newspapers are generally printed on large rolls of newsprint, which are then trimmed and folded to the correct size.

• A fashion magazine or catalog requiring accurate color reproduction. *Four-color* printing refers to mixing the four process ink colors (cyan, magenta, yellow, and black, or CMYK) for printed output. When accurate color reproduction is required, printing is done on a printing press using CMYK inks. CMYK inks can reproduce a good amount of the visible color spectrum, with the exception of neon or metallic colors. You'll learn more about color models in the next section.

About printing devices

Now that you've looked at several types of publications and different ways to reproduce them, you'll begin learning basic printing concepts and printing terminology.

Halftone screens

To reproduce any type of artwork, a printing device typically breaks down the artwork into a series of dots of various sizes called a *halftone screen*. Black dots are used to print black-and-white or grayscale artwork. For color artwork, a halftone screen is created for each ink color (cyan, magenta, yellow, and black); these then overlay one another at different angles to produce the full range of printed color. To see a good example of how individual halftone screens overlay each other at different angles on a printed page, look at a color comics page through a magnifying glass.

The size of the dots in a halftone screen determines how light or dark colors appear in print. The smaller the dot, the lighter the color appears; the larger the dot, the darker the color appears.

Enlarged detail showing dots in halftone screen

Screen frequency

Screen frequency (also called line screen, screen ruling, or halftone frequency) refers to the number of rows or lines of dots used to render an image on film or paper. In addition, the rows of dots are broken down into individual squares, called *halftone cells*. Screen frequency is measured in lines per inch (lpi) and is a fixed value you can set for your printing device.

As a general rule, higher screen frequencies produce finer detail in printed output. This is because the higher the screen frequency, the smaller the halftone cells, and subsequently, the smaller the halftone dot in the cell.

However, a high screen frequency alone does not guarantee high-quality output. The screen frequency must be appropriate to the paper, the inks, and the printer or printing press used to output the artwork. Your printing professional will help you select the appropriate line screen value for your artwork and output device.

Low-screen ruling (65 lpi) often used to print newsletters.

High-screen rulings (150–200 lpi) used for high-quality books.

Output device resolution

The *resolution* of a printing device describes the number of dots the printing device has available to *render*, or create, a halftone dot. The higher the output device resolution, the higher the quality of the printed output. For example, the printed quality of an image output at 2400 dots per inch (dpi) is higher than the printed quality of an image output at 300 dpi. Adobe Illustrator is resolution-independent and will always print at the printing device's highest resolution capability.

The quality of printed output depends on the relationship between the resolution of the output device (dpi) and the screen frequency (lpi). As a general rule, high-resolution output devices use higher screen frequency values to produce the highest quality images. For example, an imagesetter with a resolution of 2400 dpi and a screen frequency of 177 lpi produces a higher quality image than a desktop printer with a resolution of 300 to 600 dpi and a screen frequency of 85 lpi.

About color

Color is produced by a computer monitor and printing device using two different *color models* (methods for displaying and measuring color). The human eye perceives color according to the wavelength of the light it receives. Light containing the full color spectrum is perceived as white; in the absence of light, the eye perceives black.

The *gamut* of a color model is the range of colors that can be displayed or printed. The largest color gamut is that viewed in nature; all other color gamuts produce a subset of nature's color gamut. The two most common color models are red, green, and blue (RGB), the method by which monitors display color; and cyan, magenta, yellow, and black (CMYK), the method by which images are printed using four process ink colors.

The RGB color model

A large percentage of the visible spectrum of color can be represented by mixing three basic components of colored light in various proportions. These components are known as the *additive colors*: red, green, and blue (RGB). The RGB color model is called the additive color model because various percentages of each colored light are added to create color. All monitors display color using the RGB color model.

The CMYK color model

If 100% of red, green, or blue is subtracted from white light, the resulting color is cyan, magenta, or yellow. For example, if an object absorbs (subtracts) 100% red light and reflects green and blue, cyan is the perceived color. Cyan, magenta, and yellow are called the subtractive primaries, and they form the basis for printed colors. In addition to cyan, magenta, and yellow, black ink is used to generate true black and to deepen the shadows in images. These four inks (CMYK) are often called *process* colors because they are the four standard inks used in the printing process.

For an illustration of RGB and CMYK color models, see figure 13-3 in the color section.

Spot colors

Whereas process colors are reproduced using cyan, magenta, yellow, and black inks, spot colors are premixed inks used in place of, or in addition to, CMYK colors. Spot colors can be selected from color-matching systems, such as the PANTONE or TOYO™ color libraries. Many spot colors can be converted to their process color equivalents when printed; however, some spot colors, such as metallic or iridescent colors, require their own plate on press.

Use spot color in the following situations:

• To save money on one-color and two-color print jobs. (When your printing budget won't allow for four-color printing, you can still print relatively inexpensively using one or two colors.)

• To print logos or other graphic elements that require precise color matching.

• To print special inks, such as metallic, fluorescent, or pearlescent colors.

Getting started

Before you begin, you must restore the default preferences for Adobe Illustrator. Then you'll open the art file for this lesson.

1 To ensure that the tools and palettes function exactly as described in this lesson, delete or deactivate (by renaming) the Adobe Illustrator 10.0 preferences file. See "Restoring default preferences" on page 4.

2 Start Adobe Illustrator.

3 Choose File > Open, and open the L13strt1.ai file in the Lesson13 folder, located inside the Lessons folder within the AICIB folder on your hard drive.

For an illustration of the finished artwork in this lesson, see the color section.

4 Choose File > Save As, name the file **Circus.ai**, and select the Lesson13 folder. Leave the Format option set to Adobe Illustrator® Document, and click Save. In the Illustrator Native Format Options dialog box, select Illustrator 10 Compatibility and click OK.

Color management

Although all color gamuts overlap, they don't match exactly, which is why some colors on your monitor can't be reproduced in print. The colors that can't be reproduced in print are called *out-of-gamut* colors because they are outside the spectrum of printable colors.

To compensate for these differences and to ensure the closest match between on-screen colors and printed colors, Adobe Illustrator includes a color management system (CMS) that lets you select profiles for your monitor and for the output device to which you'll print. Selecting a color profile controls the conversion of RGB values to CMYK values at print time. To select a color profile, you use the Color Settings command.

1 Choose Edit > Color Settings.

2 In the Color Settings dialog box, choose U.S. Prepress Defaults from the Settings menu.

In this lesson, you'll use one of the predefined sets of color management settings provided in Adobe Illustrator. Each set has corresponding color profile and conversion options designed to preserve consistent color for a particular publishing workflow under typical conditions. For more information on color management settings, see "Using predefined color management settings" in online Help or Chapter 7 in the Adobe Illustrator User Guide.

3 Leave the settings and options at their default values. Click OK.

Printing black-and-white proofs

As a general rule, you should print black-and-white proofs of all your documents at different stages of your work to check the layout and to verify the accuracy of text and graphics before preparing the document for final output.

Now you'll print a draft of the Circus.ai file.

1 In the Circus.ai file, notice the *crop marks*, the pairs of lines at each corner of the artwork. Crop marks define where the artwork is trimmed after it is printed. The crop marks indicate a *bleed,* the area of artwork that falls outside the crop marks, and which will be removed when the printed artwork is trimmed. The bleed is used to ensure that the artwork prints to the edge of the trimmed page. For more information on bleed, see "Specifying the bleed area" on page 414.

You can set crop marks where you want them directly in the artwork. See "Setting crop marks and trim marks" in online Help or Chapter 16 in the Adobe Illustrator User Guide.

2 If you're not connected to a black-and-white printer, go on to the next section.

3 Choose File > Print, and click OK (Windows) or Print (Mac OS).

The circus logo is printed in black, white, and shades of gray. Next, you'll soft-proof the color on your monitor screen.

Soft-proofing colors

In a color-managed work flow, you can use the precision of color profiles to soft-proof your document directly on the monitor. Soft-proofing lets you preview on-screen how your document's colors will look when reproduced on a particular output device.

The reliability of soft-proofing completely depends, however, on the quality of your monitor, your monitor profile, and the ambient lighting conditions of your workstation area. For information on creating a monitor profile, see "Creating an ICC monitor profile" in online Help or Chapter 7 in the Adobe Illustrator User Guide.

1 Choose View > Proof Setup > Custom. The profile is set to U.S. Web Coated (SWOP) v2. Leave it set to this profile and click OK.

The View > Proof Colors option is selected by default (indicated by a check mark) so that you can view the artwork as it will look when printed to the selected standard—here, U.S. Web Coated (SWOP) v2.

Next, you'll change the profile to see what the image will look like if printed on a different output device.

2 Choose View > Proof Setup > Custom.

3 Use the Profile menu to select Euroscale Uncoated v2, and click OK. Because the view is still set to Proof Colors, the image preview automatically shifts colors to display what it would look like were it printed according to the Euroscale Uncoated profile.

You'll now return the settings to the SWOP settings.

4 Choose View > Proof Setup > Custom. Set the profile to U.S. Web Coated (SWOP) v2 and click OK.

5 Choose View > Proof Colors to turn off the soft-proofing preview.

Next, you'll work with printing color artwork.

Using the Document Info command

Before you take your color artwork to a prepress professional or begin the process of creating color separations on your own, use the Document Info command to generate and save a list of information about all the elements of your artwork file. The Document Info command displays a palette of information on the objects, linked or placed files, colors, gradients, patterns, and fonts in your document.

If you're working with prepress professionals, be sure to provide them with the Document Info list before delivering your files; they can help you determine what you'll need to include with your artwork. For example, if your artwork uses a font that the prepress house does not have, you'll need to bring or supply a copy of the font with your artwork.

1 Choose Window > Document Info. The Document Info palette appears.

2 In the Document Info palette, select different subjects about the document from the palette menu in the upper right corner. The list box displays information about each subject you select.

3 If you have an object selected in the artwork, choose Selection Only from the Document Info palette menu to display information only on that selected object. A check mark indicates that the Selection Only option is turned on.

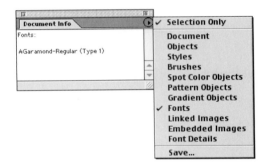

You can also view or print the entire contents of the Document Info palette by saving it and then opening it in a text editor.

4 To save the Document Info text, choose Save from the palette menu, enter a name for the Document Info file, and click Save. You can open the file in any text editor to review and print the contents of the file.

5 When you have looked through the information on the file, you can leave the Document Info palette open on-screen or close it.

Creating color separations

To print color artwork on a printing press, you must first separate the composite art into its component colors: cyan, magenta, yellow, and black, and any spot colors, if applicable. The process of breaking composite artwork into its component colors is called *color separation.*

You set separation options in the Separation Setup dialog box. It's important to note that before setting separation options, you need to discuss the specific requirements of your print job with your printing professional. (You cannot separate to a non-PostScript® printer.)

For an illustration of color separations, see figure 13-1 in the color section.

1 Make sure that the Circus.ai artwork is still open.

2 Select the selection tool (↖) in the toolbox. Then click various objects in the artwork to select them.

As you select different objects, notice that the Color palette reflects the current color's attributes. For example, if you click the flag atop the tent, a PANTONE color swatch appears in the Color palette; if you click the red or green stripe in the clown, the color is mixed using CMYK values.

3 Choose File > Separation Setup.

In this lesson, you'll work with the Separation Setup dialog box until you're ready to print the file.

Important: *To be able to continue with this section, your computer must be connected to a PostScript printer. If you are connected to an ink-jet printer or not connected to a printer, the Separation Setup option will be dimmed in the File menu.*

The Separation Setup dialog box includes options for specifying how the color in the artwork should be separated into its component colors, the output device and line screen to which the artwork will be printed, and whether the separation should be a positive or negative image. Before you can see a preview of your artwork, you must select a printer description file to indicate which output device will be used to print your artwork.

Selecting a printer description file

PostScript Printer Description (PPD) files contain information about the output device, including available page sizes, resolution, available line screen (frequency) values, and the angles of the halftone screens.

1 In the Separation Setup dialog box, click Open PPD.

2 Navigate to the General.ppd file, located in the Lesson13 folder, inside the Lessons folder within the AICIB folder on your hard drive. Click Open.

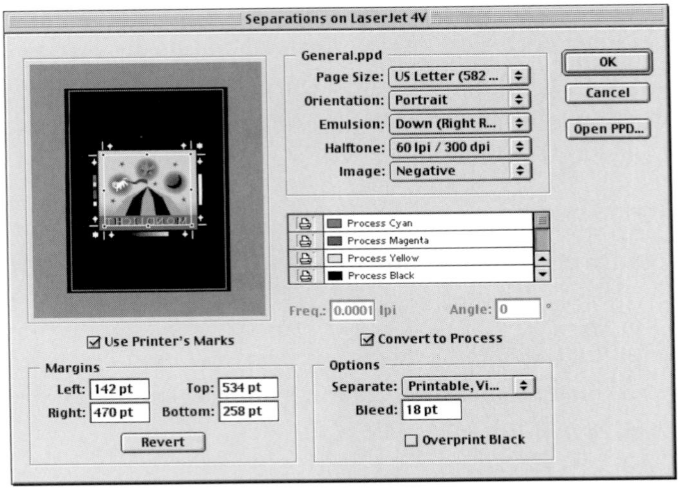

Note: A PostScript Printer Description file with limited selections has been placed in the Lesson13 folder for this exercise. When you install Adobe Illustrator, two PPDs are automatically installed in the Utilities folder within the Adobe Illustrator folder, and additional PPDs are provided on the Adobe Illustrator CD.

The Separation Setup dialog box is updated with general printer parameters, and a preview of your artwork is displayed on the left side of the dialog box. (The preview of your artwork depends on the page size selected in the Page Size menu. Each output device has a variety of page sizes available; select the desired page size from the Page Size menu in the Separation Setup dialog box.)

In addition, printer's marks surround the preview of your artwork. Printer's marks help the printer align the color separations on the press and check the color and density of the inks being used. The preview also includes the crop marks and bleeds from the artwork file. The bleeds are set to 18 points, the default setting (indicated in the Options section of the Separation Setup dialog box).

*A. Star target B. Registration mark
C. Crop mark D. Progressive color bar*

Specifying the bleed area

Bleed is the amount of artwork that falls outside of the printing bounding box, or outside the crop marks and trim marks. You can include bleed in your artwork as a margin of error—to ensure that the ink is still printed to the edge of the page after the page is trimmed or to ensure that an image can be stripped into a keyline in a document. Once you create the artwork that extends into the bleed, you can use Illustrator to specify the extent of the bleed.

Changing the bleed moves the crop marks farther from or closer to the image; however, the crop marks still define the same size printing bounding box.

Small bleed   Large bleed

To specify bleed:

1. Choose File > Separation Setup.

2. In the Options section of the Separation Setup dialog box, enter an amount in the Bleed text box.

By default, Illustrator applies a bleed of 18 points. This means that the artwork extends 18 points beyond the crop marks on your film. The maximum bleed you can set is 72 points; the minimum bleed is 0 points.

The size of the bleed you use depends on its purpose. A press bleed (that is, an image that bleeds off the edge of the printed sheet) should be at least 18 points. If the bleed is to ensure that an image fits a keyline, it needs to be no more than 2 or 3 points. Your print shop can advise you on the size of the bleed necessary for your particular job.

3. Specify other separation options, or click OK.

–From online Help and the Adobe Illustrator User Guide, Chapter 17

Separating colors

The circus artwork is composed of process colors and spot colors, which are displayed in the Separation Setup dialog box. By default, all spot colors are converted to their process color equivalents.

		Process Yellow
		Process Black
		PANTONE 116 CVU
		PANTONE 185 CVC

Indicates spot color will be separated into process color equivalents.

To the left of the process color names, a printer icon is displayed, indicating that a separation will be generated for each color. To the left of the spot color names, a process color icon is displayed, indicating that the spot colors will be converted to their process color equivalents. If you were to print color separations at this point, all the colors, including the spot colors in the artwork, would be separated onto the four process color (CMYK) plates or pieces of film.

Composite image

Cyan separation

Magenta separation

Yellow separation

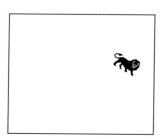

Black separation

As you learned earlier, you can print separations using process colors or spot colors, or you can use a combination of both. You'll convert the first spot color (PANTONE 116) to a process color because a precise color match isn't necessary. The second spot color, PANTONE 185 CVC, will not be converted to a process color because a precise color match is desired.

To modify how individual spot colors are separated, you must first deselect the Convert to Process option in the Separation Setup dialog box.

1 In the Separation Setup dialog box, deselect the Convert to Process option.

2 To convert the first spot color (PANTONE 116) to a process color, click the printer icon next to its name in the list of colors.

If you were to print at this point, five separations would be generated: one each for the cyan, magenta, yellow, and black plates (including the spot color converted to a process color); and a single plate for the PANTONE 185 CVC spot color. (This job would require a more specialized press, capable of printing five colors, or the paper would have to be sent back through the press to print the fifth color.)

Composite image   Cyan separation   Magenta separation

Yellow separation   Black separation   Spot separation

Specifying the screen frequency

At the beginning of this lesson, you learned that the relationship between the output device resolution and the screen frequency determines the quality of the printed output. Depending on the output device you select, more than one screen frequency value may be available. Your printing professional will direct you to select the screen frequency appropriate to your artwork.

1 In the General.ppd section of the Separation Setup dialog box, choose 60 lpi/300 dpi from the Halftone menu. The first value, 60, represents the screen frequency (lpi), and the second value, 300, represents the output device resolution (dpi).

Additional separation options, such as Emulsion Up/Down and Positive or Negative film, should be discussed with your printing professional, who can help you determine how these options should be set for your particular job.

2 Click OK to exit the Separation Setup dialog box.

[?] For more information, see "Step 5: Set separation options" in online Help or Chapter 17 in the Adobe Illustrator User Guide.

Printing separations

Before printing your separations to a high-resolution output device, it's a good idea to print a set of separations, called *proofs*, on your black-and-white desktop printer. You'll save time and money by making any needed corrections to your files after reviewing the black-and-white proofs.

1 Choose File > Print.

2 In Mac OS, choose Adobe Illustrator 10 from the pop-up menu.

3 In Windows and Mac OS, choose Separate from the Output menu.

4 In Mac OS, select Printer in the Destination section of the Print dialog box.

5 Choose Separate from the Output pop-up menu.

6 Click OK (Windows) or Print (Mac OS) to print separations. Five pieces of paper should be printed—one each for cyan, magenta, yellow, and black, and one for the spot color.

Note: Depending on your chosen printer, you may get a warning message that your PPD doesn't match the current printer. Click Continue to print the proofs.

7 Choose File > Save. The Separation Setup settings you entered are saved with your artwork file.

8 Close the Circus.ai file.

Working with two-color illustrations

As you learned earlier, two-color printing generally refers to black and one spot color, but may also refer to two spot colors. In addition to printing the two solid colors, you can print tints, or *screens*, of the colors. Two-color printing is much less expensive than four-color printing and lets you create a rich range of depth and color when used effectively.

Editing a spot color

In this section, you'll open a two-color version of the circus illustration containing black, a spot color, and tints of the spot color. Before you separate the illustration, you'll replace the current spot color with another from the PANTONE color library. Illustrator lets you make global adjustments to spot colors and tints of spot colors using a keyboard shortcut.

1 Choose File > Open, and open the L13strt2.ai file in the Lesson13 folder, located inside the Lessons folder within the AICIB folder on your hard drive.

Because you have set up Illustrator to work with a color management profile, you will be prompted each time you open a new file if you want to change how that file is color managed.

2 At the prompt, select Assign Current Working Space, and click OK.

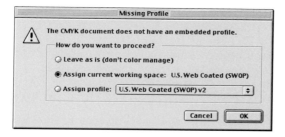

3 Choose File > Save As, name the file **Twocolor.ai**, and select the Lesson13 folder. Leave the Format option set to Adobe Illustrator® Document, and click Save. In the Illustrator Native Format Options dialog box, select Illustrator 10 Compatibility and click OK.

4 Make sure that the Color palette and the Swatches palette are open and visible; if they aren't, use the Window menu to display them. Click the Swatches tab to bring the palette to the front of its group.

5 Select the selection tool ( ) in the toolbox. Then click any colored part of the circus tent. Notice the PANTONE 116 C swatch in the Color palette.

Next, you'll replace every instance of the spot color (including any tints of the color) with another spot color.

6 Choose Select > Deselect or click away from the artwork to deselect it.

7 Choose Window > Swatch Libraries > PANTONE Solid Coated. The PANTONE swatch library appears.

You can choose new spot colors from the swatch library by typing the number of the color you want to use.

8 Click in the Find text box of the PANTONE Coated palette and type **193**. PANTONE 193 C is selected in the palette, as indicated by the white outline around the swatch.

Next, you'll replace the current PANTONE color with the new PANTONE color.

9 If necessary, drag the title bar of the PANTONE Solid Coated swatch library to view the Swatches palette.

10 Hold down Alt (Windows) or Option (Mac OS), and drag the PANTONE 193 C swatch from the PANTONE Solid Coated swatch library onto the PANTONE 116 swatch in the Swatches palette.

As you Alt/Option-drag the swatch, the pointer changes to a crosshair.

The PANTONE 193 C replaces the PANTONE 116 swatch in the Swatches palette, and the artwork is updated with the new PANTONE Solid color.

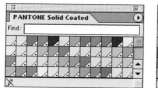

Open PANTONE Solid Coated swatch library.

Select PANTONE 193 C swatch.

Alt/Option-drag onto swatch to replace in Swatches palette.

Notice that the updated red swatch still is named PANTONE 116. You need to rename the updated swatch to avoid confusion about the spot color when your artwork is printed by a commercial press.

11 In the Swatches palette, double-click the updated swatch (still named PANTONE 116), and rename the swatch to match its color, PANTONE 193 C. Click OK.

Separating spot colors

As you learned in "Separating colors" on page 415, you can convert spot colors to their process color equivalents, or you can output them to their own separation. When you're working with a two-color illustration, separating spot colors into their process color equivalents is less cost-effective than outputting the spot color to its own separation (converting to four CMYK plates versus one plate for each individual spot color). You'll deselect the Convert to Process option in the Separation Setup dialog box to output each spot color to its own separation.

Composite image

Separation 1: Black

Separation 2: Spot color

1 Choose File > Separation Setup.

2 Deselect the Convert to Process option. Notice that Process Black and the spot color PANTONE 193 C now have printer icons to their left in the list of colors for the artwork. The printer icon indicates that a single separation will be printed for each color. No icons appear next to cyan, magenta, and yellow in the list of separations, because the artwork contains no cyan, magenta, or yellow values.

	Process Magenta
	Process Yellow
🖶	Process Black
🖶	PANTONE 193 C

3 Click OK to exit the Separation Setup dialog box.

4 Choose File > Save to save the separation settings with your file.

5 Close the Twocolor.ai file.

Creating a trap

Trapping is used to compensate for any gaps or color shifts that may occur between adjoining or overlapping objects when printing. These gaps or color shifts occur from *misregistration*, the result of the paper or the printing plates becoming misaligned during printing. Trapping is a technique developed by commercial print shops to slightly overprint the colors along common edges.

Gap created by misregistration

Gap removed by trapping

About traps

When overlapping painted objects share a common color, trapping may be unnecessary if the color that is common to both objects creates an automatic trap. For example, if two overlapping objects contain cyan as part of their CMYK values, any gap between them is covered by the cyan content of the object underneath.

Note: *When artwork contains common ink colors, overprinting does not occur on the shared plate—that is, the topmost overlapping printing ink appears opaque.*

There are two types of traps: a spread, in which a lighter object overlaps a darker background and seems to expand into the background; and a choke, in which a lighter background overlaps a darker object that falls within the background and seems to squeeze or reduce the object.

You can create both spreads and chokes in the Adobe Illustrator program.

Spread: Object overlaps background. *Choke: Background overlaps object.*

It is generally best to scale your graphic to its final size before adding a trap. Once you create a trap for an object, the amount of trapping increases or decreases if you scale the object (unless you deselect the Scale line weight option in the Scale dialog box). For example, if you create a graphic that has a 0.5-point trap and scale it to five times its original size, the result is a 2.5-point trap for the enlarged graphic.

–From online Help and the Adobe Illustrator User Guide, Chapter 17

Although trapping sounds simple enough, it requires a thorough knowledge of color and design and an eye for determining where trapping is necessary. You can create a trap in Adobe Illustrator using two methods: by applying the Trap filter or Trap effect, for simple artwork whose parts can be selected and trapped individually; and by setting a Stroke value for individual objects you want to trap. Like printing, creating a trap is an art that requires time and experience.

📃 For more information on creating a trap, see "Step 3: Create a trap to compensate for misregistration on press" in online Help or Chapter 17 in the Adobe Illustrator User Guide.

Now you'll practice creating a simple kind of trap called overprinting.

Overprinting objects

When preparing an image for color separation, you can define how you want overlapping objects of different colors to print. By default, the top object in the Illustrator artwork *knocks out*, or removes the color of, underlying artwork on the other separations and prints with the color of the top object only. Misregistration may occur when you knock out colors.

Composite image   *First plate*   *Second plate*

You can also specify objects to *overprint*, or print on top of, any of the artwork under them. Overprinting is the simplest method you can use to prevent misregistration (gaps between colors) on press. The overprinted color automatically traps into the background color.

Composite image   *First plate*   *Second plate*

For an illustration of overprinting, see figure 13-2 in the color section.

You'll select an object in the circus illustration and apply the overprint option. Then you will preview the overprint on-screen.

1 Choose File > Open. Locate and open the Circus.ai file, which you saved in the Lesson13 folder, inside the Lessons folder within the AICIB folder on your hard drive.

2 In the Missing Profile dialog box, select Assign Current Working Space: US Web Coated (SWOP) v2, and click OK.

The color version of the circus illustration appears.

3 Choose View > Zoom In to zoom in on the lion. You'll be able to see the overprint lines better if you magnify the view of the image. (We zoomed in to 400%.)

4 Select the selection tool ( ) in the toolbox. Then click the lion to select it.

5 Click the Attributes tab to bring the palette to the front of its group. (If the Attributes palette isn't open, choose Window > Attributes.)

6 In the Attributes palette, select Overprint Fill.

Now you'll see an approximation of how overprinting and blending will appear in the color-separated output.

7 Choose View > Overprint Preview to see the effect of the overprinted objects. The effect is subtle; look closely at the tip of the flag to see the overprinting.

If an object has a stroke, you can also select the Overprint Stroke option to make sure that the stroke overprints on the object below it as well. Next you'll add a stroke to an object to create a trap.

8 With the selection tool ( ), select the yellow flag to the left of the lion.

9 Click the Color tab to bring the palette to the front.

10 In the Color palette, drag the yellow fill swatch onto the Stroke box to stroke the flag with the same color as its fill.

11 Click the Attributes tab to bring the palette to the front of its group. Select the Overprint Stroke option.

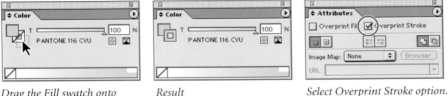

Drag the Fill swatch onto   Result   Select Overprint Stroke option.
the Stroke box.

Depending on what you have discussed with your printing professional, you may want to change the amount of trap specified. You'll try out changing the specified trap now.

12 Select the flag shape with the overprint stroke.

13 Click the Stroke tab to bring the palette to the front of its group. Change the Stroke Weight, and then choose View > Overprint Preview to see the results.

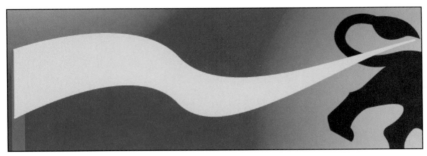

No Overprint preview

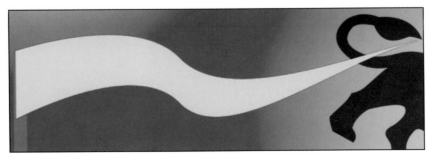

Overprint preview

Strokes are centered over the object's path. This means that if an object is stroked with the same color as its fill, only half of the stroke weight actually overprints. For example, if your printing professional wants a 0.5-point trap added to the yellow flag, you would use a 1-point stroke weight to achieve the trap. Half the stroke will appear inside the fill area and half will appear outside the fill area.

14 Choose File > Save. Choose File > Close to close the file.

You've finished the lesson. In an ordinary workflow situation, you would now be ready to send your artwork to a commercial press to be printed. Include proofs of color separation setups when you send your electronic file to a printer. Also tell your printer about any traps you created in the artwork. Keep in mind that you must remain in close communication with your printing professional for each print job. Each print job has unique requirements that you must consider before you begin the process of color separation.

Review questions

1 How do the RGB and CMYK color gamuts affect the relationship between on-screen colors and printed colors?

2 How can you create a closer match between your on-screen colors and printed colors?

3 What is the benefit of printing interim drafts of your artwork to a black-and-white desktop printer?

4 What does the term *color separation* mean?

5 What are two ways to output spot colors?

6 What are the advantages of one- or two-color printing?

7 What is trapping?

8 What is a simple method you can use to create trap?

Review answers

1 Each color model has a gamut of color that overlaps, but does not precisely match the others. Because monitors display color using the RGB color gamut and printed artwork uses the smaller CMYK color gamut, there may be times when a printed color cannot precisely match an on-screen color.

2 You can select one of Illustrator's built-in color management profiles to better simulate the relationship between on-screen colors and printed colors. You can choose View > Proof Setup and select an output device profile. Then choose View > Proof Colors to get an on-screen version of how the artwork will look when printed to the selected device.

3 It's a good idea to print black-and-white drafts of your artwork on a desktop printer to check the layout and the accuracy of text and graphics in your publication before incurring the expense of printing to a color printer or imagesetter (for separations).

4 Color separation refers to breaking down composite artwork into its component colors—for example, using the four process colors (cyan, magenta, yellow, and black) to reproduce a large portion of the visible color spectrum.

5 You can convert a spot color to its process color equivalents if a precise color match is not required, or you can output a spot color to its own separation.

6 One- or two-color printing is less expensive than four-color printing, and you can use spot colors for precise color matching.

7 Trapping is a technique developed by commercial print shops to slightly overprint the colors along common edges, and it is used to compensate for any gaps or color shifts that may occur between adjoining or overlapping objects when printed.

8 You can specify objects to overprint, or print on top of, any of the artwork under them. Overprinting is the simplest method you can use to create trap, which compensates for misregistration on press.

Lesson 14

14 | Combining Illustrator Graphics and Photoshop Images

GAMING AROUND

ANNUAL DIGITAL CHESS TOURNAMENT
CONVENTION CENTER
WEST WING

You can easily add an image created in an image-editing program to an Adobe Illustrator file. This is an effective method for seeing how a photograph looks incorporated with a line drawing or for trying out Illustrator special effects on bitmap images.

In this lesson, you'll learn how to do the following:

- Differentiate between vector and bitmap graphics.
- Place embedded Adobe Photoshop graphics in an Adobe Illustrator file.
- Create a clipping mask from compound paths.
- Make an opacity mask to display part of the image.
- Sample color in a placed image.
- Replace a placed image with another and update the document.
- Export a layered file to Adobe Photoshop and edit the type.

Combining artwork

You can combine Illustrator artwork with images from other graphics applications in a variety of ways for a wide range of creative results. Sharing artwork between applications lets you combine continuous-tone paintings and photographs with line art. Even though Illustrator lets you create certain types of raster images, Photoshop excels at many image-editing tasks; once done, the images then can be placed in Illustrator.

To illustrate how you can combine bitmap images with vector art and work between applications, this lesson steps you through the process of creating a composite image. In this lesson, you will add photographic images created in Adobe Photoshop to a postcard created in Adobe Illustrator. Then you'll adjust the color in the photo, mask the photo, and sample color from the photo to use in the Illustrator artwork. You'll update a placed image and then export your postcard to Photoshop to complete the type treatment.

Vector versus bitmap graphics

Adobe Illustrator creates *vector graphics*, also called draw graphics, which are made up of shapes based on mathematical expressions. These graphics consist of clear, smooth lines that retain their crispness when scaled. They are appropriate for illustrations, type, and graphics such as logos that may be scaled to different sizes.

Bitmap images, also called raster images, are based on a grid of pixels and are created by image-editing applications such as Adobe Photoshop. In working with bitmap images, you edit groups of pixels rather than objects or shapes. Because bitmap graphics can represent subtle gradations of shade and color, they are appropriate for continuous-tone images such as photographs or artwork created in painting programs. A disadvantage of bitmap graphics is that they lose definition and appear jagged when scaled up.

Logo drawn as vector art

Logo rasterized as bitmap art

In deciding whether to use Illustrator or a bitmap image program such as Photoshop for creating and combining graphics, consider both the elements of the image and how the image will be used. In general, use Illustrator if you need to create art or type with clean lines that will look good at any magnification. In most cases, you will also want to use Illustrator for laying out a design, because Illustrator offers more flexibility in working with type and with reselecting, moving, and altering images. You can create raster images in Illustrator but its pixel-editing tools are limited. Use Photoshop for images that need pixel-editing, color correcting, painting, and other special effects.

Getting started

Before you begin, you'll need to restore the default preferences for Adobe Illustrator. Then you'll open the finished art file for this lesson to see what you'll create.

1 To ensure that the tools and palettes function exactly as described in this lesson, delete or deactivate (by renaming) the Adobe Illustrator 10.0 preferences file. See "Restoring default preferences" on page 4.

2 Start Adobe Illustrator.

3 Choose File > Open, and open the L14end.ai file in the Lesson14 folder, located inside the Lessons folder within the AICIB folder on your hard drive.

4 Choose View > Zoom Out to make the finished artwork smaller, adjust the window size, and leave it on-screen as you work. (Use the hand tool (🖐) to move the artwork where you want it in the window.) If you don't want to leave the image open, choose File > Close.

🔵 For an illustration of the finished artwork in this lesson, see the color section.

Now you'll open the start file to begin the lesson.

5 Choose File > Open, and open the L14strt.ai file.

The file has been prepared with three layers: the Text layer, and two additional layers, Layer 1 and Checkerboard, on which you'll place images. Checkerboard also contains objects that you'll make into a mask.

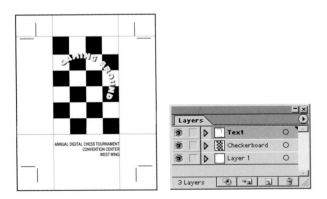

6 Choose File > Save As, name the file **Postcard.ai**, and select the Lesson14 folder. Leave the Format option set to Adobe Illustrator® Document, and click Save. In the Illustrator Native Format Options dialog box, select Illustrator 10 Compatibility and click OK.

Placing an Adobe Photoshop file

You'll begin by placing a Photoshop file in the Illustrator document as an *embedded* file. Placed files can be embedded or *linked*. Embedded files are added to the Illustrator file, and the Illustrator file size increases to reflect the addition of the placed file. Linked files remain separate, external files, with a link to the placed file in the Illustrator file. (The linked file must always accompany the Illustrator file, or the link will break and the placed file will not appear in the Illustrator artwork.)

1 Resize the Layers palette so that you can see all of the layers.

2 In the Layers palette, select the Checkerboard layer.

When you place an image, it is added to the selected layer. You'll use the Checkerboard layer for the placed image, because the layer includes artwork for a mask for the image that you'll create later in the lesson.

3 Choose File > Place.

4 Navigate to the Chess.psd file (in the Lesson14 folder inside the Lessons folder in the AICIB folder on your hard drive), and select it. Do not double-click the file or click Place yet.

5 In Mac OS, in the Place dialog box click Link to deselect the option.

In Mac OS, placed files are linked by default; in Windows, placed files are embedded by default. Deselecting the Link option embeds the placed file and makes it part of the Illustrator file.

The advantage of embedding a file is that the file is permanently included in the Illustrator artwork, and no link can be broken. The advantage of linking a file is that the Illustrator file size does not become as large (because the linked file is not included in the Illustrator file).

6 Click Place.

7 In the Photoshop Import dialog box, select the Convert Photoshop Layers to Objects option. Click OK.

Rather than flatten the file, you want to convert the Photoshop layers to objects because the Chess.psd file contains two layers and one layer mask. You will use them later in the lesson.

Now you'll move the placed image, using the guides in the artwork to place the image precisely.

8 Select the selection tool ( ) in the toolbox. Drag the placed image at its edge (but don't grab a bounding box handle because that will resize the image), and drag the image onto the guides provided in the artwork. Release the mouse button when you have aligned the image with the guides.

You can use the arrow keys to nudge the selection into place.

The placed image covers up the squares in the Checkerboard layer. The placed image was added as a sublayer to the Checkerboard layer because it was selected when you choose the Place command.

9 Choose File > Save

Now you will move the image below the squares and duplicate it.

Placing files

The Place command places files from other applications into Illustrator. Files can be embedded, or included in, the Illustrator file, or they can be linked to the Illustrator file. Linked files remain independent of the Illustrator file, resulting in a smaller Illustrator file. Depending on a preference you set for updating links, the linked image in the Illustrator file may change when the artwork in the linked file changes.

By default, the Link option is selected in the Place dialog box. If you deselect the Link option, the artwork is embedded in the Adobe Illustrator file, resulting in a larger Illustrator file. The Links palette lets you identify, select, monitor, and update objects in the Illustrator artwork that are linked to external files. (See Managing linked and embedded images.)

Placed bitmap images can be modified using transformation tools and image filters; placed vector artwork is converted to Illustrator paths (embedded images only).

If you place a Photoshop file and deselect the Link option, the Photoshop Import dialog box appears. For information on options in the Photoshop Import dialog box, see Opening Photoshop files in Illustrator in online Help.

Note: *Do not place an EPS file containing mesh objects or transparency objects if it was created in an application other than Illustrator. Instead, open the EPS file, copy all objects and then paste in Illustrator.*

–From online Help and the Adobe Illustrator User Guide, Chapter 2

Duplicating a placed image

You can duplicate placed images just as you do other objects in an Illustrator file. The copy of the image can then be modified independently of the original.

Now you'll reposition and duplicate the Chess.psd image in the Layers palette.

1 Click the Expand triangle (▶) to the left of the Checkerboard layer to expand it. Enlarge the Layers palette so that you can see all the contents of the Checkerboard layer.

2 Drag the Chess.psd layer down the list until it is at the bottom of the Checkerboard layer, and then release the mouse button when the indicator bar appears between the last <Path> layer and Layer 1.

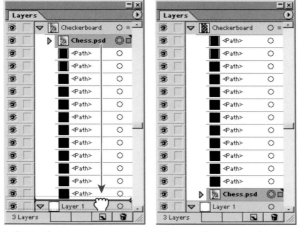

Indicator bar   Chess.psd layer moved

3 Click the triangle to the left of the Chess.psd layer to expand it. Notice that the Chess.psd layer has two sublayers, Masked King and Background. You will now duplicate the Background layer.

4 To duplicate the Background layer, drag its thumbnail onto the New Layer button at the bottom of the Layers palette. Another layer called Background is created.

5 Double-click the lower Background layer and rename it **Blue Chess.psd.** Click OK. You will change the color of this image later in the lesson.

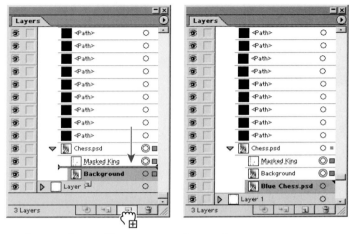

Duplicate Background layer.   Rename layer.

6 Choose File > Save.

Adjusting color in a placed image

You can use filters to modify colors in placed images in a variety of ways. You can use filters to convert to a different color mode (such as RGB, CMYK, or grayscale) or to adjust individual color values. You can also use filters to saturate or desaturate (darken or lighten) colors, or invert colors (create a color negative).

For information on color modes and modifying colors with filters, see "Color modes and models" and "Using filters to modify colors" in online Help or Chapter 6 in the Adobe Illustrator User Guide.

In this section, you'll adjust colors in the Background layer. Later in the lesson, you'll apply a mask to this image and then adjust colors in the Blue Chess.psd layer so that the two layers appear in contrasting colors through the mask.

For an illustration of color filters, see figure 14-1 in the color section.

1 In the Layers palette, select the Background sublayer.

2 Click the eye icon to the far left of the Masked King layer to hide it.

When you hide a layer, all objects on that layer are deselected, hidden, and locked.

3 In the Layers palette, click the selection column to the far right of the Background layer to select its contents quickly.

Masked King layer hidden and contents of Background layer selected

4 Choose Filter > Colors > Adjust Colors.

5 In the Adjust Colors dialog box, select Preview so that you can see the color changes. Drag the sliders or enter values for the CMYK percentages to change the colors in the image. You can press Tab to move between the text boxes. (We used the following values to create an orange cast: C=**–23**, M=**20**, Y=**74**, and K=**–52**.)

6 When you are satisfied with the color in the image, click OK.

7 Click outside the artwork to deselect the Background image, and then choose File > Save.

[?] Besides using filters to adjust colors, you can also use filters to apply special effects to images, distort images, produce a hand-drawn appearance, and create other interesting effects. See "Using filters and filter effects on bitmap images" in online Help or Chapter 11 in the Adobe Illustrator User Guide.

⬤ For an illustration of special effects filters applied to bitmap images, and RGB and grayscale images, see figure 14-2 in the color section.

Masking an image

Masks crop part of an image so that only a portion of the image appears through the shape of the mask. You can make a mask from a single path or a compound path. You can also import masks made in Photoshop files.

Creating compound path and opacity masks

In this section, you'll create a compound path from the checkerboard pattern on the Checkerboard layer and create an opacity mask from the compound path, so that the Background layer appears through the mask. Then you'll adjust the colors in Blue Chess.psd to contrast with the Background layer. You'll also use an opacity mask that was created in Photoshop and saved as a layer mask.

1 Select the magic wand tool (✎) in the toolbox.

2 Using the magic wand tool, click the upper left black square in the checkerboard pattern to select all of the black squares. This action selects the checkerboard and deselects the background.

[?] You can use the magic wand tool to select all objects in a document with the same or similar fill color, stroke weight, stroke color, opacity, or blending mode. See "Using the magic wand tool" in online Help or in Chapter 4 of the Adobe Illustrator User Guide.

3 Choose Object > Compound Path > Make.

Notice how all the squares have been placed onto one layer, called <Compound Path>, in the Layers palette.

The Compound Path command creates a single compound object from two or more objects. Compound paths act as grouped objects. The Compound Path command lets you create complex objects more easily than if you used the drawing tools or the Pathfinder commands.

4 With the checkerboard still selected in the artwork, in the Layers palette Shift-click the selection column to the far right of the Background layer to select it and add it to the <Compound Path> selection. (The selection indicator (■) will appear and the Background layer will be added to the selection.)

Both the masking object and the object to be masked must be selected in order to create a mask.

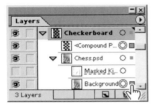

Background and <Compound Path> selected

5 Click the Transparency palette tab to bring it to the front of its group. (If the Transparency palette isn't visible on-screen, choose Window > Transparency.)

6 From the Transparency palette menu, choose Show Options to expand the palette fully.

Now you'll mask the Background layer with an opacity mask that lets you use the change in luminosity in the overlying checkerboard to affect the background. Similar to a clipping mask, an opacity mask lets you make color and other fine adjustments that you can't make with a clipping mask.

7 From the Transparency palette menu, choose Make Opacity Mask. Select both the Clip and Invert Mask options.

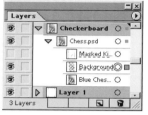

Dotted line indicates mask   *Preview includes opacity mask*

The checkerboard pattern is assigned a fill and stroke of None, and the Background layer is masked with the checkerboard pattern, as indicated by the dotted underline beneath the layer name. The Blue Chess.psd layer appears through the masked sections of the Background layer.

Now you'll apply the Adjust Colors filter to the Blue Chess.psd layer to create a stronger contrast between the two images.

8 In the Layers palette, click the selection indicator for the Blue Chess.psd layer to select only its contents.

9 Choose Filter > Colors > Adjust Colors.

The most recently used filter (in this case, Adjust Colors) appears at the top of the Filter menu, letting you easily reapply the filter. (Choosing Filter > Apply Adjust Colors would apply the filter with the same settings used on the Background layer.)

10 Click Preview to preview changes in the artwork.

11 Drag the sliders for the CMYK values to change the colors in the image. (We used the following values to create a blue cast: C=**12**, M=**–10**, Y=**–74**, and K=**–31**.) You can compare the color in Blue Chess.psd to that in the Background layer to choose a color that contrasts effectively.

12 When you are satisfied with the color, click OK. Click outside the artwork to deselect the Blue Chess.psd image.

13 Choose File > Save.

Editing an imported mask

You've made an opacity mask from artwork created in Illustrator. Now you'll use a mask that was created in Photoshop and imported when you placed the Chess.psd file. You'll experiment with changing the color of the image and then adjusting the transparency of the opacity mask to tone down the effect.

1 In the Layers palette, click the eye column to show the Masked King layer.

2 Click the selection indicator (▪) for the Masked King layer to select its contents. (The dotted line under its layer name indicates that the Masked King layer has an opacity mask applied to it.)

3 Choose Filter > Colors > Adjust Colors.

4 In the Adjust Colors dialog box, click Preview to preview changes in the artwork. Drag the sliders for the CMYK values to change the colors in the image. (We used the following values to create a strong purple cast: C=**60**, M=**60**, Y=**−46**, and K=**−60**.) Click OK.

5 In the Transparency palette, change the opacity setting to 75% for the Masked King layer.

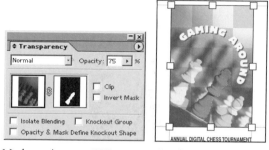

Mask opacity set to 75%   *Result*

For a dramatic effect you will now invert the opacity mask. This will subdue the Background and Blue Chess.psd layers and make the Masked King layer pop visually.

6 In the Transparency palette, select the Invert Mask option to reverse the effect of the opacity mask.

Mask inverted   *Result*

7 Click outside the artwork to deselect the Masked King layer.

8 Choose File > Save.

Sampling colors in placed images

You can *sample*, or copy, the colors in placed images, to apply the colors to other objects in the artwork. Sampling colors enables you to easily make colors consistent in a file combining Photoshop images and Illustrator artwork.

Copying attributes between objects

You can use the eyedropper tool to copy colors from any object in an Illustrator file—from a paint swatch or from anywhere on the desktop, including from another application. You can then use the paint bucket tool to apply the current paint attributes to an object. Together these tools let you copy the paint attributes from anywhere on-screen to other objects.

By default, the eyedropper and paint bucket tools affect all paint attributes of an object. You can use the tool's options dialog box to change the object's attributes. You can also use the eyedropper tool and paint bucket tool to copy and paste type attributes.

–From online Help and the Adobe Illustrator User Guide, Chapter 6

In this section, you'll use the eyedropper tool to sample colors from the placed image, and apply the colors to selected type on the Text layer.

1 Use the selection tool (▶) to click in the text at the bottom of the artwork to select the entire text block.

2 Select the eyedropper tool (⚟), and Shift-click in the image to sample a color to be applied to the selected text. (We chose a medium-purple color near the center of the image, between the king and queen chess pieces.)

The color you sample is applied to the selected text.

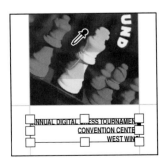

3 Choose File > Save.

Replacing a placed image

You can easily replace a placed image with another image to update a document. The replacement image is positioned exactly where the original image was, so you don't have to align the replacement image. (If you scaled the original images, you may have to resize the replacement image to match the original image.)

Now you'll replace the Blue Chess.psd image with the Chess2.psd image to create a new version of the postcard.

1 Choose File > Save As, name the file **Postcard2.ai**, and select the Lesson14 folder. Leave the Format option set to Adobe Illustrator® Document, and click Save. In the Illustrator Native Format Options dialog box, select Illustrator 10 Compatibility and click OK.

2 Click the Links tab to bring the Links palette to the front of its group. (If the Links palette isn't visible on-screen, choose Window > Links.)

3 Click the last link in the Links palette to select it. (These links don't have names because we embedded them instead of linking them.)

4 Click the Replace Link button at the bottom of the Links palette.

5 In the Place dialog box, navigate to the Chess2.psd image in the Lesson14 folder and select it. Make sure that the Link option is deselected. Click Place to replace the Blue Chess.psd image with the new one.

The replacement image appears in the Chess.psd layer with no color adjustments applied. When you replace an image, color adjustments you made to the original image are not applied to the replacement. However, masks applied to the original image are preserved. Any layer modes and transparency adjustments you've made to other layers also may affect the image's appearance.

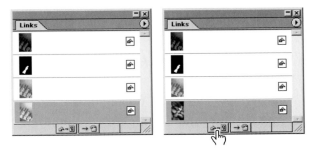

Select image in Links palette.   Click Replace Link button to replace with new image.

6 Choose File > Save.

You have completed the lesson. If you want to learn how to open and manipulate a layered Illustrator file in Photoshop, continue. If not, skip to "Exploring on your own" on page 453.

Exporting a layered file to Photoshop

Not only can you open layered Photoshop files in Illustrator, but you can also save layered Illustrator files and then open them in Photoshop. Working with layered files between Illustrator and Photoshop is very helpful when creating and editing Web graphics. You can preserve the hierarchical relationship of the layers by selecting the Write Nested Layers option when saving your file. You can also open and edit type objects.

Now you'll adjust the Text layer and then you'll export the file, change its color mode and save it in layered Photoshop format so that you can edit it in Photoshop.

1 Click the Layers tab to bring the palette to the front of its group.

2 In the Layers palette, click the triangle (▶) to the left of the Text layer to expand its list.

3 Drag the Annual Digital Chess sublayer out of and above the Text layer. It is now its own layer instead of a sublayer nested in the Text layer.

To keep the Illustrator type layer editable when opened in Photoshop, the type layer must reside by itself on the topmost layer and not be nested inside another layer. Illustrator also cannot export area type, type on a path, or multicolored type to Photoshop as editable text.

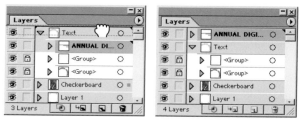

Select sublayer.   Drag out of nested hierarchy to own layer.

4 Choose File > Export.

5 Navigate to the folder where you'll save the file, and name the file **Postcard2.psd**. Changing the file name preserves your original Illustrator file.

6 Choose Photoshop (PSD) from the Save as Type (Windows) or Format (Mac OS) pop-up menu, and click Save (Windows) or Export (Mac OS).

7 In the Photoshop Options dialog box, choose RGB as the Color Model, select Screen (72 ppi) for Resolution, and make sure that Anti-alias, Write Layers, and Editable Text options are selected. Click OK.

The Anti-alias option removes jagged edges in the artwork. The Write Layers option lets you export each Illustrator top-level layer as a separate Photoshop layer. Nested layers are flattened into the top-level layer during export, unless you've also selected the Nested Layers option. You're not exporting any nested layers from the Postcard file.

8 Start Adobe Photoshop.

9 Open the Postcard2.psd file that you exported in step 7.

10 If prompted to update text layers, click Update.

You'll edit the text you just exported to shorten it and increase its type size.

11 Select the type tool in the toolbox.

12 Click the type tool within the *ANNUAL DIGITAL CHESS* text, and choose Select > All to select all of the text.

13 In the Options bar, click the Palettes button to display the Character palette. In the Character palette, edit the type by changing the point size to **24 pt** and the Leading to **24 pt**.

14 In the Options bar, click the Flush Left button to move the text flush left.

15 Using the type tool, select and delete the *CONVENTION CENTER WEST WING* text. (You may have to scroll to see the text.)

16 In the image, use the selection tool to move the type so that its left edge aligns with the left edge of the image.

17 Choose File > Save. Choose File > Close to close the file.

You've completed the lesson on combining Illustrator graphics and Photoshop images, and learned how easy it is to work between the two applications.

Exploring on your own

Now that you know how to place and mask an image in an Illustrator file, you can place other images and apply a variety of modifications to the images. You can also create masks for images from objects you create in Illustrator. For more practice, try the following:

• Repeat the lesson using the Chess2.psd image in place of the Chess.psd image. In addition to adjusting color in the copies of the image, apply transformation effects, such as shearing or rotating, or filters or effects, such as one of the Artistic or Distort filters/effects, to create contrast between the two images in the checkerboard pattern.

• Use the basic shapes tools or the drawing tools to draw objects to create a compound path to use as a mask. Then place the Chess.psd image into the file with the compound path, and apply the compound path as a mask.

• Create large type and use the type as a mask to mask a placed object.

Review questions

1 Describe the difference between linking and embedding a placed file in Illustrator.

2 How do you create an opacity mask for a placed image?

3 What kinds of objects can be used as masks?

4 What color modifications can you apply to a selected object using filters?

5 Describe how to replace a placed image with another image in a document.

Review answers

1 A linked file is a separate, external file connected to the Illustrator file by an electronic link. A linked file does not add significantly to the size of the Illustrator file. The linked file must accompany the Illustrator file to preserve the link and ensure that the placed file appears in the Illustrator file. An embedded file is included in the Illustrator file. The Illustrator file size reflects the addition of the embedded file. Because the embedded file is part of the Illustrator file, no link can be broken. Both linked and embedded files can be updated using the Replace Link button in the Links palette.

2 You create an opacity mask by placing the object to be used as a mask on top of the object to be masked. Then you select the mask and the objects to be masked, and choose Make Opacity Mask from the Transparency palette menu.

3 A mask can be a simple or compound path. You can use type as a mask. You can import opacity masks with placed Photoshop files. You can also create layer clipping masks with any shape that is the topmost object of a group or layer.

4 You can use filters to change the color mode (RGB, CMYK, or Grayscale) or adjust individual colors in a selected object. You can also saturate or desaturate colors or invert colors in a selected object. You can apply color modifications to placed images, as well as to artwork created in Illustrator.

5 To replace a placed image, select the placed image in the Links palette. Then click the Replace Link button, and locate and select the image to be used as the replacement. Then click Place. The replacement image appears in the artwork in place of the original image.

Lesson 15

15 Creating a Web Publication

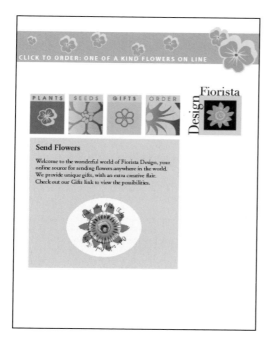

It's easy to design Web-ready, HTML pages in Illustrator that load quickly in browsers and maintain the artwork's integrity. Using slices, you can divide artwork and optimize it for size and quality in different Web file formats—including GIF or PNG-8 file format for flat-color art, JPEG or PNG-24 for continuous-tone photos and gradients, SWF for sound and animation, and HTML for text. You can animate slices, link them to URLs, or use them as HTML text.

In this lesson, you'll learn how to do the following:

• Determine which file format to use to publish different styles of artwork on the Web.

• Use Web-safe colors in your artwork.

• Link objects to URL addresses.

• Export different styles of artwork to GIF and JPEG formats.

• Create artwork for a simple animation and export it to the Macromedia® Flash™ (SWF) format.

• Export your Illustrator design as a completed HTML page with a folder of images ready to post to a Web site.

• Update artwork created in Adobe Illustrator in Adobe Photoshop, and then update your Web site with the edited image.

Important: During this lesson, you can preview the Web page, including links to URLs, on your local computer via your browser. However, you can only preview links to external URLs if your browser has a live connection to the Internet.

About Web format and compression options

Creating small graphics files is key to distributing images on the World Wide Web. With smaller files, Web servers can store and transmit images more efficiently, and viewers can download images more quickly. You decrease file size by saving your artwork in one of several compressed file formats like GIF, JPEG, or PNG.

Other formats used on the Web include SVG (Scalable Vector Graphics), Macromedia Flash (SWF), and HTML. SVG is an XML-based language for describing interactive, animated, two-dimensional graphics. The SVG format supports vector graphics (lines and curves), but it also supports text and raster images. Its feature set includes transformations, transparency, clipping paths, and filter effects. SVG files can easily be combined with HTML and JavaScript in Web pages.

For publishing vector artwork and sound in interactive Web sites and animations, the Macromedia Flash (SWF) file format works well with HTML and JavaScript.

The following table describes the file formats generally recommended for displaying specific types of artwork on the Web. Keep in mind, however, that the file format you choose for your artwork may also be determined by the quality and size of the image you want to place on the Web.

Slice format	Advantages and compression options
HTML	Ideal for plain HTML text.
GIF	Standard for logos and art with solid flat color. Choose dithering options, set transparency and interlacing.
JPEG	Standard format for photos and images with transparency and gradient color. Specify compression quality, whether the image loads progressively, and optimization controls.
PNG	Ideal for images when transparency is required. Specify whether to use PNG-8 or PNG-24 format, as well as other options including color reduction controls, dithering options, and more.
SVG	Ideal for vector-based graphics, especially when collaborating with developers. Choose whether fonts and image are embedded or linked as well as other compression options.
SWF	Ideal for vector-based graphics.

For more information on exporting images for the Web, see "About exporting artwork" in online Help or Chapter 14 of the Adobe Illustrator User Guide.

Image quality versus compression

There's always a trade-off between image quality and amount of compression: Higher quality images use less compression (and thus take longer to download) than lower quality images. The JPEG format uses a *lossy* compression method, in which data is discarded during compression. The JPEG compression method can degrade sharp detail in an image, such as type and line drawings. You specify the amount of compression to be applied by choosing a quality setting. A higher quality setting results in less data being discarded.

Note: *Data is discarded from a JPEG image each time you save the file. You should always save JPEG files from the original artwork, not from a previously saved JPEG file.*

The GIF format uses a *lossless* compression method, in which no data is discarded during compression. You can save a GIF file multiple times without discarding data. However, because GIF files are 8-bit color, optimizing an original 24-bit image (artwork created on a system displaying millions of colors) as an 8-bit GIF can degrade image quality.

The PNG-8 format is similar to the GIF format in that it is lossless and uses 8-bit color. It uses a more advanced compression scheme than GIF and depending on the image's color patterns, some PNG-8 files can be 10% to 30% smaller than GIF files. The disadvantage to using PNG-8, however, is that not all browsers support it. Thus, it may be advisable to avoid this format if your image needs to be accessible to the widest possible audience.

Using Web-safe colors to prevent dithering

Most images viewed on the Web are created using 24-bit color displays, but many Web browsers are on computers using only 8-bit color displays, so that Web images often contain colors not available to many Web browsers. Computers use a technique called *dithering* to simulate colors not available in the color display system. Dithering adjusts adjacent pixels of different colors to give the appearance of a third color. (For example, a blue color and a yellow color may dither in a mosaic pattern to produce the illusion of a green color that does not appear in the color palette.)

Dithering can occur when you export artwork to GIF or PNG-8 formats if Illustrator attempts to simulate colors that appear in the original artwork but don't appear in the color palette you specify. It can also occur in GIF or JPEG images when a Web browser using an 8-bit color display attempts to simulate colors that are in the image but not in the browser's color palette. You can minimize dithering by shifting individual or groups of colors to their closest Web-palette equivalent. You can also control dithering done by Web browsers by painting your artwork with Web-safe colors from the Web palette. Web-safe colors can be displayed by any browser that uses an 8-bit or 24-bit color display.

For an example of dithering that occurs in a GIF image that has not been painted with Web-safe colors compared to a GIF image that has been painted with them, see figure 15-1 in the color section.

Getting started

In this lesson, you'll create an HTML Web page along with a folder of images. You will optimize Web graphics by creating slices. The page will include links from several buttons to a URL, and a simple animation for a Web banner using symbols.

You'll start by previewing the completed Web page in your Web browser.

1 Launch your Web browser.

2 From the desktop, navigate to the Flwrhome.html file, located in the L15Web folder, inside the Lesson 15 folder that is inside the Lessons folder within the AICIB folder on your hard drive. Drag and drop the Flwrhome.html into your browser. Notice the animation at the top, and the links in the navigation bar.

3 If you have a live Internet connection, click one of the navigation buttons to jump to its link.

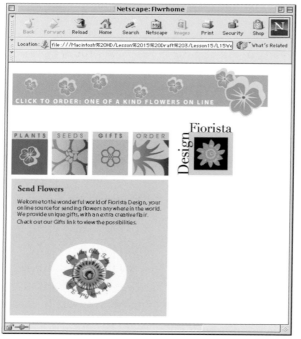

Flowerhome.html

4 When you have finished exploring the page, close the browser window or exit the browser.

5 To ensure that the tools and palettes function exactly as described in this lesson, delete or deactivate (by renaming) the Adobe Illustrator 10.0 preferences file. See "Restoring default preferences" on page 4.

6 Start Adobe Illustrator.

7 Choose File > Open, and open the L15comp.ai file in the L15Start folder, located in the Lesson15 folder that is inside the Lessons folder within the AICIB folder on your hard drive.

The artwork in this file is a design mock-up of a Web home page. The design for the completed page includes several styles of artwork, including flat-color, continuous-tone, and gradient-filled artwork.

L15comp.ai

8 If the Layers palette isn't visible on-screen, choose Window > Layers to display it.

9 Using the selection tool ( ), click the various components in the artwork to examine them. Notice in the Layers palette which layers correspond to the styles of artwork in the design, as follows:

- Navigation bar. The four buttons incorporate two flat-color artwork and two gradient backgrounds. All four are made into buttons that link to a URL address.

- Sticker. This artwork includes a placed photograph, which is a continuous-tone bitmap image imported from Adobe Photoshop.

- Text. This layer is placeholder text for HTML text.

- Animation, created in Illustrator at the top of the page.

10 If you like, choose View > Zoom Out to make the design mock-up smaller, adjust the window size, and leave it on your screen as you work. (Use the hand tool ( ) to move the artwork where you want it in the window.) If you don't want to leave the artwork open, choose File > Close.

For an illustration of the finished artwork in this lesson, see the color section.

Now you're ready to begin the Web page design.

Slicing artwork for Web pages

You'll create slices in the Web design to define its different Web elements. *Slicing* a design into small pieces lets you designate areas in an image as different file formats for different Web elements (such as GIF for a logo and JPEG for a gradient), to make the Web page load more quickly and to assign special behaviors, such as links to sections of a page.

When you save the artwork as a Web page, you can save each slice as an independent file with its own format, settings, and color palette. Using these slices, Illustrator creates an HTML table or cascading style sheet to contain and align the slices. (If you want, you can generate an HTML file that contains the sliced image along with the table of cascading style sheets.)

Creating slices from objects

You can create slices based on objects (or layers). Illustrator updates these slices automatically if you move or edit the selection, and uses these auto slices to create a valid HTML table if you save artwork as a Web page.

1 Choose File > Open, and open the L15strt1.ai file in the L15Start folder, located in the Lesson15 folder.

2 Choose File > Save As, rename the file **Flwrhome.ai**, and select the L15Start folder. Leave the Format option set to Adobe Illustrator® Document, and click Save. In the Illustrator Native Format Options dialog box, select Illustrator 10.0 Compatibility and click OK.

You'll start by slicing the buttons on the navigation bar.

3 In the Layers palette, Alt-click (Windows) or Option-click (Mac OS) the eye icon to the left of the Navigation Bar layer to hide all layers except the navigation bar. (Hiding the layers also locks them.) You won't use the hidden layers just yet.

The navigation bar contains two buttons with gradations and two buttons with flat color. You'll slice the buttons to optimize them individually with different format and compression settings.

4 Click the triangle next to the Navigation Bar layer to expand it. If necessary, resize the Layers palette to see all of the layers.

5 Select the selection tool (▸) in the toolbar. Then select the Gifts button in the artwork. Like the other buttons, the Gifts button elements have been grouped.

6 In the Layers palette, notice the blue square to the right of the layer, indicating that the sublayer is selected. You'll define your first slice based on this sublayer.

Selected sublayer

7 Press Ctrl+spacebar (Windows) or Command+spacebar (Mac OS) and click once or twice to zoom in to 150% on the artwork.

Now you'll create a slice that matches the boundary of one of the buttons in your artwork using the Make Slice command. This command defines the size of the slice according to a selection's rectangular bounding box.

8 Choose Object > Slice > Make. A series of numbered red outlines appear to indicate the position and order of the slices.

The Make Slice command creates *auto slices* for any areas of your artwork not already defined by slices.

9 Notice the semitransparent pink slices. These are subslices, also generated automatically by Illustrator, to indicate how overlapping slices will be divided.

Although subslices are numbered and display a slice symbol, you cannot select them separately from the underlying slice. Illustrator regenerates subslices every time you arrange the stacking order of slices.

10 Using the selection tool, move the Gift button to underneath the Plants button. Notice that the slices move with the object.

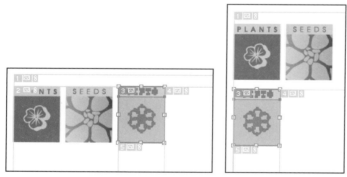

Sliced button   *Slice updated on moving object*

11 Return the slice to its original position by choosing Edit > Undo.

   If you inadvertently create a slice from the wrong selection, you can delete the slices and start over. Simply choose Object > Slice > Delete All.

Creating slices from a selection

You can also define slices based on selections in the image, guides, or by using the slice tool. Now you'll create slices using several other techniques to define the remaining buttons on the navigation bar.

1 In the Layers palette, click the triangle to the left of the Navigation Bar layer to collapse the sublayers. Then click the eye column to the left of the Sticker layer to make it visible.

2 Click the triangle next to the Sticker layer to expand it. Resize the Layers palette so that you can see the layer and its sublayers.

3 Choose View > Fit in Window to see the sticker clearly.

4 With the selection tool, in the artwork, select the sticker. Its artwork, like the buttons, is grouped.

You can create slices from selections, guides, or objects—called *custom slices*. You can also define the slice dimensions separate from the underlying artwork.

5 Choose Object > Slice > Create from Selection.

Custom slices appear as items in the Layers palette, labeled as <Slice>. You can move, resize, and delete them in the same way as other vector objects. However, custom slices do not update automatically if you move them.

6 In the Layers palette, notice the sublayer <Slice>, the custom slice you just created.

7 Select the remaining navigation buttons in turn, and repeat steps 4 and 5 to create a slice from the selection.

Now you'll try another way to create slices using the manual slicing tools—the slice tool and slice select tool. Manual slices don't update automatically. But they let you dissect a single object into multiple slices or create slices that aren't tied to a specific object or group.

8 Position the pointer on the slice tool ( ) in the toolbox. Drag to the right to select the small triangle to the right of the slice tools, and then select the triangle to tear off the tools.

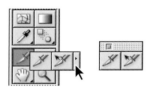

💡 *To separate a group of hidden tools from the toolbox, select the small triangle that appears at the right end of the group.*

9 In the Layers palette, click the eye column to the left of the Logo layer to make it visible. Then select the Logo layer in the palette.

10 Using the zoom tool ( ), zoom in to 150%.

11 Select the slice tool in the tear-off slice tools. The slice tool defines rectangular areas in your image as slices.

12 Position the pointer at the lower left corner of the logo artwork, below the *Design* text. Then drag diagonally up to draw a rectangle around the logo and its type, getting as close as possible to the shape to minimize the image size.

When you use the slice tool, Illustrator creates auto slices for all the undefined areas surrounding the slice you drew. You can adjust a slice after you've drawn it.

13 Select the slice select tool (), and position it at the edge of the slice rectangle. The pointer changes to a double-headed arrow. Drag to adjust the size of the slice.

Note: *If you make a mistake, delete the slice by selecting the slice with the slice select tool and pressing Delete; then redraw the slice.*

Draw the slice with the
slice tool.

Drag with slice select tool
to adjust slice.

Result

14 Choose Select > Deselect, and then choose File > Save.

Before you set optimization settings for these slices, you'll make sure that the colors are Web-safe.

Exporting flat-color artwork

Flat-color artwork with repetitive color and sharp detail, such as line art, logos, or illustrations with type, should be exported to GIF or PNG-8 format. Flat-color artwork appears best on the Web without any *dithering*—mixing colors to approximate those not present in the palette. To prevent computers from dithering colors, use Web-safe colors in your artwork.

In this part of the lesson, you'll prepare the artwork to be exported in the GIF format.

Painting with Web-safe colors

You'll start by painting the flat-color buttons in the navigation bar with Web-safe colors.

1 In the Layers palette, Alt/Option-click the Logo layer to turn on all layers. Turning on the layers also unlocks them.

You'll hide the slices so that they don't distract you.

2 Choose View > Hide Slices.

You'll select multiple objects and paint them with Web-safe colors.

3 Choose View > Zoom In to zoom in on the artwork to 200%.

4 Choose View > Pixel Preview to see the artwork as it will look in a Web browser. Notice that graphics that appeared smooth in the Preview view are now pixelated in the Pixel Preview. This is how your graphic will appear when it is placed in a Web page.

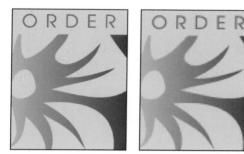

Preview   Pixel preview

You've been looking at a zoomed-in view of the graphic. Web browsers don't let you zoom in on graphics. You'll look at the graphic at actual size to see how the pixelization will appear.

5 Choose View > Actual Size to get a 100% view of the artwork.

You can continue to work in Pixel Preview for the rest of this lesson, or choose View > Pixel Preview to turn off the preview.

For more information, see "Working in pixel preview mode" in online Help or in Chapter 14 of the Adobe Illustrator User Guide.

6 If necessary, scroll to the Plants button in the artwork.

7 Using the direct-selection tool ( ), select the purple background of the Plants button.

8 Choose Select > Same > Fill Color to select all the objects in the artwork that are painted the same color as the selected object.

9 In the Color palette, choose the Web Safe RGB option from the palette menu in the upper right corner. (If the Color palette is not visible on-screen, choose Window > Color.)

Select purple background.

Auto-select objects with same fill color.

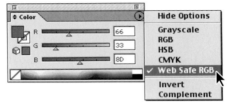

Change Color palette to Web Safe RGB.

The Web palette contains 216 RGB colors that are shared by both Windows and Mac OS platforms, so they can be viewed by anyone who has a system displaying at least 256 colors. If you have used a color that is not Web-safe, the Color palette displays a cube below the stroke and fill boxes in the Color palette and a small color swatch next to the cube containing the closest Web-safe color.

Now you'll select and correct the colors in the artwork that are not Web-safe.

10 In the Color palette, click the Out of Web Color Warning button to change the fill color to the nearest Web-safe color.

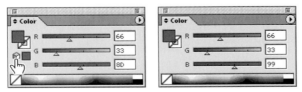

Click Out of Web Color Warning button to substitute nearest Web-safe color.

11 Press Ctrl+spacebar (Windows) or Command+spacebar (Mac OS) and click to zoom in on the Navigation buttons in the artwork.

12 Select the light blue rectangle behind the word *Plants*, and choose Select > Same > Fill Color to select all the objects with the same color.

13 In the Color palette, click the Out of Web Color Warning cube to change the fill color to the nearest Web-safe color.

The remaining objects in the artwork have already been painted with Web-safe colors.

14 Choose Select > Deselect. Then choose File > Save to save the changes to the artwork.

Creating slices for text and text formatting

Like flat-color artwork, type should be exported in the GIF or PNG-8 format. Now you'll create slices for text on the page.

1 Choose View > Show Slices to redisplay the slices.

2 In the Layers palette, click the eye column to the right of the Text layer to show the layer. Then select the Text layer.

3 With the selection tool ( ), click the paragraph of type to select it. This text is not outlined and is intended to be HTML text.

4 Choose Object > Slice > Make.

To create a slice with HTML Text content, you must select the text object and then use the Make Slice command. You cannot create HTML Text content using any other slicing method.

Next, you'll create a slice for the *Send Flowers* headline text. You'll create this slice as an image slice so that you can control its typeface in a browser.

5 With the slice tool, drag a rectangle around the text *Send Flowers*, being sure to include the yellow box behind the text. Start at the top left, and drag all the way to the edge of the yellow box. Do not drag on top of the slice you just made for the paragraph of text. If you drag slowly, the slice will snap to the top edge of the paragraph slice.

Selecting headline text

Because you used the slice tool to create the slice, by default it is an image slice and cannot be used for HTML text.

6 Choose File > Save to save the changes to the artwork.

Setting GIF export options

Now that you've created all the slices in your artwork to designate different Web elements, you're ready to *optimize* the artwork—that is, select export file settings that best trade off image quality, compression, and download speed.

1 Choose File > Save for Web.

The Save for Web dialog box displays all the slices of visible layers and lets you set optimization at the same time. Take a moment to familiarize yourself with this dialog box, using tool tips to identify the options. In Web production, you'll use this dialog box often.

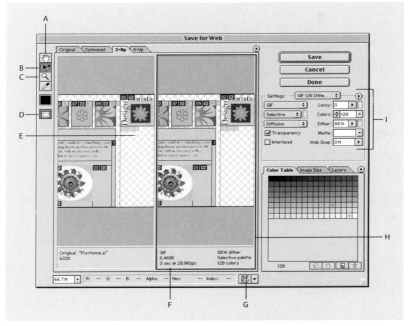

*A. Hand tool **B.** Slice select tool, **C.** Zoom tool **D.** Toggle Slice Visibility
E. Transparency checkerboard **F.** File size/Download speed **G.** Preview in Browser
H. Selected view **I.** Optimization settings*

2 Click Done to close the Save for Web dialog box.

You'll start by optimizing the navigation bar.

3 In the Layers palette, Alt-click (Windows) or Option-click (Mac OS) the eye icon to the left of the Navigation Bar layer to hide all layers but that layer.

4 Choose File > Save for Web.

The View options in the Save for Web dialog box let you switch easily between optimized and original (nonoptimized) versions of an image and view up to four versions of an optimized image simultaneously. The different views let you try out different settings before saving an optimized version.

5 Click the 2-Up tab.

Now you'll select two of the slices with flat color and select one of the preset optimizations available in Illustrator.

6 Make sure that the bottom (or right) preview (the Optimized view) is selected, as indicated by the black outline around the window.

7 In the Save for Web dialog box, select the slice select tool (✐). In the Optimized view, click the Plants button to select its slice. A selected slice is outlined in yellow.

8 In the Settings pop-up menu, choose GIF 128 Dithered.

9 Notice the file size in the bottom left corner of the window and the Color table in the bottom right corner.

10 Try GIF Web Palette from the Settings menu. The number of colors and file size decrease, but you have not lost any quality in this flat color button. You can compare the new setting on the bottom to the original on top.

11 Select the Toggle Slices Visibility button (▦) to turn off the numbering of each slice, so that you can clearly see all the buttons.

12 Click the Toggle Slice Visibility button again to turn on the slicing.

13 In the bottom or right Optimized view, select the Gifts button. In the Settings pop-up menu, choose GIF Web Palette.

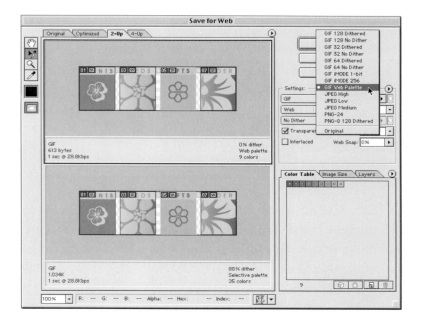

14 Click Done (not Save) to remember the current settings and close the dialog box. You won't save the settings until you've finished determining the settings for all of the slices.

15 Choose File > Save to save the file.

? You can also create your own custom settings. For more information on creating custom settings see "Applying optimization settings" in online Help or Chapter 13 in the Adobe Illustrator User Guide.

Exporting continuous-tone and gradient artwork

Next you'll optimize the logo and the sticker slices, and then optimize the remaining continuous-tone buttons in the JPEG and PNG-24 formats and compare these options.

To preserve the quality of continuous-tone and gradient-filled artwork, it's recommended that you use the JPEG image file format. Illustrator saves JPEG files using different compressions based on the specified image quality. The compression option you select determines how the color information in the artwork is preserved, which affects the size and quality of the image. It is important to keep in mind that JPEG doesn't support transparency.

Note: Transparency makes it possible to place a nonrectangular graphic object against the background of a Web page. Background transparency, supported by GIF and PNG formats, preserves transparent pixels in the image, allowing the Web page background to show through in a browser.

You can also export continuous-tone artwork to PNG-24 format—for example, to use background transparency or background matting with an image. However, not all browsers support the PNG-24 format. An image in the PNG-24 format usually is larger than in the JPEG format, because the PNG-24 format uses the same lossless compression method as the PNG-8 format, in which no data is discarded.

You'll start by selecting the logo and applying transparency.

1 In the Layers palette, Alt/Option-click the eye icon next to the Navigation Bar layer to display and unlock all layers.

2 Choose File > Save for Web.

3 In the Save for Web dialog box, select the hand tool and scroll so that you can see the Logo slice in the upper right corner.

4 Select the slice select tool, and then click the Logo slice in the Optimized view to select the slice.

5 Choose JPEG High from the Settings pop-up menu. Notice the white showing up in the open areas of the logo.

This color show-through—similar to color show-through in printing when colors aren't trapped—sometimes occurs when images are on top of a background.

White in JPEG preview indicates color show-through.

The JPEG format maintains good quality in an image, but does not support transparency; if you choose the JPEG setting, the white background will show through in a browser.

If your image contains transparency and you do not know the Web page background color, or if the background will be a pattern, you should use a format that supports transparency (GIF, PNG-8, or PNG-24).

Now you'll try a file format that supports transparency, and see if it can also maintain the image quality.

6 In the Settings pop-up menu, choose GIF 128 Dithered. Notice the background display is now transparent, as indicated by the checkerboard, because the transparency option has been selected.

GIF 128 Dithered setting maintains transparency.

Next you'll optimize the sticker slice with the same setting.

7 Select the Zoom tool or Hand tool, and drag the sticker to bring it into view.

8 Using the slice select tool in the Optimized view, select the sticker slice. Choose GIF 128 Dithered from the Settings pop-up menu.

Now you'll compare the JPEG and PNG optimization settings.

9 Using the Zoom tool and the Hand tool in the dialog box, zoom in to 200% on the Seed button preview in one of the frames and center the Seed button slice in the preview window.

Selecting or editing an object in one frame updates its preview in all frames.

You can also use the keyboard shortcuts to get the hand and zoom tools while in the Save for Web dialog box. Press the spacebar to get the hand tool. Press Ctrl/Command+spacebar and click to zoom in on a preview. Press Alt+Ctrl+spacebar (Windows) or Option+Command+spacebar (Mac OS) and click to zoom out.

10 Click the 4-Up tab at the top of the Save for Web dialog box, so that you can preview four different settings. The original version appears in the upper left corner.

11 In the Save for Web dialog box, select the slice select tool, and then click the Seed button in the upper left of the dialog box to select the button. Make sure that a yellow outline appears around the Seed button, indicating it is selected.

First you'll compare JPEG settings.

12 Click the upper right version, and choose JPEG High from the Settings menu.

13 Click the lower right version, and choose JPEG Medium from the Settings menu.

14 Click the lower left version, and choose JPEG Low from the Settings menu.

15 Notice the difference in image quality between the four versions, particularly around the edges of the shapes where the colors blur.

16 Also note the file sizes of the different versions (approximately 2.752K for the JPEG High version, 1.61K for JPEG Medium, and 1.16K for JPEG Low).

The JPEG Low version will download more quickly than the JPEG High or Medium versions, but like the JPEG Medium version, is seriously compromised. Only the JPEG High version maintains the image quality.

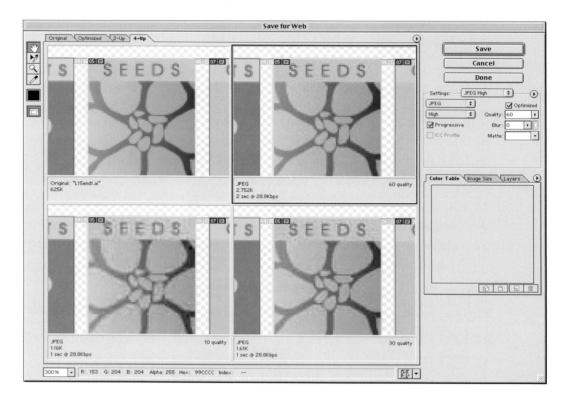

Now you'll compare the image quality and file size for the PNG-24 setting.

17 Click the lower left version if it is not already selected. Choose PNG-24 from the Settings pop-up menu.

Notice that the image quality of the PNG-24 version is very good, but the file size is now approximately 4.56K. Even though the image quality is slightly better than the JPEG High version, the increased file size will slow the Web site download time.

18 Choose JPEG High from the Settings pop-up menu.

You'll apply the same settings to the Order button.

19 Click the Optimized view tab. Double-click the Zoom tool to view the images at actual size.

20 In the dialog box, use the slice select tool to select the Order button.

21 Choose JPEG High from the Settings menu.

You'll continue working in the Save for Web dialog box to set up links to URLs.

Linking slices to URLs

When designing Web pages, it's useful to attach links to objects that will load the specified Web page. You can link any object you create in Adobe Illustrator to a Uniform Resource Locator (URL) address, transforming the object into a button that links to an Internet Web site.

You can use either slices or image maps to link one or more areas of an image—called *hotspots*—to a URL. When a user clicks the hotspot in the resulting Web page, the Web browser loads the linked file. Slices with hotspots can link only to rectangular areas.

[?] Image maps can link to polygonal or rectangular areas in your artwork. For more information on image maps, see "Creating image maps" in online Help or Chapter 14 of the Adobe Illustrator User Guide.

Now you'll add URLs to the navigation bar slices.

1 Using the slice select tool ( ), double-click the first button (Plants) to display the Slice Options dialog box. The Name text box lists the slice name, the default file name when you save the Web page.

You'll specify a URL to make the slice area a hotspot in the resulting Web page.

2 In the URL text box, type the URL for the destination of the link. You can enter a relative URL, a full URL (including http://), or choose a previously created URL from the pop-up menu. (We used **http://www.adobe.com**). Click OK to apply the changes.

```
                        Slice Options
  ┌─────────────────────────────────────────────────┐
  │  Slice Type: [ Image      ◆ ]                     │
  │                                    ┌──────────┐   │
  │       Name: [User_03            ]  │    OK    │   │
  │                                    └──────────┘   │
  │        URL: [http://www.adobe.com  ▼]             │
  │                                    ┌──────────┐   │
  │     Target: [                    ▼]│  Cancel  │   │
  │                                    └──────────┘   │
  │    Message: [                     ]               │
  │                                                   │
  │        Alt: [                     ]               │
  │                                                   │
  │                                                   │
  │              Background: [ None  ▼]               │
  └─────────────────────────────────────────────────┘
```

3 Double-click the remaining buttons (Seeds, Gifts, and Order) in turn to select and display the Slice Options dialog box. Repeat step 2, typing in another URL to link the slice to a second destination URL. You can also select a URL from the URL pop-up menu. Click OK.

🔆 *To clear the URLs shown in the pop-up menu, delete the Adobe Save For Web AI Prefs file located in the Illustrator 10 folder (Windows) or the System folder (Mac OS).*

After assigning the URLs to the buttons, you can test whether the URLs are valid.

4 If you have a live Internet connection, click the Preview in Browser button in the bottom right corner of the Save for Web dialog box. Valid URLs will jump to the address you entered in the URL text box.

Note: *Testing these URLs requires that you have a live Internet connection via your browser. If you don't have a live connection, testing the link will generate an error message. You can also enter a URL to your local computer in step 2 and test it locally.*

5 Close your browser window to quit the preview.

Now you'll have Illustrator remember the current settings in the Save for Web dialog box.

6 In the Save for Web dialog box, press Alt (Windows) or Option (Mac OS) and click Remember to remember the current settings and keep the dialog box open. Holding down Alt/Option changes the Done button to Remember.

Setting HTML text options

Next you will replace the placeholder paragraph of text with HTML text.

Creating a slice as HTML text lets you capture text and basic formatting characteristics (such as the background color) of the text object in Illustrator. Text in HTML pages varies according to each browser setting. To control the exact typeface and size of a font you must convert text to an image.

1 In the Save for Web dialog box, click the Optimized tab if it is not already selected.

2 With the slice select tool, double-click the paragraph of text to display the Slice Options dialog box.

3 For Slice Type, choose HTML Text from the pop-up menu. The slice type and options determines how the content of the slice will look and function on the Web.

The text for HTML Text slices appears in the Slice Options dialog box, but you can't edit the content in the dialog box. To edit the text for HTML Text content slices, you must update the text in your artwork.

Note: *You can make HTML text editable in the Slice Options dialog box by changing the slice type to No Image. This breaks the link with the text object on the artboard.*

By default, the background color of the slice is none. You'll assign it a background color.

4 Using the Background pop-up menu at the bottom of the Slice Options dialog box, choose Other. The Color Picker appears.

5 In the Color Picker, select Only Web Colors. In the # text box, enter **FFCC00** for the background color. Click OK. Click OK again in the Slice Options dialog box.

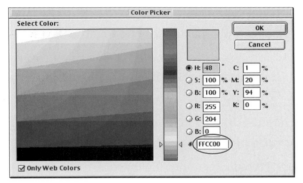

Selecting a background color

Selecting a Web color as the background color

6 To view the HTML text, click the Preview in Browser button at the bottom of the Save for Web dialog box to launch your browser.

7 Look closely at the paragraph of text in the browser window. As HTML text, the font can change depending on the font preferences viewers have set for their browsers. (You can test how the font can change by changing the font preferences in your browser and seeing its effect on this text.)

8 Close your browser window to quit the preview.

Controlling the look of your type

You cannot control exactly how browsers display HTML text; you can only control the text size and weight, such as bold. The way to control the look of type—for example, if a design's look depends on using a specific typeface—is by setting a slice to be an image.

1 In the Save for Web dialog box, use the slice select tool and double-click the slice containing the words *Send Flowers* to display the Slice Options dialog box.

This slice includes both the text box and the background color that you selected when you created the slice, and is defined as an image. By default, slices are defined as images. When text is specified as an image slice, the text will be rasterized in the HTML page and the typeface will be maintained. However, you can't edit the headline text unless you return to Illustrator.

To see how text will appear in a browser when it's not specified as an image, you'll try another slice setting.

2 For Slice Type, choose No Image from the pop-up menu. In the Text Displayed in Cell text box, type the words **Send Flowers**. A No Image slice won't display text unless you enter it in the Text Displayed in Cell text box.

3 For Cell Alignment, select Horizontal Center and Vertical Middle. For Background, choose Other to display the Color Picker, change the background color to **FFCC00** in the # text box, and click OK. Click OK again in the Slice Options dialog box.

The No Image slice type lets you specify text or a solid color on the resulting Web page. You can't view No Image content in Illustrator; you must use a Web browser to preview it.

4 Click the Preview in Browser button at the bottom of the Save for Web dialog box to launch your browser. Notice that the headline type is now HTML text and follows the formats you set in the Slice Options dialog box.

5 Exit the browser.

Because it's important to control the typeface of this headline, you'll specify this slice as an image.

6 In the Save for Web dialog box, use the slice select tool to double-click the slice containing the words *Send Flowers* and display the Slice Options dialog box.

7 For Slice Type, choose Image from the pop-up menu. Click OK.

8 In the Settings pop-up menu, choose GIF 32 No Dither.

9 Click the Preview in Browser button at the bottom of the Save for Web dialog box to launch your browser. Notice that the type is exactly as you viewed it in Illustrator, Adobe Garamond Semibold.

Headline as HTML Text loses formatting.

Headline as an image maintains typeface.

10 Exit the browser.

11 Alt/Option-click the Remember button to remember the current settings and keep the Save for Web dialog box open.

Saving your Web page as an HTML file with images

Once you've completed slicing your page for the Web, you are ready to save your page and create the HTML file with all your optimized images. The last artwork to optimize are the remaining auto slices that are filled with the yellow color.

1 In the Optimized view, use the slice select tool to double-click one of the long vertical yellow auto slices below the left edge of the heading *Send Flowers*. This action selects the slice and displays the Slice Options dialog box.

2 In the Slice Options dialog box, for slice type choose No Image, set the background color to yellow by choosing Eyedropper Color from the Background pop-up menu to display the Color Picker. Select Only Web Colors, and then enter **FFCC00** in the # text box. Click OK to close the Color Picker; then click OK again.

You can also set the eyedropper color to FFCC00 by clicking the background of the yellow paragraph text, and then choosing Eyedropper Color from the Background menu in the Slice Options dialog box.

3 Repeat steps 1 and 2 for the remaining yellow auto slices.

You've completed optimizing the file for the Web, and you're ready to save your settings.

4 In the Save for Web dialog box, click Save.

5 Click the New Folder button and navigate to your desktop. Create a new folder on your desktop for the HTML file and images, and name it **FlwrSite**.

6 In the Save Optimized As dialog box, for Format choose HTML and Images to generate all files required to use your artwork as a Web page.

Note: If you want to fine-tune HTML settings, you can click Output Settings and select Include Adobe GoLive code to allow further editing.

7 Click Save. Illustrator generates the HTML file and separate folder of image files within the folder you specified in step 5.

The HMTL file contains information that tells a Web browser what to display when it loads the page. It can contain pointers to images (in the form of GIF, PNG, and JPEG files), HTML text, linking information, and JavaScript code for creating rollover effects.

8 From the desktop, open the folder you just created, FlwrSite. Notice that the folder contains a folder of GIF and JPEG images, numbered according to the slices you created.

You now have the necessary elements to post your Web site to a server or hand it over to a developer for further enhancements.

9 Launch your browser. Then drag and drop the HTML file from the FlwrSite folder into your browser window to view the completed page. Close the browser window to quit the preview.

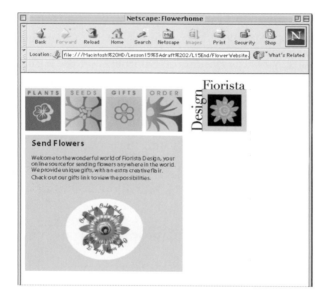

10 Return to Illustrator.

11 Choose File > Save to save the Flowerhome.ai file. Then choose File > Close.

Creating a Flash animation from symbols

To attract viewers to your site, you'll create a Web banner with an animated flower made up of symbols. You can also incorporate this artwork into your Web page.

Using symbols in your artwork minimizes file size. When you export a file containing symbols, the symbol is defined only once, resulting in smaller file sizes that are more Web-friendly.

1 Choose File > Open, and open the L15strt2.ai file in the L15Start folder, located in the Lesson15 folder.

The document contains a rectangular guide in the standard dimensions of a Web banner, 468 pixels by 60 pixels.

2 Choose File > Save As, name the file **Animate.ai**, and select the L15Start folder. Leave the Format option set to Adobe Illustrator® Document, and click Save. In the Illustrator Native Format Options dialog box, select Illustrator 10 Compatibility and click OK.

You'll start by creating your artwork using symbol instances.

3 Click the Symbols tab to bring the Symbols palette to the front. (If the Symbols palette isn't open on-screen, choose Window > Symbol.)

You'll place a symbol instance in the artwork using the Symbols palette. You can also place multiple symbol instances as a set using the symbol sprayer tool.

4 In the Symbols palette, expand the palette to see all of the symbols. Then select the Blue Flower symbol (the last symbol in the palette.)

5 Drag the symbol and place it inside the Web banner near the left edge. The symbol instance appears selected in the artwork with a bounding box around it, similar to grouped artwork.

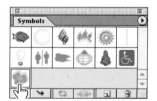

Placing symbol instance in artwork

Symbol instances placed using the Symbols palette are exact replicas of the original.

Now you will duplicate this symbol instance.

6 Using the selection tool ( ), Alt-drag (Windows) or Option-drag (Mac OS) the symbol instance to the right of the first symbol. Do this several times (we used seven symbols) to fill in the banner with the flowers.

You'll change the size of some of the flowers. (We enlarged the symbols of the right end and reduced the symbols on the left).

7 Move the pointer over any corner of the selected symbol. The pointer changes to a double arrow. Hold down Shift as you drag to enlarge or decrease the symbol size.

8 Continue resizing the flowers until you're satisfied with the arrangement.

Symbol instances added to artwork and resized

You're ready to set up the animation. To animate the artwork, you'll expand it so that each flower is placed on its own layer and becomes a separate frame in the animation.

9 In the Layers palette, click the triangle ( ) next to the Animation layer to display the symbol instances you created. (If the Layers palette isn't open, choose Window > Layers.)

To place the flowers, background, and text on separate layers and make each flower a different frame in an animation, you *release* the flowers to their own layers.

10 In the Layers palette, select the Animation layer.

11 In the Layers palette, choose Release to Layers (Build) from the palette menu. Each flower is now on its own layer, and all layers have been named and numbered.

Releasing flowers to their own layer   *Result*

The Release to Layers command instantly distributes all of the objects on one layer into separate, individual layers. You can use this feature to prepare files for Web animation applications that support layers, such as Macromedia Flash. For example, you can prepare different frames of an animation by first applying blend options to objects or by using the scatter brush to paint repeated copies of an object along a path. You can then release each object in the blend or scattered path to a separate layer and export the file as a Flash (SWF) file or to Adobe ImageReady™ 3.0 to set up the animation.

Now you'll export the layered file to the SWF format. You can then open the animation in a browser and see the flowers dance across the page.

12 Choose File > Export. Choose Macromedia Flash (SWF) from the Save as Type (Windows) or Format (Mac OS) menu, name the file **Animate.swf**, and select the L15Start folder. Create a new folder inside the start folder titled **Banner**. Click Save (Windows) or Export (Mac OS).

Other formats that support symbols include SVG.

13 In the Macromedia® Flash™ (SWF) Format Options dialog box, choose AI Layers to SWF Frames from the Export As menu. Adjust the Frame Rate and Resolution if desired (We used a frame rate of 6 fps, selected Looping, and entered a resolution of 72 ppi.) Click OK.

```
┌────────────────────────────────────────────────────┐
│        Macromedia® Flash™ (SWF) Format Options       │
├────────────────────────────────────────────────────┤
│  ┌─Export Options──────────────────┐   ┌────────┐   │
│    Export As: │ AI Layers to SWF Frames ▼ │  │   OK   │   │
│                                         └────────┘   │
│    Frame Rate: │ 6      │ fps           ┌────────┐   │
│                                         │ Cancel │   │
│               ☑ Looping                 └────────┘   │
│               ☑ Generate HTML                        │
│               ☐ Read Only                            │
│               ☐ Clip to Artboard Size                │
│    Curve Quality: │ 7  ▶ │                           │
│  ┌─Image Options───────────────────┐                │
│    Image Format: ● Lossless                          │
│                  ○ Lossy (JPEG)                      │
│    JPEG Quality: │ Medium ▼ │ │ 3 ▶ │                │
│        Method: ● Baseline (Standard)                 │
│                ○ Baseline Optimized                  │
│    Resolution: │ 72     │ ppi                        │
└────────────────────────────────────────────────────┘
```

Illustrator creates two files, a SWF and an HTML file.

14 To view the Flash animation, open the Animate.html file in your browser window. Close the browser window to quit the preview.

Note: Viewing the Flash animation requires the Shockwave plug-in. You can download the latest plug-in at http://www.macromedia.com/shockwave.

15 Return to Illustrator.

16 Choose File > Save to save your work. Close your file.

You've completed the lesson in building a Web page. If you'd like more practice, you can continue fine-tuning your artwork using Adobe Photoshop, in the next section.

💡 *If you plan to convert several files to Web images or want to create animations from your artwork, consider Adobe ImageReady, Adobe GoLive®, or Adobe LiveMotion™—all programs for optimizing your graphics for the Web. For more information on these Adobe products and capabilities, visit the Adobe Web site at http://www.adobe.com.*

Exploring on your own with Adobe Photoshop

Adobe applications are integrated so that you can go back and forth between them to fine-tune your artwork, depending on your design needs. Choose Adobe Illustrator for its tools for drawing and editing individual shapes, and for the full editing control it gives you over contours, scaling, and crisp, hard edges. When you want to blend photographic images and illustrative elements, choose Adobe Photoshop to let you integrate them visually by adjusting color, shading, transparency, and lighting.

Exporting an Illustrator image to Photoshop

Now you'll have a chance to work with Adobe Photoshop to alter the look of the sticker image at the bottom right of the flower Web page. This sticker was created in Adobe Illustrator and Adobe Photoshop. As you move a file between the two applications, layers, masks, and opacity settings are preserved. Follow the steps in this section to replicate the image for a Web page.

1 In Illustrator, choose File > Open, and open the L15strt3.ai file in the L15Start folder, located in the Lesson15 folder.

2 Choose Window > Layers to display the Layers palette.

3 Notice that the sticker flat-color artwork is separated into four separate layers—Type, Star, Flower, and Oval. All of the objects in the artwork are painted with Web-safe colors.

Now you'll export the artwork in the Photoshop format.

4 Choose File > Export. In the Export dialog box, choose Photoshop (PSD) from the Save as Type (Windows) or Format (Mac OS) menu, name the file **Sticker2.psd**, and select the L15Start folder inside the Lesson15 folder. Click Save (Windows) or Export (Mac OS).

5 In the Photoshop Options dialog box, choose RGB for Color Model and Screen (72 dpi) resolution. Leave the Anti-Alias and Write Layers options selected, and click OK.

You'll switch to Photoshop, and then return to Illustrator to complete the lesson.

Adding a mask and applying effects in Photoshop

You'll work in Photoshop to create a mask for the sticker artwork and optimize it for the Web.

1 Start Adobe Photoshop.

2 In Photoshop, choose File > Open and open the file you just exported, Sticker2.psd, in the L15Start folder, located in the Lesson15 folder.

3 If the Layers palette isn't visible on-screen, choose Window > Show Layers. Notice how the layers in the artwork remain intact in the exported file.

4 Choose File > Open, and open the Flower.psd file in the L15Start folder, located in the Lesson15 folder. This file contains the bitmap image of a passion flower.

Note: *If the Missing Profile dialog box appears, click the Leave As Is (Don't Color Manage) option.*

5 Choose Select > All, and then choose Edit > Copy to copy the flower image to the Clipboard.

6 In the Sticker.psd file, choose Edit > Paste to paste the photo image into the sticker artwork. A new Layer 1 appears at the top of the Layers palette in the Sticker.psd file.

7 In the Layers palette, drag Layer 1 down between the Star and Flower layers.

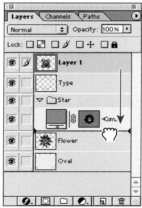

Paste flower into Sticker file.

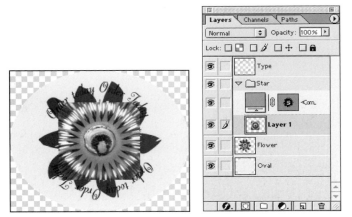

Move Layer 1 down between Star and Flower layers.

You'll mask the flower to replicate the artwork in the finished Web page.

8 Select the elliptical marquee tool (○) under the rectangular marquee tool (□) in the toolbox.

9 Position the pointer in the center of the flower. Hold down Alt+Shift (Windows) or Option+Shift (Mac OS), and drag to draw a circle centered within the square photo.

10 Reposition the marquee within the square photo by positioning the pointer over the selection to change the cursor to a hollow pointer; then move the selection into place without moving pixels. Or press the arrow keys on the keyboard to nudge the selection into place.

11 With Layer 1 (the flower) active, choose Layer > Add Layer Mask > Reveal Selection. Now the image of the flower is masked within the circle.

Next you will adjust the color and simulated depth of the masked photograph.

12 In the Layers palette, select the layer thumbnail of the flower on Layer 1.

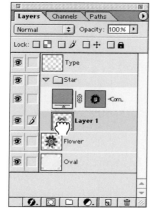

Selecting layer thumbnail of flower

You'll adjust the color cast of the center of the flower, to complement the star points.

13 Choose Image > Adjust > Hue/Saturation. In the Hue/Saturation dialog box, select Colorize, and drag the sliders to adjust the Hue and the Saturation. (We selected a Hue of 124 and Saturation of 20, for a sea-green color.) Click OK.

Now you'll apply a live effect to give the flower a rounded embossed effect.

14 Choose Layer > Layer Style > Bevel and Emboss to apply a live filter to the image. In the Layer Style dialog box, change the Depth to **141%** and the Soften to **4** pixels. Click OK.

15 Choose File > Save to save the Sticker2.psd file.

16 Quit Adobe Photoshop.

Optimizing a Photoshop file for the Web

You can optimize the sticker using the Save for Web dialog box in either Photoshop or Illustrator. The Save for Web feature has similar controls in both applications. In this case, you'll return to Illustrator to place the sticker artwork you just revised and then optimize the artwork.

1 Start Illustrator if it is not already running.

2 Choose File > Open, and open the file Flwrhome.ai in the L15Start folder, located in the Lesson15 folder.

3 If the Layers palette isn't visible on-screen, choose Window > Layers to display it.

4 Choose View > Show Slices to turn on the slices so that you can see their boundaries.

5 Select the Sticker layer. Click the triangle to the left of the Sticker layer to expand it.

6 To the right of the <Group> sublayer, click the target indicator (o) to target only the sticker. You'll leave the slice and background sublayers intact.

7 Press Backspace or Delete to delete the sticker.

Next, you'll place the file you adjusted in Photoshop and scale the sticker so that it fits inside the existing slice.

8 Choose File > Place and locate the Sticker2.psd in the L15Start folder, located in the Lesson15 folder.

9 Using the selection tool, align the bottom left corners of the slice and the sticker. Then Shift-drag the top right corner to scale the sticker to fit within the slice.

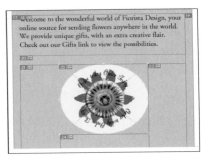

Scaling the sticker to fit within the slice

Now you're ready to optimize the sticker image.

10 Choose File > Save for Web.

11 Using the slice select tool, select just the sticker slice. (A selected slice appears darker than other slices.)

12 Choose GIF 128 Dithered from the Settings pop-up menu. You can also try the GIF 64 Dithered and GIF 32 Dithered setting.

You'll create a new folder for the HTML file and its updated images.

13 In the Save for Web dialog box, click Save.

14 Click the New Folder button and navigate to your desktop. Create a new folder on your desktop for the HTML file and images, and name it **FlwrSite2**.

15 In the Save Optimized As dialog box, for Format choose HTML and Images to generate all files required to use your artwork as a Web page. Click Save.

16 Quit Illustrator.

17 To view the edited Web page, drag and drop the FlwrSite.html file onto your browser window.

You can integrate your Web production process by working in both Illustrator and Photoshop to fine-tune your Web pages.

You can also open Photoshop files directly in Adobe GoLive 5.0. Slices, URLs, and other Web features in Photoshop files are accessible in GoLive for management and editing. Alternatively, you can open Photoshop files in GoLive as page templates. Page templates display as a shaded preview and provide a visual guide for building a Web page in GoLive. For more information on using GoLive, see the *Adobe GoLive 5.0 User Guide*.

Review questions

1 What determines the file format you should use when saving images for Web publication?

2 Name three styles of artwork that require different file formats for publication on the Web.

3 What is the benefit of selecting the Web palette when preparing images for publication on the World Wide Web?

4 What does the transparency option in a GIF file format do?

5 Does JPEG support transparency?

6 Describe how to select multiple objects and paint them with the same Web-safe colors.

7 Describe how to animate artwork for the Web.

8 Name some objects that lend themselves to animation.

Review answers

1 The style of artwork you're working with determines the file format you should use to save an image for publication on the Web. In addition, file size and image integrity may also affect which file format you use. In general, you should try to maintain the integrity of the image and keep the file size down.

2 Different styles of artwork include the following:

• Flat color (such as line art, logos, or illustrations with type).

• Full-color continuous-tone (such as bitmap images and photographs).

• Gradient-filled.

• Continuous-tone grayscale.

• Black and white.

• Animation.

• Artwork with URL links embedded in it.

3 Selecting the Web palette ensures that your images are displayed using the same color palette, regardless of the platform on which the image is displayed.

4 Transparency makes all the unpainted areas of the artwork transparent in a Web browser. You cannot select specific areas to be transparent; only the unpainted areas are defined as transparent.

5 The JPEG file format does not support transparency. When you save an image as a JPEG file, transparent pixels are filled with the Matte color specified in the Optimize palette.

6 Select an object and choose Edit > Select > Same Fill Color/Stroke Color/Paint Style to select the fill, stroke, or both of all the objects in the artwork that are painted the same color. Then choose Web Safe RGB from the Color palette menu, and click a color to apply it to the selection. You can also click the Out of Web color warning cube in the Color palette to automatically switch to the nearest Web-safe color.

7 To animate artwork, you select the objects you want to animate and then expand them so that each object is placed on its own layer and becomes a separate frame in the animation. You can use the Release to Layers command to distribute all objects on one layer into separate, individual layers, for Web animation applications that support layers, such as Macromedia Flash (in the SWF format) or to Adobe Photoshop 6.0 to set up the animation.

8 To prepare different animation frames, you can begin by applying blend options to objects; by using the scatter brush to paint repeated copies of an object along a path; or by spraying symbols in your artwork.

Index

Production Notes

This book was created electronically using Adobe FrameMaker®. Art was produced using Adobe Illustrator, Adobe ImageReady, and Adobe Photoshop. The Minion® and Frutiger® families of typefaces are used throughout the book.

Photography Credits

These photographic images are intended for use only with the tutorials.

Adobe Image Library: Lesson 7 (figure of woman, from Exercise and Wellness, EWE_095; clouds, from Endless Skies, ESK_076); Lesson 14 (chess pieces, from Business Symbols, BSY_058 and BSY_066).

Passion flower: Lesson 15 (Kim Meuli Brown).

The Adobe Image Library contains compelling images to make your ideas stand out in any media. For more information, visit the U.S. Web site at http://www.adobestudios.com.

Adobe Typefaces Used

Lesson 6: Bossa Nova™

Lesson 7: Adobe Garamond

Lesson 8: Sassafras™

Lesson 9: Penumbra™

Lesson 12: Bossa Nova, Emmascript™

Lesson 14: Mezz™ MM

Lesson 15: Adobe Garamond, ITC Avant Garde Gothic®, Linotype Didot™

The Adobe Type Library

Adobe Certification Programs

Adobe® Certified Expert

What is an ACE?

An Adobe Certified Expert (ACE) is an individual who has passed an Adobe Product Proficiency Exam for a specified Adobe software product. Adobe Certified Experts are eligible to promote themselves to clients or employers as highly skilled, expert level users of Adobe Software. ACE certification is a recognized standard for excellence in Adobe software knowledge.

ACE Benefits

When you become an ACE, you enjoy these special benefits:

- Professional recognition
- An ACE program certificate
- Use of the Adobe Certified Expert program logo

Adobe® Certified Training Provider

What is an ACTP?

An Adobe Certified Training Provider (ACTP) is a Training professional or organization that has met the ACTP program requirements. Adobe promotes ACTPs to customers who need training on Adobe software.

ACTP Benefits

- Professional recognition
- An ACTP program certificate
- Use of the Adobe Certified Training Provider program logo
- Listing in the Partner Finder on Adobe.com
- Access to beta software releases when available
- Classroom in a Book in Adobe Acrobat PDF
- Marketing materials
- Co-marketing opportunities

For more information on the ACE and ACTP programs, go to partners.adobe.com, and look for these programs under the Join section.